HOUSE OF COMMONS LIBRARY

LOCATION    ML 920 STEPHENSON G

AUTHOR      *George* DAVIES

Acc DATE    25 AUG 2004

STEPHE

TO BE
DISPOSED
BY
AUTHORITY

D0318759

*For James Davies of Cambuslang*

# *George* STEPHENSON

## THE REMARKABLE LIFE OF THE FOUNDER OF THE RAILWAYS

### HUNTER DAVIES

SUTTON PUBLISHING

This book was first published in 1975 by Weidenfeld and Nicolson

This new revised edition first published in 2004 by
Sutton Publishing Limited · Phoenix Mill
Thrupp · Stroud · Gloucestershire · GL5 2BU

Copyright © Hunter Davies, 1975, 2004

All rights reserved. No part of this publication may be reproduced,
stored in a retrieval system, or transmitted, in any form, or by any
means, electronic, mechanical, photocopying, recording or
otherwise, without the prior permission of the publisher and
copyright holder.

British Library Cataloguing in Publication Data
A catalogue record for this book is available from the British
Library

ISBN 0 7509 3795 5

Typeset in 11/12pt Goudy.
Typesetting and origination by
Sutton Publishing Limited.
Printed and bound in Great Britain by
J.H. Haynes & Co. Ltd, Sparkford.

# CONTENTS

# ACKNOWLEDGEMENTS

I am grateful to Professor Jack Simmons of Leicester University for his help and advice and most of all for agreeing to read through the finished manuscript; to Lord Wardington for access to his collection of books about the Pease family; to Herbert Simon for endless encouragement; to the librarians, staff and officials at Darlington, Newcastle, Liverpool and Chesterfield public libraries; and at the Institution of Mechanical Engineers, the Science Museum and the Public Records Office, and all others who made railway and other documents available, and gave willingly of their time. I am also grateful to all those who gave me permission to reproduce material. Not forgetting Samuel Smiles for all his good work.

# INTRODUCTION

George Stephenson was one of the greatest ever Britons. Such claims are often wildly thrown around, and not always sustainable or deserved, but there are not many people about whom it can be said that he changed the world into which he was born – literally. As the Father of Railways, George Stephenson left the world a totally different place. Since the dawn of civilisation, man had moved at the speed of the fastest horse. After Stephenson, life on the planet was never the same again. Motor cars, aeroplanes, space rockets, might have come along since, and gone faster, further, but mechanical transportation began with the railways.

Railways affected everything. People lived differently, worked differently, ate differently, had holidays differently. Suburbs were created because people no longer needed to live on top of their work. Fresh fruit and vegetables could be brought hundreds of miles. The Grand Tour for the nobs or a day trip to the seaside for the workers was open to everyone who could afford the fare. The original railways were steam fired, but they created an early form of the electric village, in that communications expanded, local times were standardised into one national time, people were brought nearer to each other, the world began to shrink.

Would railways have arrived without Stephenson? Probably, in due course, but he was the single most important element. He did not invent the locomotive engine – no one person can truly take the credit for that – but he was the one who created railways in the sense that he perfected the primitive locomotive engines, got them to run on rails which no one had successfully done before, carved out the routes, laid down the tracks, built the bridges, and created the world's first passenger railway.

And yet his work, his contribution, continues to be undervalued, underappreciated. Some folks confuse him with Robert Louis Stevenson, thinking he might have written *Treasure Island*. And if they do get him right, they might remember the *Rocket* from their school days, but then are likely to imagine him as merely a horny handed engine driver rather than an engineer of genius.

He didn't even make the top twenty in a recent poll which the BBC ran to find the Greatest Britons. His great rival Isambard Kingdom Brunel, who was far less influential in the birth of railways, did much better, being voted number two, behind Winston Churchill. Brunel, for some reason, has increasingly emerged over the decades as a much more glamourous figure. He did wear that awful distinctive stove pipe hat, which has helped his image and identification. He was also educated, son of a famous knighted father, southern born and polished while Stephenson was uneducated, Northern and rough.

This biography of Stephenson first came out in 1975 and has been out of print for the last fifteen years or so, much of course to my personal fury. But I see it as part of a wider slur. The book was meant for the general public, accessible to all, even for those with little technical knowledge or interest. There hasn't been another general biography of him since that time, as far as I can gather, looking on the internet, checking in Waterstones, though there has been a good biography of his son Robert.

Part of the problem is that the literary and publishing establishment appears more interested in memoirs of minor literary or aristocratic figures from the Victorian age than its great engineers. You can more easily be commissioned to do yet another biography of Wordsworth, which I myself have done, than any of our great scientists, inventors and engineers. Most of our writers, publishers and literary editors are roughly from the same mould, with an English degree or similar, so they know all about Wordsworth, but try to interest them in a Victorian engineer who never went to school and their eyes are liable to go glazed.

And yet over the years, while this book has been out of print, I have had so many requests for it. Colin Welland, who wrote *Chariots of Fire*, came to talk to me about him, very excited at the possibilities of a George Stephenson film. There are some dramatic visual events in Stephenson's life, as you will discover, such as the death of a famous person at the opening of the Liverpool-Manchester Railway. Some great rows, family feuds, a brilliant baddy in George Hudson, and you could work up the romantic angle with the ever so pretty Fanny Kemble. It could make another British blockbuster for Hollywood, or not. As I write nothing has happened.

I then had a visit from the actor Jimmy Nail, the star of *Auf Wiedersen Pet*, who was very keen to do a TV series about Stephenson, with himself, being a fellow Geordie, as George. That project too seems to be dormant, if not dead.

I also had a visit from the novelist Ken Follett, who was researching a novel set in Victorian England which had a railway element and wanted to know more about Stephenson. That did come out.

When people do the smallest bit of research about life today, in what we like to think are modern times, they soon realise that the birth of railways, though it happened over 175 years ago, had effects and repercussions which are still with us now. And if they do a little more digging, they will discover that there were some larger than life figures behind the creation and development of railways, notably George Stephenson.

I must admit I knew very little about George Stephenson when I first started this book. I suppose I must have learnt about him at school, then I forgot about him.

In 1972 I was walking Hadrian's Wall and went to look at Newburn Church, a few miles west of Newcastle, to inspect their Roman remains. Like so many buildings either side of the Wall, it contains stones stolen from Hadrian's Wall. In the records of the church, I saw that George Stephenson had been married there, not just once but twice. They don't teach you about people's marriages at schools.

From then onwards I kept coming across George's tracks, literally and metaphorically, following the railway lines from Newcastle, following the road that *Rocket* took on its way to Liverpool for the Rainhill Trials and wondering constantly about what sort of man George Stephenson must have been, and not just because he'd been married twice. In reading about him, I discovered a third marriage, but all of them red herrings, at least as far as scandalous stories were concerned.

In Carlisle I read old railway records about the days when there were seven rival railway companies in the town, all fighting for passengers, and I began to realise the extent of Railway Mania. I read up on the history of other towns and their railways, about the dramas and passions aroused by the arrival of railways. I hadn't really realised that in such a short space of time railways had not only arisen from almost nowhere but spread across the face of the world. All of it, or a great deal of it, was due to George Stephenson. I wanted to find out more about him. Not just his railways and his engines but about George Stephenson, the man.

I spent three years retracing his steps, trying to piece together the elements that formed his character, reading his letters, looking for clues to his actions, attempting to build a picture of him as a human being. Over the previous 150 years his railways had been exhaustively written about, yet the man himself had remained a shadowy figure. Samuel Smiles, in his great biography of Stephenson in 1857, attributed most of the known virtues to him, leaving unstated the many faults which his enemies certainly felt he had, and turned him into a Victorian legend. Since Victorian times, almost every writer on the subject of railways has been specifically a *railway* writer, an expert writing mainly for other experts, not primarily concerned with the home life of their heroes or even how they felt as they saw their creations cover the world. It was a difficult job to find George Stephenson's feelings. His letters, for reasons which will be explained, tell little, but even this has been largely ignored by railway writers.

As an outsider, I did not enter into arguments or even discussions about gauges and blasts and tubular boilers. I have kept railway technicalities to the minimum but I hope this attempt at a biography, though meant for the general reader, will perhaps throw some new light on the personality of the Father of Railways which railway fans might have missed.

Since the book came out, railways themselves have been disappearing fast as the process of closing branch lines, accelerated by Dr Beeching in the 1960s, came to a climax. In 1948, when British Rail was born, it inherited roughly 19,000 route miles. Today, when British Rail has long gone and we are back to a handful of independent railway operators, for the moment anyway, there are only 10,000 miles. So 9,000 miles of track have vanished. One good side effect of this has been the appearance of new walks and cycle tracks, all over the country, converted from old railway lines.

But the railway system, despite everything, is as strong and popular as ever, politically and economically seen as vitally important to the nation, if a bit slimmer than it used to be. We now have the Channel Tunnel and Eurostar, whisking us from London to Paris in 2½ hours, which even old George Stephenson could never have envisaged. Billions if not trillions have gone into the new railway terminus at St Pancras, which will open up Europe to even more millions who prefer the train to take the strain.

Steam is still with us, though in a period, folksy form. The moment steam began to disappear from the network, some fifty years ago, it became an art form. Today, the various railway preservation lines carry a total of nine million passengers a year. And steam itself might come back as engineers are working on something called a 5AT, a steam locomotive which looks a bit like those Stephenson built locos, but without the grime and smoke, more economical and environmentally friendly, yet capable of 200 kph.

These locos might never get built, steaming no further than the drawing board, but it's pretty clear that railways are here to stay. The end of the line is not yet nigh. What George Stephenson created is still running. So, I am absolutely thrilled this book is back in print. I hope it will help a new generation to learn something about he did it.

Perhaps I exaggerated when I suggested he might have been forgotten. In 2004, a life size statue of him, holding a miniature Locomotion No 1, was erected in Chesterfield, where he died, outside the railway station.

Even more exciting, from 1990 till 2003, we all had the pleasure of looking at his face every day, passing his image over the counters, carrying his name in our wallets. Thank you Bank of England for honouring him on your £5 notes. Now, once again, you can read about the man behind the name.

Hunter Davies,
London,
2004

# 1

# EARLY YEARS

George Stephenson was born in the village of Wylam, about nine miles west of Newcastle-upon-Tyne, on 9 June 1781. It was not a particularly great year for Britain. At home, Lord North's Tory government was about to fall, after twelve years of power. Abroad, there was trouble in India, in the West Indies and in North America. It was in 1781 that Cornwallis, the British general, surrendered at Yorktown and American Independence was assured. George III refused to believe that the United States could ever survive, and fully expected them to come begging to be allowed back in the Empire, but he soon had other things on his mind, like getting out of his carriage in Windsor Great Park and addressing an oak tree as the King of Prussia.

Up in Wylam, Britain's foreign affairs were not a matter of great concern to the villagers, though they would doubtless have enjoyed any gossip about the king going mad, but that was being kept from them for as long as possible. Up in Wylam, life revolved round the pit.

Taking coals from Newcastle had been going on for centuries, since Shakespeare's day, but the industrial revolution, now well under way, had greatly increased the demand for coal and the means of providing it. James Watt was still busily improving the simple steam pumping machines, which Newcomen had invented earlier in the century, and these new machines were being installed in all the latest pits. With a steam pump, working at the coal face, you could pump out water and increase the length of the field. With a steam winding machine, set up at the top of the shaft, you could haul more men, materials and coal and greatly increase the depth. Tyneside coal was not only responsible for heating and powering Tyneside but the endless coal boats, sailing from the mouth of the Tyne down the east coast, were providing the heat and power for London, now a city with a population of almost a million.

Despite the national importance of coal, the colliers were amongst the most deprived of the deprived labouring classes, amongst the last to be enfranchised, the last to be freed from the bonds by which the colliery owners had complete control over their work and their lives. There was admittedly plenty of work, compared with some parts of the country, but an aging collier could easily be displaced, as thousands of agricultural labourers flocked into the new industrial areas. The relief was fortnightly, on pay nights, when according to Smiles, Tyneside experienced a saturnalia of 'cock fighting, dog fighting, hard drinking and cuddy races'.

Robert Stephenson, George's father, was working at Wylam colliery on one of the primitive steam pumping machines. He was officially classed as a fireman, which meant he shovelled on the coals, while the plugman was the man in charge. His wage was twelve shillings a week. There was a tradition in the family that originally the Stephensons had come across the border from Scotland, but no one knew for sure. His wife Mabel was a local girl, daughter of a dyer. Like her husband she could neither read nor write and signed her name with an X in the marriage register. They were both of slender build. Robert was described as all skin and bone and his wife as rather delicate. From all accounts, George, the second of their six children (two girls and four boys) was a throwback to earlier generations, being big, strong and healthy.

Wylam today is a pretty, residential village on the banks of the Tyne. It has been cleaned up, the slag heaps levelled and must now look very much as it did before the Stephensons and the other mining families came to live there. In their day, and for the next one hundred years or so, it was one filthy, industrial slag heap. This transplanting of industry onto a rural scene was very much a characteristic of the early days of the industrial revolution. The advent of industrialisation left the towns virtually untouched but the surrounding villages were ruined, turning into slums almost overnight. Most of the industrial workers had rural origins – in fact out of a population of just under ten million at the turn of the century, well over half were still employed in agriculture.

The feudal traditions continued in these new industrial communities. The mine and the mill took over from the castle as the centre of power, and the worker was dependent on the master for his cottage, his pub, his chapel, his shop, and of course his job. When a mine was worked out, or it became impossible to exploit it further, the masters would look for a new mine, or winning as it was called, and the whole force would have to up and go. This happened several times to Robert Stephenson and his young family, though for the first eight years of George's life they remained at Wylam.

None of the children went to school. The family was too poor. As one of the older children, George had to help from an early age with the younger ones, making sure they didn't stray on to the wooden train way which went past their front door. His first paid job was at eight when an old widow gave him tuppence a day to keep her cows off the line. Horses pulled the coal wagons along these wooden rails from the pit to the riverside staiths, or loading stations. From there they went into keels, or coal barges, down the Tyne and then into the seagoing coal boats for London. As his father moved around the area, George got various jobs at the different pits. He started about the age of ten driving one of the horses for tuppence a day, becoming a picker at sixpence a day – picking stones and dross out of the coal – until the age of fourteen, when he was employed no longer as a boy worker but as an adult, becoming assistant fireman to his father on one shilling a day.

He had set his heart on working on a pumping engine with his father and there are numerous stories about the hours he spent as a boy making scale models in clay of his father's engine and of the other engines he had seen at work in the collieries. From his father he developed a great love for the countryside. It was very easy to get quickly out of the colliery into open unspoiled fields and woods. But you had to be careful. Disturbing game, let alone trying to capture any, was an offence which could result in transportation, if not hanging. There were 220 offences for which the death penalty could be imposed, ranging from sheep stealing and pickpocketing to murder. (It was only in 1808 that pickpocketing goods to the value of one shilling or more ceased to be a capital offence.) The landed gentry clung to their estates and their privileges, making life for the poor very harsh, terrified that the workers would be influenced by the revolution which had begun in France.

George was eight when it began and he grew up whilst England was at war with revolutionary France and then Napoleon. He and his three brothers were now at work full time in the mine with their father, and bringing home their extra incomes, but they were well aware of the effects of the war. The price of wheat shot up and corn riots were frequent. In his biography of Stephenson, Samuel Smiles relates that by 1800 the price of wheat had become 130 shillings a quarter whereas in 1795 it had only been fifty-four shillings.

George spent all his spare time working on the engine, even though he was only the assistant fireman, taking it to pieces after his work was over and putting it together again. The pit where he and his father both worked soon failed and around sixteen George went to a different pit on his own, as a fireman in his own right. When he was seventeen, George met up with his father once again at a new winning at Newburn – this time with George as plugman.

George's eagerness to learn was not limited to the pumping machines he worked on but extended to all of the machinery in the mine. At the age of seventeen he had already got further than his father had done in a lifetime, but he was not content to be simply a plugman, even though he was now in charge of the pump and his father. (When the water level went down in the pit and the suction stopped, it was the plugman's job to go to the bottom of the shaft, plug the pipe and get the suction I started again.) He was constantly being called to mend other machines, such as the winding engine which controlled the cage up and down the shaft, a job considered much more important and difficult than manning a pump. He managed to persuade a friend to let him have a go at being the brakesman, the man in charge of the winding machine, so called because the most difficult part was stopping the machine at the exact time. The established brakesmen were annoyed and one of them went so far as to stop the working of the pit, saying that not only was young George untrained, he couldn't do the job properly and would break his own arms stopping the machine and bump all the men in the cage. But George, our hero, managed to persuade the viewer of the pit, as the manager was called, that he could do the job properly. Soon afterwards he was promoted to being a fully fledged brakesman.

At Black Callerton, the colliery where in 1801 he was made a brakesman, there was a pitman called Ned Nelson who complained about the way that George, as brakesman, drew him out of the pit. He challenged George to a fight after work and George agreed. From an early age, he had been proud of his strength, wrestling with village boys, but no one thought that he would have a chance against the much older and tougher Ned Nelson. George hammered him. Another triumph.

It is to Samuel Smiles' biography, which appeared in 1857, that we are indebted for these touching early stories of George as a pit boy growing up. Every anecdote finishes with a long homily about George's virtues, such as bravery and fortitude. Smiles went back to the pit villages in the 1850s and picked up these stories from old miners, still working away, and set great store by them in his biography. There is no doubt about George's great ingenuity and aptitude as an engineman, but reading between the lines his character could be interpreted in different ways from the same stories. We have to take Smiles' word for it that Ned Nelson was 'a roystering bully, the terror of the village', but from the way George was going around doing other people's jobs, telling them how he could do it better, he must have struck many older pitmen as a real know-all, too cocky by half. Even though he was certainly clever at repairing engines, a certain humility might have been more suited to his years.

Until the age of eighteen he was completely illiterate. He was a grown man, earning around £1 a week, the top pay in the colliery for an untrained mechanic, but he realised that he could never improve further, least of all call himself a skilled mechanic, unless he could read and write. It wasn't that he wanted to be up to date with Miss Austen's amusing novels, Sir Walter Scott's romantic epics, or Wordsworth's lovely poems that the gentry were currently enthusing over; he realised the simple fact that there was an easier way of discovering the principles of engines than taking them to pieces. People like Nicholas Wood, a young viewer who was soon taking a great interest in his work, pointed out that it was all written down in the books, Wood was a properly qualified engineer, in other words his middle-class parents had been able to pay not just for his schooling but for his apprenticeship to an established colliery engineer, the men who designed and built the engines, leaving them to the likes of George Stephenson to run.

George began night classes with a man in the nearby village of Walbottle, going three nights a week at a cost of threepence a week, practising his pot hooks on a slate in spare moments at work. A local farmer gave him extra coaching and by the age of nineteen, much to his pride, he could write his own name. Sums came easier than writing. He hired boys to rush back and forward with his slate full of homework to have it corrected. By about the age of twenty or twenty-one, he understood the simple elements of reading and writing. They never came easily to him. Even from the earliest days he paid or persuaded other people to write letters for him and read to him from books. Many letters and documents belonging to George Stephenson have come to light since Smiles' day, and still more are being found, but it is rare for them to be in George's own hand.

Having become an engine mechanic and desperately if belatedly trying to become educated, he now managed to find some time for courting. His first recorded girl friend was Elizabeth Hindmarsh, the daughter of the largest farmer in the Black Callerton parish. He met her secretly in her father's orchard and she seems to have had a fancy for him, but the family would have none of it. They had no intention of allowing their daughter to marry a poor, uneducated pitman, even if he was trying to better himself; and they certainly were not going to let him better himself at their daughter's expense. She was being prepared for a much smarter catch. The romance was forcibly broken off by the Hindmarsh family, to the disappointment of Elizabeth herself. She declared she would never marry anyone else – and she didn't.

George meanwhile bounced back very quickly and started going out with another farmer's daughter, though their family farm was much smaller than Hindmarsh's and this time there was no dowry to add to the attractions. Her name was Ann Henderson and she was a domestic servant in the farmer's house where George had taken lodgings. George made her a handsome pair of leather shoes – one of his many spare-time occupations to make more money – which she accepted, but she refused his marriage proposal. He then proposed to her older sister Frances, who worked as a maid at the same farm. Fanny, as she was called, was twelve years older than George, who was just twenty-one, and she was already thought of as an old maid.

Fanny had worked as a servant in the farm for over ten years, before in fact the present owner had taken over. He'd inherited her and her reference which told him: 'Frances Henderson is a girl of sober disposition, an honest servant and of good family.' Some years previously she'd been engaged to the village school master in

Black Callerton but he'd died when she was twenty-six leaving her, so the villagers thought, with no prospects of getting married. She jumped when young George offered and they were married on 28 November 1802, at Newburn Church. Mr Thompson, the farmer who employed her, promised his young lodger and his faithful servant that he would be their witness and that they could have their wedding breakfast back at the farm.

Newburn Church, a handsome Norman building, was in those days the centre of a large and affluent parish. The couple were married by a curate, not the vicar himself, but they did both sign the marriage register, though George may have signed Fanny's name as well. George's own signature in the register is badly smudged and endearingly child-like.

Not long afterwards, they moved to Willington Quay, this time east of Newcastle, where George was to be brakesman in charge of a new winding machine that had just been installed. It was here, in their one room in a cottage by the Quay furnished out of Fanny's savings, that their only son Robert was born on 16 October 1803. Fanny was considered in those days almost too old at thirty-four to have a first child, and she was ill for some time afterwards. The miners' cottages, owned by the colliery, were continuously being divided up as more families moved in, until several families were crowded together into one cottage. At Wylam, for example, the Stephenson family of eight had been crowded into two rooms with unplastered walls and clay floors, while three other families shared the rest of the cottage.

As George was now reasonably well paid for a working man, he managed to hang on to his one room and was soon able to afford two and then three rooms in the cottage, but he was always very canny and never threw his money around. He was still making shoes to supplement his earnings as well as mending clocks for the pitmen. Having a clock was a great status symbol, and of great use for a shift-working pitman.

Samuel Smiles continually stresses how sober the young George Stephenson was, so much so that one almost suspects he was a drunkard. It has to be remembered that in the early nineteenth-century, drink was the mass escape. There were scores of gin and beer rooms in all these new industrial slum villages. Working as they did twelve, sometimes sixteen, hours a day, six days a week, all the year round except Christmas Day and Good Friday, worrying constantly about the rising price of bread, unable to strike or press for better conditions for fear of terrible reprisals, thanks to the Combination laws, it was hardly surprising that so many took solace in drink, the cheapest and almost the only form of escape. The stern Victorian morality with its continual theme of temperance from people like Smiles might today seem rather extreme. It was extreme because the problem was extreme.

George was certainly sober. He could hardly have had time for boozing with working on his engines, making shoes, mending clocks and doing his homework. While most pitmen did spend their spare time drinking, or watching prize fights, or cock fighting, George was one of the new breed of self-made mechanics who were consumed and excited by the wonders of the modern world, especially all the new inventions, and wanted to know more about them.

One of the newest wonders of the world was the canal. Since 1761, when the Duke of Bridgwater's canal halved the price of coal in Manchester, canals had been spreading throughout the country. By 1815 there were 2,600 miles of canals in England, most of them built by sweated Irish labour, the land navigators as they were called, because they directed the passage of ships across the land, later to be known universally as navvies. Crowds gathered to watch canals being opened across hills like the Pennines, wondering at man's ingenuity, forgetting of course that the Romans had first built canals in East Anglia over 1,500 years previously, though the secret had died with them.

At the same time, roads were being greatly improved by engineers like Telford and McAdam. The newspapers were full of the new speeds achieved by the flying coaches on the new improved turnpike roads. In 1754 it had taken four and a half days by coach from London to Manchester. By 1788 this had been reduced to twenty-eight hours. But it wasn't cheap. The working man couldn't afford it. Sir Walter Scott, when he travelled down from Edinburgh to London by coach, reported that the price was £50. That was a year's wages for someone like George Stephenson. When George and his wife Fanny set up home, they were lucky enough to borrow a farm horse to get themselves the fifteen miles to their new cottage at Willington. Normally George, like every other working man, walked everywhere. Or he stayed at home.

The local wonder of the day, which was what attracted George in

Willington, were the attempts by colliery engineers to use the stationary steam engines, so far used for pumping and winding, for drawing the coal wagons to the riverside. Steam engines were being placed beside any hilly bits of the tramways and used to pull the coal wagons on ropes or chains up the hill, letting them roll down the other side by gravity. On the flat, horses still pulled the wagons.

There was one such machine at Willington, built by a well-known Tyneside enginewright, Robert Hawthorn, who had recommended George for the job as its brakesman. Like Nicholas Wood, the educated viewer, Hawthorn was an early patron of Stephenson's, recognising his talent and giving him great help, though George gave him little thanks. He liked to think he mastered everything on his own. Stephenson felt that Hawthorn was jealous but as the latter was the boss he took care not to quarrel.

In 1804 George moved to yet another pit, this time at Killingworth, seven miles north of Newcastle, again as a brakesman. Fanny's health for a time improved and it was here that she gave birth to a daughter, also called Fanny. The baby died after three weeks and Fanny's own health deteriorated again. She died of consumption the following year, at the age of thirty-seven. George was a widower of twenty-five, left with a two-year-old son to look after. By all accounts he was devoted to the baby, but not long afterwards he set off alone for Montrose in Scotland, on foot, to work on a new Watt engine. There is little record of George talking much about this expedition to Scotland in later life, though he often regaled people with the hard times he'd had at Killingworth. Smiles says he was invited to Montrose, which is surprising considering he was an obscure Northumbrian mechanic. Other Victorian writers, trying equally hard to preserve the image of George as some horny-handed saint, have said that he was so heartbroken by his wife's death, distraught by all the sad memories in the little cottage, that he just had to get away. But in fact no one knows what his precise motivation was, and an attempt to draw nice morals from his every action is unnecessary. Perhaps he'd lost his job, through quarrelling with Hawthorn, and had been forced to seek work further afield. Someone like Hawthorn had influence throughout many Tyneside collieries. George was an ambitious young man and off he went, feeling sad about having to leave Tyneside, for whatever reasons, but no doubt feeling excited about the prospect of new experiences.

He came back after a few months, walking home with the large sum of £28 which he'd managed to save. He'd left his baby Robert at home with a neighbour who acted as housekeeper. He found his cottage deserted on his return, much to his surprise and alarm. In his absence the neighbour had married one of George's brothers and had taken the baby with her. George moved back into his old cottage and soon his unmarried sister Eleanor moved in to look after him and his son Robert. It was Eleanor who brought Robert up, and he referred to her always as Aunt Nelly.

Nelly was three years younger than George and had been badly disappointed in love. She had gone to London to work as a domestic servant till a boyfriend back in Northumberland wrote and asked her to marry him. She sailed home to the Tyne, after a long passage which cost all of her savings, to find that the boyfriend had married someone else. She developed a passion for Methodism, taking young Robert to chapel with her, though failing to interest George. She sounds a bright cheerful soul and took Robert on many outings into the country. His aunt Ann (sister of his mother Fanny, the one who accepted George's shoes but not his proposal) had married a farmer and lived in some style. Robert always remembered that when he visited her house he got a whole boiled egg to himself, not just the top of his father's, plus a little butter.

On his return from Scotland George also found that his father had met with an accident. While mending an engine a fellow workman had suddenly let out the steam and the blast had blinded his father. His sight never returned and he was forced to leave work. Since the accident he had run up many debts which George paid off on his return. He moved his father and mother to a cottage near his at Killingworth and supported them until their death. George's savings finally disappeared when not long afterwards he received another blow – he was drawn for service in the militia. Britain was waging war single-handed against Napoleon, and in 1808 Lord Castlereagh ordered local militia to be drawn up in every town, amounting to a total of 200,000.

Press gangs went round strong-arming or bribing men into the navy while the army recruited its men by ordering a quota from every district. If you were drawn there was only one way out: you could pay someone else to go in your place, if you had the money. As long as the correct number was made up, the recruiting officer was happy. George paid for a substitute and that was the last of his Scottish savings. Not unnaturally he was rather miserable and depressed around this period. What with his family problems and his lack of money, his engineering ambitions seem to have been temporarily halted, though fortunately he was taken back as a brakesman at Killingworth. He said later in a speech that he'd seriously considered emigrating. 'Not having served an apprenticeship, I had made up my mind to go to America, considering that no one in England would trust me to act as engineer.'

It wasn't uncommon to leave for America – his other sister Anne, who'd married a John Nixon, had recently done so. (She had six children but records of them have not survived, though other branches of the American Nixons did reasonably well.) George settled down again at Killingworth and his career once more moved forward. His capability with every sort of machine, running or repairing them, eventually brought him to the personal attention of the owners of the pit, a group of masters known as the Grand Allies.

One of George's more important triumphs, lovingly related by Smiles, concerned a Newcomen pumping machine that had been installed in a new and expensive pit at Killingworth but for a year had given endless trouble. George used to walk across in spare moments and look at it, boasting that he could get it working if asked, though he was just a common brakesman. Eventually when the engine was deemed a failure, the head viewer, Mr Dodds, came personally to George, saying that as everyone else had failed he could try. George's only condition was very characteristic – he wanted to select his own workmen. The men on the job, all older and more experienced than George, weren't pleased, but Dodds told him to go ahead. For three days and nights George and his team worked on the machine, taking it to pieces and getting it working, clearing out the water and sending the men to the bottom of the pit for the first time. Dodds presented George with £10 and promised him promotion.

In 1812, at the age of thirty-one, he was made colliery enginewright, in charge of all the machines, at a salary of £100 a year. He not only looked after the Killingworth machines but built and supervised stationary engines for the Grand Allies at their other pits – even being permitted to do freelance work for other collieries.

At the same time, thanks to his increased income, he was devoting his attention to the education of his son Robert, perhaps one of the most interesting phases of his early years at Killingworth.

For a long time he'd realised that his own lack of education was a serious handicap. Perhaps it was this which brought out the aggressive and dogmatic side of his nature, a quality which never left him. He thought he knew as much as, if not more than, the educated engineers and viewers who were his bosses, though his knowledge had been of necessity picked up by trial and error. He hated them flaunting their academic knowledge and, worst of all, telling him something he didn't know. At the root of his aggression no doubt lurked an element of inferiority. It wasn't simply that he wanted Robert to have all the advantages that he himself had missed, the age-old ambition of the self-made man, whether a property tycoon sending his son to Eton, or a jumped-up mechanic wanting his son to go to grammar school. George Stephenson's other aim was that his son Robert should be the tool of his own self-improvement. Through Robert's education, he too would be educated.

Robert was sent first of all to the village school at Long Benton, one and a half miles away from their Killingworth cottage. He was a sickly child, inheriting his mother's physique rather than his father's, but he grew up wiry and resolute. The school fees were only fourpence a week and many of the children came barefooted. When he was eleven, Robert was transferred to Dr Bruce's private academy in Newcastle. This was considered much smarter even than the Newcastle Royal Grammar School. It was very much a middle-class establishment and at first Robert was rather teased for his broad Northumberland accent and his pit village manners. But over the next four years he lost most of his country dialect and could pass for the son of a Tyneside gentleman, like his other school fellows. Later on, Robert was able to mix easily in every society, but his father never lost the broad Northumberland accent, which most people outside the area found on first hearing almost unintelligible.

The round trip to Newcastle was ten miles, rather a long walk for a thin limbed, delicate looking boy, so George bought him a cuddy. He needed a horse not just to save his legs but for all the books he was constantly bringing home. Along with his son, George was struggling with the basic elements of chemistry and physics. Robert, a far better reader than his father, would read aloud the theoretical principles, and then, together, they would discuss and come to an understanding of them. Having done that they would try some practical experiments. The pair of them constructed a sundial which actually worked, building it above the front door of their Killingworth cottage, where it can still be seen.

When they exhausted the school syllabus George enrolled Robert in Newcastle's Literary and Philosophical Society at a fee of three guineas a year. Together they moved onto more advanced books. When the books were too valuable for Robert to be allowed to take home on his donkey he was instructed to copy out the vital bits, especially any diagrams, and take them home for his father. One of the secretaries at the Lit and Phil, realising what an eager young member Robert was becoming, went out of his way to help him, recommending books and making instruments available. Eventually George plucked up courage to go into Newcastle himself and enter the imposing building with his son. Robert would easily have developed on his own, thanks to his expensive schooling, but without Robert, George might have taken years to gain the theoretical knowledge. George's nature, being proud and self-opinionated, made it hard for him to learn from another adult. But with his son, so much his junior in years, they could study and work together with Robert almost unaware that in effect he was being used to teach his father.

Robert's education shows how relatively well off George had become. The four years' schooling at Dr Bruce's Academy came to just £40 in all, a large amount for an ordinary working man. George's basic annual salary was still £100 but every year he was decreasing his Killingworth hours and increasing his freelance work. He devised some stationary engines for underground work which so successfully hauled the coal carts that his masters at Killingworth, the Grand Allies, were able to reduce the number of pit ponies from a hundred to fifteen. They allowed him, at his own profit, to do the same for other colliery owners.

He was endlessly working on other less commercial inventions at work and at home. He built a clockwork scarecrow in his garden whose arms flew round and round, scaring all the birds and most of the neighbours. He invented a way of fastening his garden door so that he could get through it but nobody else could. He designed a baby's cradle which automatically rocked by means of the smoke from the chimney stack. (It's not clear how this worked, but Samuel Smiles says the women of the village remembered his ingenious invention for many years.) He devised a lamp which burned under water and he amused a local colliery owner's family by going into their fish ponds at night and using his lamp to catch all their fish. His cottage was crammed with all sorts of finished and half-finished models and inventions. He was obsessed at the time, as so many of the new mechanics were, by the idea of perpetual motion, a problem which had baffled inventors for centuries. But even George couldn't solve that one.

He was becoming known throughout the Tyneside pits by owners and managers as a highly skilled engineer with an inventive turn of mind, a rather strong-minded, obstinate character, full of strange facts and weird theories, but an enthusiast, an optimist who was confident he would get things done. He'd done very well for himself, having risen from assistant fireman to enginewright in just sixteen years, and he was now riding round on a company horse, one of the perks that went with being made enginewright. His share of the cottage was now four large rooms. All the same, he was still very much a working man in his manner and life style, unchanged and unaffected, despite his new income and his new position. He would still take part in daft bets of strength such as throwing hammers or lifting weights, along with any pit lads who cared to challenge him.

When Robert left school George apprenticed him to his friend Nicholas Wood, who'd now become head viewer at Killingworth. Although some years younger than George, Nicholas Wood had recognised George's talents from the moment he arrived at Killingworth as an underviewer. They'd progressed together, helping each other, though Wood was in every way the professional, highly educated and cultured engineer, with George his rough and ready protégé. It was a good start for Robert, being apprenticed to one of the best men in the area. From an early age there were signs that he had inherited his father's inventiveness and he was obviously going to be much more than his father's tool. Unbeknown to his father, he once tried an electricity experiment on his own, having read a paper on harnessing lightning. He almost set fire to the cottage but fortunately the only damage was to his donkey, who was knocked over by the electric shock.

Not long after Robert had started his apprenticeship in 1818, when he was fifteen, his Aunt Nelly left home and got married. It looks very much as if she'd deliberately stayed on, acting as his locum mother, until his education was over. There is not the slightest indication that George had any relations with other women during the thirteen years since Fanny had died, not that one would expect Samuel Smiles to breathe a word of such things. He was certainly attractive to women, big and strong, full of energy, enthusiasm and excitement, always good company as long as you didn't cross him. But throughout his life he appears to have thrown all his energies into his work. Just over a year after his sister Nelly left, George remarried. His bride this time was Elizabeth Hindmarsh, known as Betty, the farmer's daughter who hadn't been allowed to marry him, all those years ago. She had stuck to her vow and had never married anyone else.

George was now an excellent catch. He was no longer a poor, obscure run-of-the-mill brakesman, lucky to make £50 a year. He was now an important enginewright, earning over £200 a year, with a large cottage, several hundred pounds in savings and investments, turning down offers and jobs all over Tyneside. He was highly thought of by his employers, Lord Ravensworth and the other Grand Allies, the most prosperous owners in the north east. This esteem was due to the fact that his inventions were saving so much money. The new mechanics, like George, were the elite workers of the day, the makers and menders of the machines which made the industrial revolution. They were much better paid than their fellow workers, with more responsibility. The owners bowed to their superior technical knowledge and gave them great freedom.

For his second marriage in 1820 he went back to the same church at Newburn, but this time he had the full treatment. The vicar himself officiated and he had the church's new violin quartet playing for the ceremony. (It played at all such ceremonies, for those who could afford it, till the church got an organ in 1834.) The marriage was by special license as he could now afford to pay to have things speeded up. (The vicar who married him, Rev J. Edmonson, came to a tragic end twelve years later. Along with sixty-six other parishioners, he died in an outbreak of cholera which swept the parish of Newburn in January, 1832).

George's signature in the marriage register book this time is strong and bold, ending with a flourish and not a trace of a smudge. He signed himself 'Geo' not George. Very businesslike. By this time he was indeed a businesslike man for by now he had begun to solve the many problems of successfully running steam engines which moved of their own accord, or locomotives as they were being called, and had taken out patents to prove it.

George Stephenson didn't invent locomotives, though in popular folklore he has been credited with doing so for the last hundred and fifty years. (Even G.M. Trevelyan, in his great classic *Social History of England*, describes George as 'the man who invented the locomotive'.) Before proceeding to what he did with locomotives, let us go back for a moment, leaving George newly married and newly affluent, travelling round on his company cuddy inspecting his engines, to investigate something which he did invent, something which, for one hundred and fifty years, popular folklore has completely credited to someone else. Every schoolboy has heard of the Davy lamp. How many know that George Stephenson got there first? It's a story with all the right Victorian morals.

# 2

# THE SAFETY LAMP ROW

The early nineteenth century was a great period for scientific discoveries and inventions. Botanists were busy cataloguing the flora and fauna, geologists were looking at the nature of soil and rocks and there was similar activity in astronomy, optics, zoology, physics and chemistry. All this activity was being watched and marvelled at by an increasingly large and knowledgeable public. For the first time, science had become a public activity rather than a private, elitist affair.

The immense sales of the new encyclopaedias, particularly the Edinburgh-based *Encyclopaedia Britannica*, and of the new scientific and mechanical journals, helped to keep a wide audience up to date. The rise of the many scientific societies in every town in the land shows how deep was the desire for knowledge. At the top end was the Royal Society, actively supported and patronised by the nobility and the Establishment. At the other end were the provincial literary and philosophic societies modelled on the original Manchester Society which had been founded in 1781. Newcastle's, founded 1793, was where George Stephenson and his son Robert picked up their early bits of learning. By 1815, almost every town of importance had its Lit. and Phil.

The two most gifted scientists of the day were John Dalton and Humphrey Davy. Both of them received their early scientific training at their local Lit. and Phil. Socs. – Dalton in Manchester and Davy in Bristol. Dalton stayed in Manchester working on his theory of atoms, teaching and living a hand to mouth existence, avoiding popular acclaim.

Davy, on the other hand, loved the limelight. His rise to fame and fortune was known by all. From fairly modest beginnings in Cornwall, the son of a Methodist preacher, he trained as a scientist in Bristol, then moved to London to lecture at the Royal

Institution. He did a long series of experiments which resulted in the discovery of sodium, potassium, magnesium and other metals as well as chlorine which was of great use in the rapidly expanding textile industry for bleaching purposes. He developed forms of fertiliser for use in agriculture. One of the things about Davy which made him such a popular figure was that, unlike Dalton, almost all his work was of practical use. No wonder the Victorians painted his career so glowingly. Not since Newton had a scientist captured the nation's imagination. He was showered with wealth and honours, first a knighthood and then a baronetcy. In 1815 he was by far and away the most powerful and most honoured scientist in the land and in 1820 became President of the Royal Society. As a brilliant public speaker, he was courted and fêted wherever he went. In public esteem, only Wellington, thanks to Waterloo, was more loved and admired.

It wasn't surprising therefore that in August 1815 when a committee of north-eastern coal owners decided to find someone to solve a scientific problem for them, they should turn to Sir Humphrey. The call went out, as if in a Hollywood thriller, and the great man agreed to come.

The problem was gas explosions. Mining is a dangerous enough occupation at the best of times but by carrying with them a naked light – either candles or oil lamps – miners were constantly in danger of being blown to pieces every time they came across a whiff of any of the dangerous gases which are present in almost every coal seam. The problem had been there for decades but with the expansion of the coal industry and the increase in size and depth of every coal mine death had similarly increased in scale.

In Killingworth colliery, where George Stephenson was working, there had been many deaths through gas explosions. Ten men died in 1806, not long after George had become a brakesman. Twelve more were killed in 1809. Every pit in the country had similar tragedies. The worst occurred in 1812 at the nearby Felling pit in Gateshead, in which ninety men and boys died, burned to death or suffocated by an explosion of fire damp, as it was known at the time. The whole country was shocked.

Sir Humphrey came up to Newcastle on 24 August 1815, aware of the nation's feelings and in response to the appeal of the owners. He looked around a few pits and then returned to London to consider the problem. On 9 November 1815, he re-emerged to give his historic paper to the Royal Society in London, *On the Fire-Damp of Coal Mines and on Methods of lighting the Aline so as to prevent its explosion*. In under three months, he had inspected, diagnosed and corrected the problem. This led to the production of his Davy Lamp which was to ensure him a place in history.

But, and here the plot thickens, was it the first miners' safety lamp? Could an unknown, uneducated, semi-literate, self-taught enginewright called George Stephenson possibly have beaten him to it?

It would be surprising if George had not had a go at solving the problem of lighting a pit without causing instant death. He had witnessed enough tragedies at first hand and we know that over the last ten years his inventive mind had been turned towards much more complicated problems. He was by now well into the problem of building an efficient steam locomotive, but he was as aware as anyone of the need to tame the problem of fire damp. By a coincidence, about the same time Davy was working on the problem in London, George Stephenson was doing the same at Killingworth, working by trial and error, experimenting in the pit and at his cottage. He too came up with a safety lamp – identical in principle to Davy's.

On 5 December 1815, George Stephenson's invention was publicly explained at a meeting at the Lit. and Phil. in Newcastle, Over eighty members turned up to watch and listen. It was George's first public appearance, the first occasion on which he was called upon to make a speech, and he did not relish the prospect. To the end of his life he was very poor at public speaking. He got his friend Nicholas Wood to act as interpreter and frontman. George stood to the side, out of sight, while the demonstration started, but when he saw slight mistakes creeping in, George couldn't bear it any longer. He appeared from the wings and took over in his strong Northumbrian accent, giving a blow by blow history of his invention. He had with him several bladders full of hydrogen, collected from the Killingworth mine, and he demonstrated by lighting his lamp that it was perfectly safe.

When Davy's lamp was eventually exhibited in Newcastle, all the Lit. and Phil. members who'd been at the meeting, and by this time many others, exclaimed that it was the same as Stephenson's. While the Davy lamp was swiftly adopted in every other coal field in the country, the miners of the north-east stuck to what they'd had first and preferred best, the Geordy lamp.

The Davy lamp received national publicity and Sir Humphrey was duly honoured by a grateful nation. Not long afterwards the country's colliery owners presented him with a sum of £2,000 for 'his invention of the safety lamp'. The Stephenson supporters had by this time tried to draw attention to his work and as a result George was awarded a consolation prize of £100 as a good effort, being just a common working man. The Stephenson supporters took this as an insult. What annoyed them most was the wording accorded to Davy as 'the inventor of the safety lamp'. It was a fierce emotional as well as scientific battle. The Davy camp saw Stephenson as a nasty upstart, trying to cash in on the great man's fame. The Stephenson camp held high the banner of their humble local workman, proud and ingenious, unfairly treated by the powerful southern establishment. George, meanwhile, had gone back to steam engines.

The dates of the various stages of Stephenson's invention are all important. While it is true that the public unveiling of his invention at the Newcastle Lit. and Phil. took place one month after Davy's first public announcement in London, the Stephenson supporters were able to reveal that he had reached his conclusions and had produced several prototypes three months before Davy uttered his first public word on the subject. This proved, they said, that Stephenson was first. For many months in 1816, and later in 1817, national and local newspapers were full of irate letters from the rival camps.

Stephenson kept calm and rather aloof, which is surprising as he was never a man known for his modesty. He stuck to his first statement, given at the Lit. and Phil. in December 1815, later produced as a pamphlet, even when the Davy supporters started to suggest that Stephenson had pinched Davy's ideas.

George wrote a very measured letter on the subject to the Philosophical Magazine on 13 March 1817, a letter written for him by his friends:

I observe you have thought proper to insert in the last number of the Philosophical Magazine your opinion that my attempts at the safety tubes and apertures were borrowed from what I have heard of Sir Humphrey Davy's researches. . . .

You cannot have read the statement I considered myself called upon to lay before the public or you would not thus have questioned my veracity. . . . The principles upon which a safety lamp might be constructed I stated to several persons long before Sir Humphrey Davey came into this part of the Country. The plan of such a lamp was seen by several and the Lamp itself was in the hands of the manufacturers during the time he was here at which period it is not pretended he had formed any correct ideas upon which he intended to act. With any *subsequent* private communication between him and Mr Hodgson I was not acquainted.

The Mr Hodgson referred to was the Rev John Hodgson, a distinguished and much admired vicar in Tyneside who had housed Davy on his visit to Newcastle. Hodgson was claiming that from the minute Davy was called in he was working on the problem and had thought of the solution long before his Royal Society pronouncements. He'd told Hodgson personally about it in letters. The allegation was that Stephenson had somehow found out about Davy's progress.

Hodgson was the main supporter of Davy's claims in the north east and was responsible for many letters to the press and attacks on Stephenson. Davy himself at this time was keeping publicly quiet, as befitted such an important personage, in a row with a mere workman. But from letters which have turned up since, we now know that Davy was absolutely furious and had been working behind the scenes to discredit Stephenson, using Hodgson as his frontman.

In a letter dated 8 February 1816, Davy wrote from Grosvenor Street, London, to Hodgson, thanking him for copies of the recent letters in the local papers, saying that Hodgson's tone is still a bit gentle considering that there is 'an attempt at *piracy* on Stevenson's part'. All the way through the letter, in which he constantly misspells Stephenson's name, he pours scorn on Stephenson's primitive grasp of the elements of chemistry and about his 'absurd lamp'. Everything is heavily underlined, showing how angry he was. 'Depend upon it Stevenson is not a man whose testimony is worth anything. The persons who have read his pamphlet here vote him a thief and not a clever thief.'

In all Stephenson's career, and there were plenty of accusations to come, there can't have been a more damning description of him. Coming from the most eminent scientist of the day, albeit in a private letter, it's little wonder that the anti-Stephenson campaign became so vitriolic.

It was Nicholas Wood who had helped Stephenson with his original statement and his pamphlet and subsequent letters to the papers. But by now many eminent north-easterners had come to Stephenson's aid, people like the Brandlings and William Losh and not least the Grand Allies, the owners of the mines where Stephenson was employed. They lent their names in advertisements in the public press calling for a subscription to award Stephenson and for a public tribunal to clear his name.

The big meeting, to set the record straight once and for all, at least as far as the Stephenson supporters were concerned, took place at the assembly rooms in Newcastle on 1 November 1817. The committee included such local heavyweights as the Earl of Strathmore, Losh and Brandling They listened to many hours of evidence and produced a report, copies of which are today kept in the Lit. and Phil., along with one of Stephenson's safety lamps, displayed on a table in a glass cage, a permanent reminder of a great Victorian row,

The report reads like a Watergate transcript. Every piece of evidence is meticulously detailed, every witness's cross-examination carefully set down. One of the first witnesses was a Mr Hogg, a tinsmith of Newcastle, who gave evidence that between 2 October and 7 October 1815, George Stephenson came to his shop and asked him to make a lamp from plans supplied by the said George Stephenson. This first version of the lamp, so other witnesses such as colliery workers asserted, had been worked on by Stephenson from as early as August. George took this prototype down the mine and conducted experiments with the dangerous gases. (Smiles has a graphic description of Stephenson's daring, going forward to the danger area while others more experienced were scared to investigate.) It was stated that Stephenson also did many experiments in his own cottage, helped by his son Robert, taking bladders of gas home. Robert later added to these stories and so did Nicholas Wood, saying that on one occasion there was an explosion at home when the gas backfired.

The date for Stephenson's second version of his lamp, according to the report, was 4 November. The third version was perfected and in use in the mine by 20 November, being publicly unveiled at the Lit. and Phil. in December.

The reason why Stephenson had so many prototypes was that he was doing all his experimenting by trial and error, watching how gas burned and trying to work out by observations and practical tests how an explosion could be avoided. It is indeed a wonder that he failed to blow himself up during his experiments as his grasp of the basic chemical principles was very sketchy.

As a result of his early tests, he decided that the gas might not explode if it was somehow split up, entering the lamp through a series of tubes. He therefore built a lamp with tubes sticking out at the bottom where the air entered and a very tall glass chimney up the middle to protect the flame itself. He didn't know why it worked, but it seemed to. Then it struck him that it was the little holes that were doing the trick, and that the length of the tubes had nothing to do with it. So he dropped the tubes and in the second version got the tinsmith simply to surround the lamp with a perforated cylinder with holes punched all the way down. (He drew his idea for this version over a drink with the tinsmith in the Newcastle Arms. Years afterwards Robert Stephenson showed this beer stained drawing to Samuel Smiles and others.)

Davy, through his knowledge of chemistry, had gone straight to a solution based on exactly the same principle. His version was even simpler – his lamp was surrounded with a wire gauze.

In the report, the committee took great pains to pay respect to Sir Humphrey, saying what a great man he was, and how brilliant a scientist. But there was an enormous amount of evidence to show that Stephenson had done practical tests from as early as August – tests witnessed and vouched for by many people. And since in the committee's view Davy had brought forward no definite proof of his lamp until November (though his supporters said he had been 'working on it privately'), the report concluded that Stephenson could not possibly have stolen any of Davy's work and that he too was entitled to a reward. A sum of £1,000 was raised and Stephenson was presented with the money and a silver tankard. The inscription on the tankard said he was the 'first to apply in construction' the safety lamp principle.

The committee obviously enjoyed putting Davy in his place, at the same time being terribly terribly fair, drawing endless time charts and drawings of the prototypes to prove their case. Most of all, they must have enjoyed defending a humble, uneducated workman against the power of the London Establishment. An anti-London campaign always appealed to most classes in the north east.

In his speech of thanks George played the ever-so-humble part that had been cast for him. With the help of friends, and his fourteen-year-old son Robert, he composed a few suitable words which he learnt by heart. These words are quoted by Jeaffreson in his 1864 biography of Robert Stephenson, who says he saw them in George's own handwriting. (This would be amongst the earliest examples of George's writings, but I have been unable to trace its whereabouts today.)

He obviously had some help with the construction of the speech but several of the spellings would appear to be genuine George Stephenson. He begins by thanking all the Gentlemen, saying how 'gratefull I feal' for their support in his efforts in 'constructing a safety Lamp' and in supporting his claims against the 'Philosopher S H Davy'. He finishes by thanking them once again:

> For when I consider the manner I have been brought up and Liv'd the mariner of which is known to many of the Gentleman present and when I consider the high station of S H Davy his high character that he holds among society and his influence on scientific men and scientific bodys. all of which Sir lays me under a Debt of Gratitude to the Gentleman of this meeting which Gratitude shall remain with me so long as ever I shall live. I shall conclude sir with my heart felt thanks to the Gentleman of this meeting for their great reward thare support in my struggle with my competitor and hear I beg leave to thank in particular R Brandling Esqr. for I believe this meeting knows well the active part he has taken in my behalf And I hear do thank him publicly for it.

At the end of the report, the committee come back once again to George's deprived background. Reading it now, it does seem to verge on the patronising. The final pages beseech the reader to 'remember the humble and laborious station in which he has been born and lived, the scanty means and opportunities he has had for pursuing the researches of science'.

Until the report Davy had kept out of the public row. But ten days afterwards, on 11 November 1817, Davy at last showed publicly how appalled he was by the support given to Stephenson, whom he still considered an impostor. He sent a letter to each of Stephenson's main supporters, flaunting his rank, accusing Stephenson of having cheated the committee. To William Losh he said:

> Sir,
>    Having seen your name in the papers connected with an opinion which every Man of Science in the Kingdom knows to be false in substance as it is absurd in expression, I wish to know if it is used with your consent.
>    The Public Scientific Bodies to which I belong must take Cognizance of this indirect attack on my Scientific fame, my honour and varacity. I wish to know my enemies on this occasion, not from any feeling of fear, but because I would not connect the names of honourable men who may have been led into this business from mistaken ideas of benevolence with those of other persons whose conduct with respect to my exertions in this cause will, I think, awaken public indignation.
>                                        I am, Sir, Your Obdt Humble Servant,
>                                                                   H. DAVY.

Losh's reply was nicely testy and rather skitty about Davy's reputation and about the grand scientific bodies:

> Your letter which I have just received is written in a style of authority, to say the least of it, very unusual in the correspondence of gentlemen. My name was undoubtedly inserted as a Member of that Committee, the objects of which appear to have given you so much offence, with my perfect approbation.
>    Satisfied as I am with my conduct on this subject I must say that I am wholly indifferent as to the cognizance which may be taken of it by the 'Public Scientific Bodies' to which you belong.
>    Notwithstanding my sense of the great benefits which you have conferred upon the public, I consider myself at perfect liberty to testify my esteem for the genius and merits of any other person in whatever way I think best.

The Earl of Strathmore, one of the Grand Allies, was equally sharp in his reply to Davy:

> I beg leave to inform you that George Stephenson is, and has been for many years, employed at Killingworth and other Collieries in which I am concerned, and that no other Safety Lamp but that of his Invention ever has been used in any of them. . . . The men who work in them are perfectly satisfied with those lamps and no explosion has taken place in any of our collieries since their introduction.
>
> Is it to be wondered at that I should be anxious to reward a very deserving, unassuming Man, who has to his employers always proved himself a faithful servant and whose abilities, if they had been aided by the advantage of education, would probably have rendered him conspicuous in the annals of Science.
>
> No man can more highly appreciate your merits than I do but at the same time I can never allow any meritorious Individual to be cried down because he happens to be placed in an obscure situation – on the contrary, that very circumstance will operate in me as an additional stimulus to endeavour to protect him against all overbearing efforts.

Sir Humphrey kept quiet after this, but he went to his grave in 1829 still considering Stephenson a cheat. His biographer Dr Paris in 1831 kept up the accusations: 'It will be hereafter scarcely believed that an invention so eminently scientific, and which could never have been derived but from the sterling treasury of science, should have been claimed on behalf of an engine-wright of the name of Stephenson – a person not even possessing a knowledge of the elements of chemistry.' At least by 1831 they were spelling his name correctly.

Goodness knows how many eminent members of the Establishment believed what Davy told them, in public and in private, and probably remembered it for years afterwards, casting doubts whenever they could about Stephenson's later inventions and successes.

The row went on for a good many years after the report was issued. It had the effect for a time of swinging the accusations the other way – with Davy being accused of having pinched Stephenson's ideas! There were a couple of letters in the local papers which said that 'Stephenson's work had been clandestinely smuggled to Sir H. Davy.' Poor old Rev Hodgson nearly had apoplexy at this, springing to Davy's defence once more and calling it a 'calumny on his character'.

Few of the letters were as vitriolic or as self-righteous as Hodgson's and luckily not anywhere as verbose. The great length of these furious newspaper letters strike the modern reader. A few of those which appeared in the *Tyne Mercury* and *Newcastle Courant* were quite amusing, poking fun at all the people in the row. One writer to the editor refers to all 'the hot air' around and what an 'explosive' subject it had become. One writer signed himself 'Simple Wire Gauze'. Another called himself 'Aladdin'.

The arguments lingered on till 1833 when a House of Commons Committee finally announced that they believed Stephenson's claim to be justified and not a fraud. It said that the principles of the safety lamp had been 'practically known to Stephenson previously to the period when Davy brought his powerful mind to bear upon the subject'. Honours were then even, though notice how even then a bit of genuflecting to Davy and his powerful mind still lingered on.

Miners of the north east continued to use the Geordy lamp for many decades and the rest of the country the Davy lamp, despite the fact that the top of the Davy lamp tended to become red hot. In 1825 it was said to have caused a fire in a pit near Leeds in which twenty-four men and boys were killed. The Geordy lamp, because of the glass holder round the flame, never overheated.

Samuel Smiles, when he came to write his biography of Stephenson in 1857, naturally took George's side, building up George's deprivations. 'One was as yet but a colliery engine-wright, scarce raised above the manual-labour class, pursuing his experiments in obscurity; the other was the scientific prodigy of his day, the most brilliant of lecturers and the most popular of philosophers.'

It is hard to know how George himself felt during all the arguments, whether he was simply pleased to be the centre of so much attention, having his humble case fought against the highest scientist in the land; or whether he, like Davy, was absolutely furious and determined to win at all costs. Stephenson's own statements are few but they show a determined calmness which cannot simply be put down to the fact that he was helped in writing them by Wood and others. In these statements he freely admitted that he was aware of others who had gone before him, and had done similar experiments on fire damp, though not of course Sir H. Davy.

It would be interesting to know how he privately felt about the patronising tone adopted by the Grand Allies and others who so nobly sprang to his defence, or whether he was even aware of their smugness and condescension. They wallowed in their own goodness in helping such a poor, inferior workman. Like many fashionable liberals today, displaying their radical chic, these high minded but guilt ridden early Victorian capitalists liked to do and be seen to be doing good for the underprivileged.

As for George himself, he might have unconsciously resented the way the nobs rushed round making the most of their protégé. It would help to explain his later antipathy towards the nobility, and many of his subsequent attitudes.

The whole affair does appear to have been one of those curious historical coincidences, one that Davy just couldn't believe, which was why he was convinced Stephenson had cheated. It is quite clear that Stephenson was the moral victor.

The only remaining query is why Stephenson chose to begin his experiments exactly at the same time as Davy. Given Stephenson's inventive nature, and given that for the previous twenty years he'd been working in the collieries and that he was more than aware of the danger of fire damp, why had he not started experimenting sooner? Why did he wait until August 1815? This was the month when Sir Humphrey Davy was called in. In all the evidence Stephenson is presented as having, quite by chance, started his experiments just a week or two before the day in August that Davy came up to Newcastle.

There is probably a simple reason. George was too busy elsewhere. He didn't begin his safety lamp work till it reached the proportions of a national scandal, which was the same reason which brought in Davy. It would explain why he did not become too furious or too involved in all the subsequent arguments and mud slinging. He simply didn't have the time. It was a huge blow to Davy's pride but to George the safety lamp was a little one-off job, an interlude from his major preoccupation. Once he had invented his lamp it probably didn't occupy his thoughts any more than in the past the clay engines had done, or the sundial, or the shoes, or the clocks or the many other small-scale, small-time devices he'd turned his mind to. By now, and throughout the whole of the safety lamp row, he had a much more ambitious, truly scientific project, a project which, as he saw it, could change the world.

# 3

# LOCOMOTION

Three elements came together to form what we now know as railways and George Stephenson invented none of them. The three elements are the wheel, the track and the power. The origins of the wheel are lost forever in antiquity. The origins of laid down rails or tracks are a little clearer, but they too go back for many centuries and no one has ever been able to date them. As for steam power the first automatic source of power in the history of civilisation – this was by comparison an overnight phenomenon. It is, however, a subject where outsiders must step very carefully. The problem is the superabundance of facts, most of them contradictory. So many people had a hand in steam and as many hands have spent lifetimes trying to sort out the facts. Luckily, the origins of the steam engine have been more than amply covered by at least a hundred books in the last forty years so there is no need to do more than list a few of the more important stages.

The use of wheels must have been a magical discovery, whenever it was made, greatly reducing the man or oxen-power that was needed to carry any object, but the idea of then running the wheels on rails was an equal stroke of true genius, or perhaps accident. In some ways, there is still a trace of magic. Scientists find it very hard to explain exactly why it is that wheels running on rails can do much more work than wheels running on ordinary ground. The early coal miners certainly didn't worry about friction or tractive forces when they observed that a horse could pull one cart on a road but manage four or even five carts along a line of rails. It is generally accepted that the use of rails was normal practice in mining from the seventeenth century, though the secret was known in medieval times, probably even Roman.

Horsedrawn wooden trucks running on wooden boards appear

in a drawing of a German mine as early as 1530, but it was in England early in the seventeenth century that the practice became widespread thanks to the sudden increase in coal mining. This was when the rise in the size of London first led to a massive demand for coal from the north east. As the demand increased, new collieries were opened, away from the immediate area of the Tyne and Wear, and horsedrawn wagon ways became the most efficient method of getting the coal to the riverside staithes. There were wagon ways elsewhere in the country, such as Ralph Allen's wooden wagon way which he had built in 1731 to carry stone from his quarry near Bath to the river Avon, but they were most numerous in the north. By 1781, when George Stephenson was born, the whole of the north east was criss-crossed by a series of colliery wagon ways, all of them privately operated by their owners seeking the quickest way to get the coal to the nearest staithe on the river Tyne.

There are many recorded incidents of disputes as colliery owners had difficulty finding a way across private estates to get to the staithes. The legal problems caused by these wayleave battles was one of the earliest reasons why collieries started to unite, fighting together to get right of way. It was a factor which led to the formation of the Grand Allies in 1726, the group of colliery owners who employed George Stephenson.

The opening of a new wagon way was a time for great rejoicing, and crowds of up to ten thousand would turn out to watch the festivities. Sykes, in his 1833 *Local Records of Northumberland and Durham*, describes several of them:

1810 (April 23) – This being the day appointed by Simon Temple, Esq, for opening his new colliery at South Shields, the morning was ushered in by the ringing of bells, &c. Eight waggons being loaded with the coals were about one o'clock drawn by one horse from the pit to the staith, preceded by the band of the East York militia, and followed by Mr. Temple, and a long procession of his friends, and two associations of shipwrights under their banners. Seven of the waggons in succession were let down by a new inclined plane to the deck of the ship Maida, belonging to Mr. Temple, which was decorated with colours. The delivery of each was succeeded by a general discharge of cannon, and three times three cheers from the surrounding multitude. The eighth waggon was given to the families of the unfortunate men belonging to South Shields, who were prisoners in France. The company then proceeded to Hylton castle, where one hundred and fifty gentlemen sat down to dinner. The high sheriff of Northumberland, the mayor of Newcastle, several of the chapter of Durham, and most of the magistrates of the district, were at the table. At eight o'clock the ball commenced. At one o'clock, near four hundred ladies and gentlemen sat down to supper; after which dancing recommenced and continued till near six, when all retired highly pleased with the entertainment and respectful attention paid to them.

All this for some horsedrawn wagons. The next stage was equally respectfully welcomed. This was the principle of self-acting planes, in which the force of loaded wagons going down a hill was used to pull empty wagons up the other side, and it was first employed in the north east in 1798 at Benwell. Around the same time brakes were being introduced and the rails themselves were being greatly improved. Up till the eighteenth century they had been made of wood but by the 1770s cast iron rails had come into use. Experiments were tried with flanges on the rails, to keep the wagons above steady when going at speed round corners, and also with the flanges on the wheels themselves. Most of these improvements in horsedrawn wagon ways were developed in the north east long before George Stephenson started work as a pit boy.

The development of steam as a source of power for stationary engines had also been developed before Stephenson was born. It was Newcomen in 1712 who had produced the first successful steam pump, a simple up and down beam engine, but it wasn't till James Watt in 1782 perfected an improved steam engine which could turn wheels that a steam engine could be used for winding and haulage. He invented a steam condenser which enabled his machines to operate at a higher speed, more reliably, and use only a third as much coal as Newcomen's.

Once steam had been harnessed as a source of stationary power it was naturally applied to the self-acting planes. Instead of devising suitable downhill places where the force of gravity could do the pulling, steam engines were fixed to the side of the tracks at uphill stretches and with the aid of lengths of ropes and chains they did the pulling. Many colliery wagon ways then became a mixture, with horses still doing the main pulling, but with stationary engines taking over for the hard uphill bits and gravity taking over down the inclined planes. This was the position when George first started in the collieries.

The next important development, the most important of all, was the invention of the locomotive, a steam engine which could run on its own power, and this had nothing to do with George Stephenson. The inventor of this is agreed by all to have been Richard Trevithick, a brilliant Cornishman who had the misfortune to be born just slightly too early for his many ideas to be put into practice.

Trevithick was born in 1771, ten years before Stephenson, the son of a Cornish tin mine captain, or manager as he would be called today. After school he became an engineer in the local mines and worked on ways of improving Watt's stationary engines which were then being used in most mines. Under Watt's patent, Watt got a royalty based on the saving in coal used in his machines compared with Newcomen's. Trevithick produced several patent steam engines of his own which didn't please Watt, who looked upon him as his chief rival in the south west of England and tried to bring actions against him.

Trevithick, like Stephenson, was big and strong and fond of showing off his muscles. He was six feet two inches high and built in proportion and became known as the Cornish giant – as much for his size as his inventions. He threw sledge hammers over the tops of engine houses, then for a follow up he would write his name on a beam six feet from the floor with half a hundredweight hanging from his thumb. In a dispute with another mining engineer, an equally big man, Trevithick picked the man up by the waist and held him upside down, his boots against the ceiling. One might expect such behaviour from a rough uneducated pitman like Stephenson but not from a trained engineer and manager's son to boot. But Trevithick was a surprising man in every way. He was headstrong, impetuous, moving on constantly from idea to idea, forever being hard up yet giving his money away the minute he had any.

He completed his first full-sized locomotive in 1801, having been experimenting with some small-scale models for a couple of years. Other engineers in France and England, working independently, had drawn plans for a locomotive and some had even made models but Trevithick was the first who got one working properly. His first locomotive ran on roads, not rails, but it didn't run for long. While going over a deep gully in the road at Camborne, Cornwall, the steering wheel broke, the locomotive got out of control and it crashed into a house. It doesn't seem to have affected the high spirits of Trevithick and his friends. One of them, Davies Gilbert, described what happened next. 'The Parties adjourned to the Hotel and comforted their Hearts with Roast Goose and proper drinks when, forgetful of the Engine, its Water boiled away, the Iron became red hot and nothing that was combustible remained either of the engine or the house.'

It is difficult to imagine Stephenson allowing such a thing to happen. He would have been down on his hands and knees, taking the machine to pieces and repairing the faults somehow, even if it had taken days, with never a thought for the inner man. But as Mr Smiles has well told us, Stephenson was nothing if not a model of Perseverance.

Trevithick went back to developing his stationary steam engines but in 1804 he successfully built another locomotive, this time to run on rails, and this time he used it to win a bet. While in Penydaren in South Wales, where he was supplying some stationary engines for the local iron works, a wager was arranged between a local ironmaster and a friend that a steam locomotive couldn't haul ten tons of iron along the colliery tramway, a distance of some nine miles. The bet was for five hundred guineas. Trevithick won it for the ironmaster, his engine and five wagons carrying seventy men as well as the load of iron. This was a historic occasion in the birth of railways. Though the engine was not used for long, as it was found far too heavy for the rails, it was the forerunner of the locomotives that Stephenson was later to build.

It is probable that Stephenson heard of Trevithick's Cornish and Welsh experiments. He was then just a simple brakesman, with another eight years to go before being promoted to enginewright, but news of the Trevithick experiments had definitely reached the north east. Christopher Blackett, the owner of Wylam colliery where Stephenson had first worked, decided to have a Trevithick locomotive built at Gateshead in 1805. Trevithick came up to Tyneside and later boasted that he'd dangled the infant Robert on his knees. (This is highly unlikely considering that Stephenson was an obscure brakesman.) A friend of Stephenson's, John Steele, helped to build the Trevithick-style engine but there is no record of George ever visiting the Gateshead workshop, though he must have known about it. The engine was tested but never left the foundry. It was found to work well enough mechanically but like the Penydaren engine it tore up the wooden rails. It was Trevithick's bad luck to have invented a machine long before the world was ready to use it.

Trevithick did try again in 1808, this time in London, and by a nice coincidence he chose a site not far from what is now Euston Station. He built a circular track and demonstrated a new engine which he called 'Catch me who can'. Admission to the enclosure was one shilling, which included a ride for those who dared. It received some publicity if only as a piece of eccentricity, but this venture failed once again because the track was not strong enough for the engine.

After 1808 Trevithick dropped the idea of locomotives without having attempted either to invent a track which could take them or alternatively reduce the weight and clumsiness of his engines. It doesn't seem to have been in his character to keep going against the odds. Other ideas beckoned and off he went. During the next fifteen years, until he died in 1833, he became involved in many projects which took him to all parts of the world but none of them ever quite came off, though many were later taken up by other inventors. He constructed a barge which had paddle wheels driven by steam, designed a steam hammer, a portable room heater on wheels, a steam rolling mill, an underwater steam-driven dredger. He suggested a mechanical means of refrigeration, a crude form of turbine engine. He worked on a tunnel under the Thames but had to give up when the water came in. (It was Sir Marc Brunel and his son Isambard who later completed the first tunnel under the Thames.) In 1811 he went bankrupt, but by 1814 he was discharged, having paid his debts. In 1816 he set off for Peru with a great fanfare, taking a machine to open up the silver mines, but got caught up in Simon Bolivar's army. He disappeared into the depths of South America for almost ten years, trying to install his high pressure steam engines, continually being drawn into other dafter and more dangerous exploits.

One of his last ideas, on his eventual return to England, was to design an enormous column to celebrate the passing of the 1832 Reform Bill. It was to be 1,000 feet high (Nelson's column, built seventeen years later, is only 185 feet high) with a lift up the middle. Several public meetings were held but the project was finally dropped. When Trevithick died the following year he was penniless and his friends had to pay for the funeral. A tragic, unfulfilled end to one of the most inventive engineers England has ever known. His early high pressure steam engines, which he successfully patented and were used for many decades in mines and factories throughout the country, lived after him, but when he gave up his experiments with locomotives in 1808 it was several years before anyone else had the heart or the energy to try again.

However, the shortage of horses and the high prices of fodder during the height of the Napoleonic wars renewed interest once again in the possibility of locomotion. Colliery owners, faced with the high cost of running horsedrawn wagon ways, encouraged their more inventive engineers to try again. It was wrongly thought at the time that one of Trevithick's problems was getting smooth wheels to run on smooth rails. Surely the engine was bound to slide or run off the line at corners? In 1812 John Blenkinsop built a rack locomotive and ran it successfully on a colliery line near Leeds. The driving wheel had cogs which fitted into a rack on the track as it moved forward, thereby keeping it on the track.

The rack was on one side of the lines which made the engine rather lopsided but Blenkinsop, a local colliery viewer, couldn't put the rack down the middle of the track to balance the engine as it would get in the way of the horses who were still the main pulling power. Despite its clumsiness and slowness, the Blenkinsop rack locomotive ran for several years and therefore must be said to be the first commercially successful locomotive. Blenkinsop sent one of his to work on the Tyne. It wasn't a success and was soon taken off but it is thought, once again, that George Stephenson must have watched it at work.

Blenkinsop paid a royalty of £30 to Trevithick for the use of some of his boiler patents but the rack idea seems to have been his own. It caused a good deal of interest, at home and abroad. In 1815 a French engineer who had seen it, published a detailed description and the Grand Duke Nicholas of Russia, later the Tsar, was so impressed when he visited the colliery on a tour of England that he had a model of the locomotive sent to him in Russia. All the same, no other engineers seem to have followed up

Blenkinsop's experiments, mainly because of the expense of installing the rack rails. None of them survive today.

In 1813 the story moves back to the north-east, though even Blenkinsop's development had north-east connections because his colliery owners, the Brandlings, were a Northumberland family. In that year William Hedley, viewer of Wylam colliery, successfully built a smooth wheeled engine. The wagon way at Wylam had now been laid with cast iron rails, replacing the wooden ones of Stephenson's boyhood, and Hedley's engines ran successfully for many years. Two of his later ones, dating from 1828 and 1832, were called the *Puffing Billy* and *Wylam Dilly* and are the two earliest locomotives in existence. (One is in London at the Science Museum and the other is at the Royal Scottish Museum in Edinburgh.) Hedley's supporters claimed he'd solved the problem of smooth wheels running on smooth tracks, therefore making Blenkinsop's rack idea obsolescent, but of course Trevithick at Penydaren had done the same nine years earlier.

There were many other lesser known colliery engineers working away, mostly unsuccessfully, trying to produce their own forms of steam locomotive. In Whitehaven, where the local collieries had been amongst the first to use the Newcomen engine, a locomotive was built in 1812, known locally as the Iron Horse, but this, like so many before and after, tore up the rails.

News travelled fast between engineers in rival collieries and when it didn't, owners had no scruples about sending out spies. Once when Sir James Lowther, owner of the Whitehaven mines, thought that the north-eastern lads had got ahead he sent across his leading engineer, Carlisle Spedding, disguised as an ordinary pitman going under the name of Dan. Unfortunately he was injured by an explosion of fire damp. Sir James naturally ordered the best medical advice in Newcastle to attend him – which was when it was realised Dan was no ordinary miner.

The north east remained the home of most new developments in the mining industry and it was here in 1812 that William Chapman invented a self-hauling chain engine which pulled itself along. William Brunton, another north-easterner, produced an even more eccentric engine which 'walked', at least it trundled itself along on sticking-out legs. Neither was successful. By around 1813 most colliery engineers were beginning to give up, sticking in the main to horses plus fixed engines for the hills. Even as late as 1830 the mainstream of the engineering and scientific professions were of the opinion that the iron horse had no future.

They had good reasons for thinking so. Since Trevithick's first attempts nobody had really solved the many technical problems – certainly not in one engine. The basic problems were the lack of sufficient steam power, the jerky motion caused by the roughly made gear wheels which made most engines fall to pieces, the difficulty of regulating the valves and gears to put an engine into reverse, the overall heaviness of the machine, its slowness, the brittle nature of the cast iron rails. It needed a man of vision and action and perseverance even to attempt to solve any one of these problems.

In 1814 George Stephenson was thirty-three years old. He had worked his way slowly but steadily up to the position of enginewright in charge of the engine work for his employers, the Grand Allies. He was living in his cottage at West Moor, beside Killingworth Colliery. His son Robert, who was still being looked after by his sister, was eleven and by now had just started at Dr Bruce's Academy.

Other local colliery owners, like the Brandlings and Blackett, had already allowed their enginewrights and viewers to experiment with a locomotive, so it was natural that the Grand Allies should do the same. It was in 1814 that George Stephenson produced his first locomotive, a little late considering so many local engineers had already tried, and a little bit like most of the locomotives they'd already produced. But a commendable effort, considering he was a late starter, a self-taught engineer, with none of their educational advantages.

He called his engine the *Blucher*, which one must presume took its name from the Prussian general who was at that time helping the British to turn the tide against Napoleon. All the same, it's a surprisingly foreign name for Stephenson to have given his first engine. Perhaps it was christened by Sir Thomas Liddell, the Grand Ally who encouraged Stephenson to start its construction. In later Northumbrian dialect, 'Blucher' became a term of passing contempt for anything big, awkward and brutish.

It first ran on 25 July 1814, on the Killingworth colliery wagon way outside Stephenson's West Moor cottage, and quite a crowd turned up to watch its progress. No contemporary drawings exist but Nicholas Wood, who wrote about it later, described it as having two cylinders, a boiler eight feet long, flanged wheels and ran on smooth edged rails. It pulled eight wagons, weighing thirty tons, at the rate of four miles an hour.

George's elder brother James was the first driver of the *Blucher*. He seems to have followed George round the various collieries as George progressed over the years. George named one of his stationary engines the *Jimmy* after him. Like George, he lived in a cottage beside the Killingworth wagon way with his wife, a large, buxom woman called Jinnie. According to one Thomas Summerside, who knew the Stephensons at the time and some fifty years later wrote a delightful memoir of those early days, *Blucher* used to break down frequently on its journey up and down the line. Jinnie was usually the one called out to give it a shove, 'Come away Jinnie and put your shoulder to her,' so her husband would shout. Then she would go back to her work beside the track, cutting the grass to feed her cows. She must have been a busy woman. It was also her job first thing in the morning at four o'clock to get up and light a fire in *Blucher*'s grate to get the steam going.

The *Blucher* was constantly developed as George Stephenson thought of new improvements. To try and get up more power and to lessen the noise of the escaping steam he turned the exhaust into the chimney and produced what became known as the blast pipe. Arguments raged for many years amongst the experts about whether this was Stephenson's own idea, or if he had seen someone else doing it, or whether perhaps he'd discovered it by accident, not realising it would increase the steam power.

Other developments on *Blucher* included new types of valves and the introduction of connecting rods on the wheels which solved some of the problems caused by having so many roughly made gears. This was the first use of such a system, a system which became a familiar sight on all steam engines for decades. Stephenson himself later abandoned it.

Two other locomotives soon appeared incorporating the new devices, both with equally impressive names. One was named *Wellington*, for obvious reasons, and the other *My Lord*. This wasn't a piece of religious genuflecting by Stephenson, who was never a churchgoer despite what many Victorians later liked to think. He was simply keeping in with his boss, Sir Thomas Liddell, who'd just been made Lord Ravensworth.

Unlike so many engineers before him who had tended to

concentrate on one side of locomotive making and give up when ancillary problems arose, Stephenson was all the time trying to develop suitably strong rails. His own engines, despite being lighter and faster, were still tearing up the track. His bosses allowed him to spend two days a week at a local Newcastle ironworks run by William Losh where he experimented on producing new types of rails. Together he and Losh patented their own make of cast iron rails and the whole of the Killingworth wagon way was relaid with them.

Losh was a highly cultivated gentleman, a friend of Humboldt, the great German naturalist and explorer who was currently being read and followed with great excitement by most of England's educated classes. Losh was known throughout Tyneside and was one of the leading gentleman defenders of George during the safety lamp row. For George's two days a week at his ironworks Losh paid him £100 per annum – which didn't affect George's £100 a year from the Grand Allies, though it reduced his time with them. George had therefore good reason to be grateful to William Losh.

The success of his Killingworth engines and his Losh–Stephenson rails led to a demand for similar lines elsewhere. Over the next five or six years Stephenson built sixteen engines at Killingworth, most being used locally but some going to Scotland in 1817 for the Duke of Portland's wagon way from Kilmarnock to Troon.

The first entirely new line laid out by George Stephenson was begun in 1819 at Hetton colliery, near Newcastle. It was eight miles long and three fixed engines provided the motive power over a hilly one-and-a-half-mile stretch, self-acting planes for three miles and the rest consisted of locomotives. There's a most elaborate description of the Hetton line by two German engineers who devoted twenty-two pages to it in a book they brought out in 1826. (A French translation came out in 1830.) They not only quoted Stephenson's measurements for each length, they paced each section out by foot to make sure he was right.

Engineers were soon coming from all over the country to see the Killingworth engines. Robert Stevenson, grandfather of Robert Louis, an eminent civil engineer in Edinburgh, wrote in 1818 that 'Some of the most striking improvements in the system of railways are the patent inventions of Mr Stephenson of Newcastle, particularly of his Locomotive Engines.'

It's interesting to note, despite the difficulty of stage coach travel, how quickly engineers in Russia, France, Germany and elsewhere got to know about scientific developments. Stephenson had begun to corner the market in the use and production of colliery locomotives, all of it rather primitive and experimental, but there were enough people still interested in the subject to come and see his progress. He was late in the field, compared with someone like Trevithick. When George started in 1814 others had given up, leaving clues for him to see but no definite guidelines. From 1814 until 1826 there are no records of anyone but Stephenson building any new locomotive engines. He produced his at such speed, each with a new development, that others waited and wondered, most either refusing to believe the stories they were hearing or convinced that it would all end in disaster once again.

Despite the mass of books and pamphlets which have been produced on the early history of railways, these vital years in George's development, when he produced those first sixteen engines at Killingworth, are still shrouded in some mystery. From 1814, with the appearance of *Blucher*, to around 1820 or 1821, no one has yet been able to tabulate exactly the stages in George's locomotive designs. Years later he did go on at great length about his Killingworth days but it was usually the same old story about his hard struggle with everyone against him. He himself seems to have forgotten how each process was reached. It was all a matter of native, brilliant genius, according to George in later life, and according to the Smiles' accounts. In reality, his progress was probably extremely rough and ready, like his safety lamp experiments, with a lot of hammering one way, then hammering the other way, till he found one way went better than another.

It was a period when George was on his own, a rather eccentric colliery engineer working away in comparative isolation. We have to rely on foreign visitors for odd details and reports, foreign engineers doing their technical grand tour, drawn to Killingworth by rumours of this odd character and his odd machines, hoping for an amusing interlude before going on to study the work of the truly great engineers of the day like Rennie and Telford, who were well known throughout Europe.

Yet there was a large lay audience willing to watch any new

spectacle, if just for the chance of seeing a few accidents or other excitements. Crowds had always gathered for any new or strange inventions. To cater for the better informed of the general public there began to appear on the scene several writers propagating and publicising the ideas of railways, in England, Europe and in North America. Fortunately for Stephenson, one of them was his closest friend and supporter, Nicholas Wood. He kept minute records of all George's experiments, lectured and wrote extensively on the subject, but it wasn't until 1825 that he produced his massive *Practical Treatise on Rail-Roads*.

Stephenson was fortunate in several ways, though he was the last person to admit such a thing. He was able to build on what had gone before, to see the mistakes of others and correct them. He was fortunate in being born in the north east, the hub of colliery wagon ways and the home of many locomotive pioneers whose experiments he must have seen at first hand. And most important of all, he benefited from the many improvements in boilers and rails which others had made in the ten years or so since Trevithick's first attempts.

However, the vast majority of those who did know about locomotives looked upon them as a purely local phenomenon, a specialist means of private transportation, confined completely to the colliery areas. Until 1825 nobody had attempted a public railway using locomotives. Until 1825 Stephenson's ten years of continuous locomotive developments had failed to produce any real national interest. His work was known locally to the colliery public in the north east but nationally only to those few interested in colliery engineering.

The growing band of writers on the subject were looked upon as dotty as the engineers themselves. Thomas Gray devoted twenty years of his life to writing about railways but was considered slightly touched and died in poverty. None of his ideas were ever put in practice, though we now realise that most of them were eminently sensible. The idea of these funny colliery engines covering the whole country came to him suddenly in 1816 and he rushed to put pen to paper, shaking with the brilliance of his own genius. 'He shut himself up in his room, secluded from his wife and relatives, declining to give them any information on the subject of his mysterious studies, beyond assurance that his scheme "would revolutionise the whole face of the material world". The result was a pamphlet which came out in 1820. Amongst other things, he drew a rail map of Britain with the big towns connected which looks little different from today's rail maps, and schemed out six lane tracks on the main lines and created turntables.

One of his motives was to relieve the suffering of horses on the fast postchaise routes. He quoted a coach proprietor as saying that on average one horse was lost every two hundred miles. It was very common, so he stated, for the legs of horses to be snapped in two while being whipped on to keep up the timetables and beat the rival coach proprietors. This cruelty to horses was immediately to be forgotten once railways did take over and the old coach era was instantly glamorised and enshrined for ever. The romance lives on in Christmas cards. The reality of the horsedrawn coach was cruel, uncomfortable, slow, cumbersome and expensive. In his pamphlet, Gray worked out that the upkeep of the 500,000 horses then employed on the turnpike roads cost a total of £173 million over a twelve-year period. By comparison he estimated that 10,000 steam engines could be run on the same routes for only £35 million.

Gray's plans for national railways were good, but unfortunately when it came to deciding which type of locomotive engine should pull them he picked a loser. He was a fan of Blenkinsop and his racked engine long after Stephenson had proved that his engines were much more efficient. He couldn't believe, along with so many others, that smooth wheels could run on smooth rails.

The trouble with most of the literary advocates of railways was that they could well see the benefits of railways – reducing unemployment was always mentioned, plus bringing fresh vegetables to the big towns – but they all differed, or were very hazy, about the precise mechanical means. They waxed romantic about locomotives easing the strain on horses and hay caused by the long drawn out Napoleonic wars, but they argued as to which locomotive would bring about the miracle. The miracle was needed because sending goods by the new canals, the only form of bulk transport, was proving slow and crowded. One minor advantage of locomotives over canals, which was seriously put forward in the 1820s, was that railways would cut down the pilfering. Apparently there was fiddling on a mammoth scale from the bales of wool as they lay in the barges. The trick was to steal half a bale and then let in some water which would be absorbed to make up the original weight.

One writer who did pick the winner, and for many years was at the forefront of railway promotion, was William James. He was a solicitor from Henley-in-Arden who became a highly successful London land agent and entrepreneur. He was forever setting up schemes for bridges, canals and railways and toured the country giving speeches, looking at sites, meeting engineers. He came to see Stephenson at Killingworth in 1821, having been to see Blenkinsop's racked engine at Leeds and many others, and was extremely impressed. Nicholas Wood was already Stephenson's technical Boswell, noting his engines in great detail, but James had a more popular and national following, He knew members of the royal family and had done jobs for the Archbishop of Canterbury. George was very impressed.

Public interest in railways had taken a long time to grow, but by the 1820s more and more people outside the purely colliery world were becoming seriously intrigued by its possibilities. One of these was a wool merchant in Darlington called Edward Pease, who had his own little plans for a railway. No one knows exactly how George Stephenson first came to Edward Pease's attention, though William James later claimed to have started it all. Certainly he wrote a glowing letter to Pease, after he'd been to Killingworth, in which he praised all Stephenson's works.

> The Locomotive Engine of Mr Stephenson is superior beyond all comparison to all other inventions I have seen. Next to the immortal Watt, I consider Stephenson's Merit in the invention of this Engine.

It was certainly high praise and no doubt Mr Pease was greatly encouraged by it, but Edward Pease had already come across Stephenson himself. Mr Pease was neither one of the romantic school of railway writers, nor yet another colliery owner trying to cut his costs. He was rather a strange figure indeed to be caught up in railways, but the major credit for backing George Stephenson and for the birth of what was to become known as the world's first public railway must be given to Edward Pease of Darlington.

# 4

# PICKING UP THE PEASES

Darlington is a small town some thirty miles due south of Newcastle and in 1825 it had a population of just over five thousand. It was known in the north east as a thriving little wool centre, with a good line in flax spinning, but as far as the nation went nobody knew or cared much about Darlington. How on earth then did it organise itself together and become the home of the world's railways?

Steering the necessary bills through parliament, as the canal builders had found, was a job which called for a great deal of money, the best lawyers and the best establishment, parliamentary and aristocratic contacts. Why wasn't the job done by Birmingham, by Manchester or Liverpool or Glasgow or Edinburgh, large towns with influential industrialists, wealthy merchants and famous MPs? Come to that, what was London doing?

Bailey, in his history of County Durham in 1810, speaks of Darlington as 'having long been famous for its huckaback diapers'. The fame of its huckaback diapers, alas, doesn't draw many tourists to Darlington today. The use of the word diaper is interesting, at least to Americans, but in 1810 it referred simply to table napkins not to babies' nappies. Huckaback was a high quality linen. Behind the huckaback diaper trade was a group of Quakers. Behind the introduction of the railway was a group of Quakers. The Quakers, in a word, were the reason why Darlington beat every other town in Britain; managed despite its smallness to conquer parliament and raise the money, and made Darlington the only true begetter of the world's railways.

For almost a hundred years there had been an interconnected group of Quaker families living in Darlington. The Peases themselves had originally come over the border from Yorkshire. Edward Pease was born in Darlington in 1767 and after attending a Quaker boarding school near Leeds he became apprenticed at fourteen in the family wool business. Like his father before him, he travelled by horse round the north and in Scotland, visiting farmers and markets, buying up the raw wool. Under him, the family wool business expanded to include a few other interests, such as some local collieries, but he had remained as he'd begun, a small town merchant living in a modest three storey, flat fronted house in a street called Northgate, a street occupied by other local merchants, by shops and by warehouses. He hadn't become a small-time landed squire, moving out and buying an estate like other moderately successful merchants. He was content to be a small-time merchant, living if not over the shop then right beside the heart of his business. Number 73 Northgate, Darlington, was his home for sixty years and it was here that he brought up his family of eight. And it was here that he was first visited by George Stephenson.

It's hard to know what Stephenson must have thought about meeting a Quaker. They were looked upon, with some justification, as very odd people. Stephenson never allied himself with any church and doesn't seem to have been interested in religion. Nonetheless, he must have been well aware of some of the myths and legends about the Quakers, perhaps even a few of the facts.

The Quakers arose in England during the civil war, part of the Puritan backlash. George Fox, their founder, was against all High Church and even Low Church ceremonies. He wanted none of it, nor priests, nor hierarchy nor any dogma. He wanted a direct communion with God, even if it took place alone and in silence. His followers called themselves Children of Light. It wasn't until 1650, three years after their foundation, that they became known as Quakers. It started when a judge in Derby referred to them scornfully as 'quaking with emotion' during their meetings. Soon afterwards the Quakers themselves started using the name, though their official name was and still is the Society of Friends.

They had continuous troubles with judges because one of their obsessions was a refusal to swear any sort of oath. This precluded them from any public office, from going to Oxford or Cambridge, or going into Parliament. They refused to pay church taxes or tithes, to serve in the army, to acknowledge the monarch as being superior to anyone else, to recognise any saints, to call anyone sir or give anyone any sort of title. They called everyone thee or thou. No one on this earth should be more equal than anyone else. But it led them into many dotty ideas and beliefs. They would never take off their hats, either for ladies or the king, as they could take their hats off only for God, not man. A true old style Quaker wouldn't dance, gamble, go to the theatre or have anything to do with music. Such activities, so they believed, could give rise to sensual thoughts.

They shunned gaudy dress, fancy furniture, any ostentation including colours, remaining faithful through the centuries to their black or grey Puritan clothes. They never had their portraits painted because that was vanity. Edward Pease, much later on, was one of the first Quakers to be persuaded to have his likeness captured for posterity. He was finally persuaded that having a photograph taken wasn't a sin. The camera, so it was argued, unlike an artist, doesn't lie.

Their passion for equality led them to the forefront of most reforming movements and they were prominent in all the nineteenth-century campaigns against social ills, as one might expect. The Fry family, apart from being model employers, worked hard for factory reforms, to stop the employment of children and for prison reform. There were Quaker leaders amongst the anti-slavery movement and in 1824, at the height of the Stockton–Darlington railway campaign, Edward Pease was popping back and forward to France, lobbying French MPs and merchants about the slave trade, though he didn't get very far. When Quakers went abroad, like William Penn in Pennsylvania, they tried to create model societies.

It was in business that the Quakers' many virtues were seen at their best. Rather surprisingly they didn't consider it a sin to make money. Idleness, sitting around doing nothing, or even worse, sitting around and enjoying yourself, that was the sin. Making money was honourable, as long as it didn't become an end in itself. The ultimate object of making money was to do good with it. You must never make money by doing bad. Because of this Quakers never dealt in wines or spirits, though they could be brewers. (Beer was harmless, so it was thought, which was true in the days when it was compared with the nation's drinking water.) They never made money by exploiting labour or by involving themselves in anything to do with armaments, though some of the Pease family had managed to fudge the line a bit back in 1744 when they supplied 1600 woollen waistcoats for the Duke of

Cumberland's army. The Darlington Quakers, so it was thought in some Quaker circles, were a bit more worldly than some of the others, less isolated, more involved in the community. Even so, Edward Pease himself was a Quaker of the old school. It was his children who were more broad minded.

In 1817 Edward Pease was fifty. In his diaries he was already castigating himself for what he considered his profligate youth, regretting the time he'd spent hunting and following other country pursuits. From then on he allowed himself no pleasures, however innocent, except gardening. Even then, in later years, his conscience began to trouble him about the self-indulgence inherent in raising prize flowers, worrying about the pleasure it was giving him. His diaries are full of his tortured soul searchings.

It is not surprising then that to ordinary pleasure-loving folk Quakers were rather funny people. In the previous century their extreme moral stands had led to persecution. Now they were tolerated, if rather mocked, behind their backs, though in some quarters they were still actively disliked for their prissiness and unrelaxing moral rectitude.

But in business, that was different. There was no one you could possibly trust more than an upright, moralising Quaker. Throughout the nineteenth century the more go-ahead Quaker families, like the Peases, were branching out into the new industrial and commercial enterprises of the local community and becoming model captains of industry. There was almost a Moral Mafia at work, with Quaker biscuit manufacturers being financed by their relations, the Quaker bankers. In a time of quick money, madcap schemes, ridiculous investments, one could be sure that if Quakers were involved, then the venture was sound. The Quaker businessmen were the first to establish the idea of fixed prices for retail goods. They maintained that the ignorance of the public must not be exploited. Often when a Quaker came up with a new invention he didn't patent it on principle, letting the community benefit as a whole. Abraham Darby, who discovered how to smelt iron with coal, never patented his revolutionary system. Many of the Quaker iron and steel masters in Sheffield produced new ideas and processes and gave them as presents to their rivals. As businessmen, the Quakers were irreproachable in their integrity. And this integrity paid good dividends. They built huge businesses which are still household names today – Cadbury, Fry, Rowntree,

Huntley and Palmer, Bryant and May. In the City, where they were particularly strong, they founded many banks, two of which eventually became Barclays and Lloyds, two out of today's big Four. The City's biggest present day accountants, Price Waterhouse, owed its success to Quaker founders.

Edward Pease might have been an unknown northern merchant in 1817 but it was the simple fact that he was a Quaker which made people, even those who'd never heard of him, think twice about his strange-sounding scheme. For it was in the year 1817 that he decided to withdraw from fulltime business and devote himself and his conscience to two causes. There was firstly the anti-slavery movement. The fact that from Darlington he managed to obtain interviews with French cabinet ministers in order to castigate them shows perseverance as well as good contacts.

His other project was the railway, a project which would benefit his home area, helping merchants and workers alike. He knew that a new and cheap form of transport between the inland coal mines of South Durham and the sea at the mouth of the Tees would bring down the price of coal for householders and manufacturers and would stimulate industry throughout Teeside. Even at Darlington, which was only twelve miles or so from the collieries and halfway to the sea, the major item in the cost of coal was the carriage.

Tyne coal, further to the north, was dominating the national market and monopolising the London trade, partly due to the fact that so many of their coal mines were situated right on the banks of the Tyne. The inland South Durham coalfield had always been beset with costly transport problems. Cheaper coal, therefore, would not only help the manufacturers of Darlington and Stockton but create a thriving export trade.

Edward Pease wasn't the first to think of a way of reducing the transport costs for coal. As early as 1768 there had been a canal planned from the coal fields across to Stockton, the highest navigable point on the Tees. James Brindley himself had been consulted, the engineer who had designed the Duke of Bridgwater's canal in 1759. A survey was made and the cost was estimated at £63,722. But nothing was done.

In 1810, at a dinner in Stockton to celebrate the opening of a short channel which had been cut to improve navigation on the Tees (a cut only 210 yards long) the whole subject of a canal came up once again. Edward Pease was one of those who argued that a horsedrawn tramway would be cheaper, direct from the coal mouth via Darlington to the Tees. Pease and some of his fellow Darlington merchants present were very keen on a tramway. Stockton, being a port, favoured a canal. Back in Darlington, Pease and his friends got up a committee which eventually asked the Scotsman John Rennie, one of the leading engineers of the day, to report on the best means of communication. Rennie was busy elsewhere building Waterloo Bridge in London and he did not report until 1813. And when he did, he recommended a canal as being best, producing an estimate of £205,618, the highest estimate so far.

Once again, nothing was done, though this time there were good reasons for it. The country was at war against France and the USA and money and materials were very scarce.

In May 1818 some merchants in Stockton decided to finance another canal survey and this time the survey advised a canal direct from the collieries to Stockton, by-passing Darlington. This was admittedly the shortest distance, the previous canal surveys having proposed a loop to take in Darlington, but it naturally didn't appeal to the good merchants of Darlington. They didn't want to be left out. This more than anything else must have upset Pease, being concerned as he was with the good of Darlington, though his exact reactions can only be guessed at. (Unfortunately his diaries are complete only from the year 1838 onwards, thereby depriving the history of railways of one of its most important firsthand sources.)

In mid-1818, Edward Pease and a group of other Quaker merchants in Darlington, most of whom he was related to, decided to get up their own committee to form a public horsedrawn railway, not a canal. It was to be called the Stockton and Darlington Railway. They put the name Stockton first, even though the committee's headquarters were in Darlington, to try to appease the canal lobby in Stockton. All the same, the Darlington lobby itself was for a time divided. Jonathan Backhouse, Darlington's leading banker and by all accounts the single most important citizen of Darlington (having more money than Edward Pease) was in favour of a railway from the collieries to Darlington, then a canal to Stockton. Pease was completely against a broken line of communication and managed, being a man of great strength and determination, to persuade Backhouse to change his mind. Backhouse was a Quaker, which helped, and his mother was a Pease, which also helped. He himself was married to a Gurney from Norwich, the same Quaker family into which Edward Pease's son Joseph married. There were no arguments – just a discussion within the family.

A surveyor was contacted and his early reports were so in favour of a railway line, all the way, that Backhouse's remaining qualms disappeared. This survey was done by a Welsh engineer called George Overton, a relation of one of the promoters and a man with long experience in laying down iron tramways in South Wales. It was he who had built the line at Penydaren, where Trevithick's locomotive had been tried in 1804.

Around the same time as Overton was doing his survey, and for some time afterwards, the committee was also taking advice from Robert Stevenson, the noted Edinburgh engineer. He'd recently built the Bell Rock Lighthouse, which doesn't sound the ideal training for a railway engineer, but in those days, when there was no such profession as a civil engineer, any sort of engineer was looked upon as good enough to give advice on railways. He was, as we know, a railway fan and was in the process of writing the pamphlet on railways, the one in which he wrote about George Stephenson's good work at Killingworth. Perhaps he might have mentioned George's name to Pease, even at this early stage.

In a letter dated 22 December 1818, Robert Stevenson wrote from Edinburgh to say he was 'much gratified' by the committee's request for his help and described their scheme as one of 'importance and consequence'. He advised against 'calling in any other engineer' but to press on as quickly as possible with their present survey if they wanted the bill before the coming session of parliament.

The reference to 'any other engineer' was presumably a dig at John Rennie, a deadly rival of Stevenson's, who had once again been contacted, even though he still favoured a canal. Rennie was much less diplomatic in his reply to the committee. He was patently annoyed at being suggested in the same breath as Stevenson and considered himself a definite cut above such a trifling enterprise. In his reply dated 26 December 1818, he says that he is far too busy with numerous public works 'of infinitely greater magnitude and importance than the Darlington Railway'.

Robert Stevenson did come down from Edinburgh to have a look at the proposed Darlington line. It is not known if he ever produced a written report or merely gave his considered opinion. Stevenson and Rennie were national figures, unlike Overton who was doing all the donkey work, so presumably the committee were anxious to involve either of them in the scheme for prestige reasons.

The Overton survey went quickly ahead and was greeted with delight by Pease and the promoters. His estimate of the cost of the railway, to run fifty-one miles in all, including branches, was £124,000. A general meeting of the Stockton and Darlington Railway committee was held in Darlington on 13 November 1818, the date usually looked upon as the official founding date of the company, in which it was decided to open a list of subscribers and go for an act of parliament.

Jonathan Backhouse gave a brilliant speech at this meeting, analysing all the possible revenue but got rather carried away, as did several others, about the likely financial success of the railway. There was talk of a return for the investors of fifteen per cent. Edward Pease, though a less brilliant speaker, insisted that in his opinion the project was perfectly safe but all he would assure subscribers was a return of five per cent. It was his more sober, sounder realism which in the event persuaded many people to subscribe.

The original list of subscribers, announced in December 1818, makes interesting reading. It teems with members of the Pease family, four in all, and Backhouses. Edward Pease himself put up £5,000 while Jonathan Backhouse put up £10,000, but the largest single subscription came from Joseph Gurney, the Quaker banker from Norwich who was related to both of there. He subscribed £14,000. The only London subscription of any size was £10,000 from Thomas Richardson, a wealthy City banker, yet another Quaker, this time Edward Pease's cousin.

The first chairman of the world's first public railway was Thomas Meynell. He missed the earlier committee meetings but wrote letters of encouragement and subscribed £3,000 when the list opened. He wasn't a Quaker, as far as can be deduced from the few scraps known about his life. He was a well-known local landowner from Yarm, near Darlington, and this made him very important to the company. The gentry and aristocracy, unlike the town's merchants and bankers, were to a man against the very idea of a railway. They didn't want such a horrid thing going through their estates. Meynell was almost the only landowner who approved of the scheme and so was vital as a figurehead. (He resigned his chairmanship in 1828 after the line had successfully been opened because he objected to a branch extension to Middlesbrough.)

Over threequarters of the original £120,000 subscribed came from the Darlington area – the rest from Norwich, London and Stockton. To keep up the appearances of it being a joint Darlington and Stockton concern, one of the company's solicitors was Leonard Raisbeck, one of Stockton's most respected citizens. He was in favour personally of the railways and subscribed £1,000, but his main use was in encouraging the people of Stockton to see that a public railway would benefit everything in the region. He looked after the legal problems at the Stockton end of the line but his duties were mainly honorary. (He resigned in 1828 with Meynell.) It was the company's other solicitor, Francis Mewburn of Darlington (subscription £300) who did most of the company's work and in 1819 he was dispatched to London to start the long and arduous job of preparing a suitable bill for parliament.

The main point of getting an act through parliament, which was the problem all the canal promoters had faced, was to enable the railway promoters to buy up the necessary land on their proposed route. Landowners naturally objected to this and usually managed to mount their own opposition in parliament. So it was necessary for the promoters to try to come to terms with as many landowners as possible beforehand. The private colliery wagon ways had never had problems on this scale. In the main, they ran on land already the property of the colliery owners.

Not only were the majority of the local landowners against any terms, their more vociferous members happened to be active members of the House of Lords who were personally going to see that the bill wasn't passed. The two strongest opponents were the Earl of Darlington (later the Duke of Cleveland) and Lord Eldon. Lord Darlington wrote to the company in February, 1819, to say that their scheme was 'harsh and oppressive and injurious to the interests of the country through which it is intended that the railway shall pass'. What he was really worried about was that the railway would go right through his fox covers.

Lord Eldon also happened to be lord chancellor and he went through the bill very carefully, making copious notes in the margin, most of them showing that he didn't quite understand what a railway was. Earl Grey, later prime minister, noticed him one morning during prayers in the House of Lords on his knees but with one eye open, making notes on his copy of the bill.

In February 1819, Edward Pease and five other promoters came down to London to canvass members of parliament. At night they went out in pairs to call on MPs at their homes. In later life, one of the promoters, a man called William Chaytor, who was not a Quaker, used to relate that his canvassing partner was Benjamin Flounders, one of the diehard Quakers who refused to accompany him to people's houses because he said that Chaytor's clothes were scruffy and his old beaver hat too seedy.

Mr Mewburn, in charge of all the legal work, wrote later that 'the difficulties, pains and anguish which I endured during my sojourn in London while soliciting the bill can scarcely be conceived'. He did manage to get a brief interview with Lord Eldon the lord chancellor but had to report to Edward Pease that it was fruitless. 'He is too sly an old fox to give his consent to one line or another.'

But the very fact of a group of such obviously solid and respectable and eminently sensible Quakers being in town on such a strange but intriguing errand began to convince several neutral members that their scheme might not be as daft as it sounded. The Earl of Darlington was so convinced that the bill hadn't a chance that he'd decided to stay at home, but the day before the second reading, his London solicitor sent an urgent message to say that 'the Quakers had made more ground' than anyone had expected and that he should come at once. He was out hunting when the messenger arrived and servants had to go on a cross-country jaunt to find him. He caught the overnight postchaise, swearing and cursing, and at four the next day was seen canvassing support in the lobby of the House of Lords.

The bill was defeated by 106 votes to 93, a majority of only thirteen, much much closer than anyone had expected. One lord was heard to remark later that 'if the Quakers in these times when nobody knows anything about railways can raise up such a phalanx as they have done on this occasion, I should recommend the country gentlemen to be very wary how they oppose them.'

The Quakers were very greatly encouraged and George Overton was induced to do a second survey. He wasn't at first very keen, never having had such drawn-out troubles or parliamentary squabbles over his colliery wagon ways back in South Wales. Also he was displeased when he heard that once again the company had sought the advice of Robert Stevenson in Edinburgh. However, he agreed to prepare a second survey for a fee of £120, payable whether or not the bill was passed.

This time Overton's survey route avoided most of Lord Darlington's land, and his beloved fox covers, and the company managed to come to a financial understanding. They were a bit worried to find that in by-passing Lord Darlington's land Overton was planning to cross the estate of another noble Lord, Lord Barrington, but he too was eventually bought over. It was obvious that with the first attempt being so close, the second had a good chance of being passed, so many landowners decided to extract as high a price as possible while they were still in a position of strength. The company even had to buy up two local quarries from the Misses Hale, which they didn't want, because they insisted that the railway would place their collieries 'in a state of inferiority as compared with other collieries', whatever that meant. The turnpike road commissioners also had to be persuaded not to raise any opposition.

The company produced a handsome prospectus with a tinted engraving of the line by Thomas Bewick, the famous Newcastle engraver. (Newcastle, after London, was producing the country's best wood engravings at this period.) It was one of the many extra expenses of the new bill, most of which went in legal fees and settling the landowners. Just before it went before the House in 1821 (having been delayed a year due to the illness and death of George III) Mr Mewburn found that he was around £10,000 short. Parliamentary standing orders of the day required that four-fifths of the share capital of a company should be subscribed before a bill went into committee. Mr Mewburn went back to the Gurney bankers in Norwich, but they would advance no more money, neither would anyone in the City. He wrote to Pease in Darlington, saying he would have to return home unless he got the money in three days. No one else in Darlington or Stockton was prepared to advance any more money. So Edward Pease, out of his own pocket, gave the necessary £10,000, saving the railway at the last hour. In the minutes for 21 March 1821, it is recorded that it was up to Mr

Pease whether he looked upon this sum as 'a loan or as further shares in the intended railway'.

The bill, sixty-seven pages long, received its royal assent on 19 April 1821, by which time Edward Pease was virtually the head of the Stockton and Darlington Railway. He'd always been the strongest and most determined personality amongst the promoters. Now he had proved himself the largest single shareholder and the one who'd saved the company's future when all others had refused.

It was also on 19 April 1821 that George Stephenson came to visit Mr Pease at his home in Darlington.

This historic meeting later assumed legendary proportions and was much loved by Victorians. Popular magazines hammered up the story, making out that George was some sort of barefoot pitman who'd walked all the way from Newcastle to Darlington in order to try to see Mr Pease, the stern old Quaker. In some versions of the saga, Mr Pease won't see poor George at first, but comes down just as George is getting depressed and ready to go home, and grants him a short interview in the kitchen. He's rather suspicious of this burly, illiterate, broadly spoken, ill-dressed workman but is completely won over when George talks of his wonderful invention. Locomotives! At once old man Pease, having thought only of horsedrawn wagons up till then, is won over. And railways are born! The magazines and broadsheets of the 1850s and 60s even had drawings to go with the story, showing George with the Pease children, helping them with their tapestry. (George, being clever with his hands, is supposed to be showing them some new stitches.)

Samuel Smiles, with his 1857 biography, is usually blamed for all these exaggerated stories and it has to be admitted that some of the conversations he reports as having taken place between Pease and George Stephenson on their first momentous meeting do sound a trifle suspicious, owing as much perhaps to hindsight as to reality.

Mr Pease liked the appearance of his visitor. 'There was,' as he afterwards remarked, 'such an honest sensible look about him and he seemed so modest and unpretending. He spoke in the strong Northumbrian dialect of his district and described himself as "only the engine-wright at Killingworth."'

But Mr Pease was scarcely prepared for the bold assertions

made by his visitor, that the locomotive engine with which he had been working the Killingworth railway for many years was worth fifty horses. 'Come over to Killingworth,' said he, 'and see what my Blucher can do. Seeing is believing, sir.' And Mr Pease promised that on some early day he would go over to Killingworth and take a look at this wonderful machine that was to supersede horses.

On Mr Pease referring to the difficulties and opposition which the projectors of the railway had had to encounter, and the obstacles which still lay in their way, Stephenson said to him 'I think, sir, I have some knowledge of craniology and from what I see of your head, I feel sure that if you will fairly buckle to this railway, you are the man successfully to carry it through.' 'I think so too,' rejoined Mr Pease; 'and I may observe to thee, that if thou succeed in making this a good railway, thou may consider thy fortune as good as made.'

After Smiles' book had been published, Nicholas Wood came out with his version, saying that Smiles was wrong to say that the meeting had happened out of the air, all unarranged and spontaneous. According to Wood, who accompanied George on the famous day, an appointment had been made and Mr Pease knew they were coming. Wood also denies that they walked from Newcastle but said that in fact they caught a coach. He also adds the rather surprising detail that the coach took them to Stockton, not Darlington, and that they then proceeded to walk the twelve miles to Darlington along the line of the projected railway. It sounds a long and slightly unnecessary walk if they really had an appointment already made with Mr Pease in Darlington.

Mr Pease's own recollection of the meeting is not known, not until his missing diaries turn up, and it is not known what he knew of Stephenson prior to this meeting, if anything. It's difficult to believe he hadn't heard of Stephenson's engineering skill, with his closeness to Tyneside, or about the eight-mile Hetton colliery line which Stephenson was building at that time. Robert Stevenson, the Edinburgh engineer, might even have spoken of him. In the three years since the Darlington scheme had begun, George Stephenson's reputation had greatly increased and so had his locomotives and rails.

From the company's minutes it looks as if Pease had become unhappy with Overton and his survey, despite its success in parliament, and that Overton was becoming disenchanted by the project, despite having put up a large subscription himself of £2,000. Whatever the reason, once George Stephenson appeared on the scene, Overton is heard of no more.

The barefoot pitman image was of course all wrong at this stage. Stephenson was by now a highly experienced engine-wright with a leading group of colliery owners, with a good salary as well as financial interests in patents and other concerns, including by this time a colliery. (In December 1820 George took a twenty-one year lease on a colliery called Willow Bridge, he and a partner each putting up £700. It sounds as if he might have been using his £1,000 safety lamp prize money.) Both he and Wood, the colliery manager, were extremely busy men. It is unlikely they would have trailed to Darlington, or Stockton, purely on spec. Perhaps Pease had made it known he would like to see George, if only as an up and coming engineer whose advice might be worth hearing, just as he had previously contacted older and more established engineers like Robert Stevenson and Rennie.

Further complications about this first meeting have been added by some notes, dictated by George Stephenson, which have recently come into the hands of the Northumberland County Record Office (first published in 1973 in W.O. Skeat's book of Stephenson letters for the Institution of Mechanical Engineers). These notes, which contain several factual mistakes, certainly look as if they were dictated by George in his old age. In these notes George says that he applied to the Darlington company on the advice of his friends, having heard about their railway. He took the coach with Wood to Stockton (which agrees with the Wood version) where they tried to see Raisbeck, one of the company's solicitors. (As we know, Raisbeck was of minor importance but someone outside applying for a job was not to know this.) Raisbeck wasn't at home so they walked in the dark to Darlington to see Mr Pease and Mr Backhouse, the two leading directors. They saw Mr Pease next day and Stephenson handed over some letters of recommendation and explained the power of his locomotive engine.

This in many ways brings us back to the Smiles version – of Stephenson arriving out of the blue. Smiles had the cooperation of Robert Stephenson in writing his book and no doubt he had heard his father's account of the first meeting.

The true background to the meeting – how much of it was chance, accident or design – will probably never now be known, but it was as a result of this meeting that Edward Pease, the socially conscious Quaker, found a way of doing some permanent good to Darlington, and to the world.

# 5

# BUILDING THE DARLINGTON LINE

The meeting between Edward Pease and George Stephenson only became momentous in retrospect. At the time George was much busier elsewhere with other projects, as his letters show, and whether or not he harangued Pease with the brilliance of his locomotives, the official intention of the Stockton and Darlington Railway promoters was still plainly to use horsedrawn wagons. The line was perhaps going to be longer than any previous one, all of twenty-five miles, if it was ever built. It was planned to be public and open to all, thanks to the altruism of its Quaker backers, but to all intents and purposes it was just another horsedrawn colliery wagon way.

There was no sign that Pease had been instantly converted to locomotives but there is every sign that he'd been instantly converted to George Stephenson. The very next day, 20 April, he wrote to George at Killingworth telling him the good news that the bill had been passed and asking if he would be free to consider doing a survey. He was writing in his private capacity and this letter has not survived, but George's reply has been preserved and is still in Darlington, in the town's library. Its highly efficient and business-like tone suggests that perhaps George had hired himself a secretary by this stage instead of using assorted friends to cover up for his lack of writing skill.

Killingworth Colliery
April 28th, 1821

Edward Pease Esq.,
Sir,

I have been favoured with your letter of the 20 Inst & am glad to learn that the Bill has passed for the Darlington Rail Way.

I am much obliged by the favourable sentiments you express

towards me: & shall be happy if I can be of service in carrying into execution your plans.

From the nature of my engagement here and in the neighbourhood, I could not devote the whole of my time to your Rail Way, but I am willing to undertake the survey & mark out the best line of Way within the limits prescribed by the Act of Parliament and also, to assist the Committee with plans & estimates, and in letting to the different Contractors such work as they might judge it advisable to do by Contract and also to superintend the execution of the Work. And I am induced to recommend the whole being done by Contract under the superintendence of competent persons appointed by the Committee.

Were I to contract for the whole line of Road it would be necessary for me to do so at an advanced price upon the Sub Contractors, and it would also be necessary for the Committee to have some persons to superintend my undertaking. This would be attended by an extra expense, and the Committee would derive no advantage to compensate for it.

If you wish it, I will wait upon you at Darlington at an early opportunity when I can enter into more particulars as to remuneration &c &c

I remain yours
respectfully
GEO. STEPHENSON

George went to Darlington and in turn Pease, accompanied by Thomas Richardson (the London Quaker banker) went to see George's engines and rails at Killingworth. One of the first results of George's arrival on the Darlington scene was that he persuaded Pease to consider the sort of smooth metal rails which were being laid down on the Netton line. All George's locomotives had the flanges on their wheels and it was obvious that if he hoped eventually to persuade the company to use locomotives, not horses, he had to have the right sort of rails. But the main reasoning at this stage was that good metal rails rather than the old style wooden ones – a subject which provoked endless discussion and letters – would be longer lasting, for horsedrawn wagons or for anything else.

Most of the company were still thinking of horses and had always agreed with Overton, their previous surveyor, that locomotives would never be any good. Overton had witnessed the failure of Trevithick's locomotive at Penydaren and as late as 1825 he was writing: 'An engine on a public railroad would be a perpetual nuisance.'

On 25 May 1821, the company formally adopted a corporate seal, a drawing of a horse pulling four wagons along a railway line, and a company motto '*Periculum privatam utilitas publica*', meaning private risk for public service. The choice of motto reflected the Quaker influence and the company trademark showed publicly that they were well and truly wedded to horses.

Pease had become privately interested in the possibility of locomotives, ever since meeting George, but at this stage there was no apparent advantage in them as far as speed went. George's colliery engines did little more than four miles an hour, which was about half the speed the new steam boats were doing down the coast from London to Newcastle. (George's sister had taken one when she was rushing home to Newcastle, thinking she was about to be married.) One of the main objects of the Darlington railway had always been to get the coal to the coast as quickly as possible and into the steam boats. The sea, not road or canal or rail, was still the quickest way to get goods from the north east to London. George did put up his speeds during his many demonstrations at Killingworth for William James or for the Darlington promoters, but his biggest concern was to prove to visitors, by plying them with facts and figures compiled by Wood and himself, that his locomotives, however ungainly and strange they might look, were four times cheaper than horses.

In July 1821 George was officially appointed by the company to survey their line. Edward Pease sent him a copy of the company's decision along with his letter telling George the news. As usual, it was in the Quaker style, using thee and thou, and with the number not the name of the month at the top of the page:

Darlington, 7th mo. 28th, 1821.

ESTEEMED FRIEND, GEORGE STEPHENSON, – Annexed are some resolutions passed at our last general meeting. We beg thee to take them into consideration, and so soon as thou can'st name thy charge for effecting all they contain which attaches to thee as engineer, drop me a line. The resolutions are so definite and comprehensive, it does not seem needful to add more, than to request that as soon as the crops are off the ground, no time may be lost, provided nothing can be done in the meantime. In making the survey, it must be borne in mind that this is for a great public way, and to remain as long as any coal in the district remains. Its construction must be solid, and as little machinery introduced as possible – in fact, we wish thee to proceed in all thy levels, estimates, and calculations, with that care and economy which would influence thee if the work was thy own; and it would be well to let comparative estimates be formed, as to the expense of a double and single railway, and whether it be needful to have it only double in some parts, and what parts; also comparative estimates as to the expense of malleable or cast iron. We shall be glad to hear from thee soon, and I am, on behalf of the committee, thy assured friend

(Signed)      EDWARD PEASE

To this characteristic letter George sent the following reply:

EDWARD PEASE, ESQ.

Sir, – After carefully examining your favour, I find it impossible to form an accurate idea of what such a survey would cost, as not only the old line must be gone over, but all the other deviating parts, which will be equal to a double survey, and, indeed, it must be done in a very different manner from your former one, so as to enable me to make a correct measurement of all the cuts and batteries on the whole line. It would, I think, occupy me at least five weeks. My charge shall include all necessary assistance for the accomplishment of the survey, estimates of the expense of cuts and batteries on the different projected line, together with all remarks, reports, &c, of the same. Also the comparative cost of malleable iron and cast-iron rails, winning and preparing the blocks of stone, and all materials wanted to complete the line. I could not do this for less than £140, allowing me to be moderately paid. I assure you, in completing the undertaking, I will act with that economy which would influence me if the whole of the work was my own.

GEORGE STEPHENSON

KILLINGWORTH COLLIERY, August 2d, 1821.

PS. If it meet your approbation, I should like as well to be paid by the day, which would be 2 guineas together with travelling expenses. The other Surveyor that will accompany me, I could not offer him much less. I shall also want 2 men to attend to the levelling staves and two to the measuring Chain.

I think we could not well go on with the Survey till after the Corn harvest.

G.S.

Meynell, the chairman who later resigned, wasn't all that keen on appointing Stephenson to survey the route all over again, not when they already had a perfectly good survey which had been passed by parliament. Pease explained that more precise information was needed, such as an estimate of what local contractors would charge, and that the Overton survey still wasn't liked by certain landowners. It seems fairly obvious that Pease had already formed a very high opinion of his esteemed friend Stephenson and was determined to have him as the surveyor, perhaps already thinking of making him engineer.

On 15 October, when the corn had been fully gathered in, George started his survey. His chief assistant was John Dixon, who was twenty-six, a young man with good local connections. Dixon's grandfather had been one of those who had worked on a survey for a Stockton–Darlington canal some fifty years earlier and his great uncle had been Jeremiah Dixon, a noted surveyor and mathematician. Jeremiah Dixon was sent out to Pennsylvania in 1763 with another Englishman called Mason to measure the limits of the province of Pennsylvania. It was this line, separating The slave states from the free, which became known as the Mason and Dixon line.

John Dixon was the son of a local coal owner who'd sold out to Backhouse. He had started work as a clerk in the Backhouse bank, moving as a clerk to the railway company when it opened its first office in Darlington. He appears to have been a Quaker himself, as he was related to the Backhouse family, but whether he was or not, the Quakers considered him a good man to help, or perhaps keep an eye on, the still rather unknown Stephenson. They became the best of friends and colleagues. John Dixon was later to become one of the best known of the early railway engineers, one of George's many pupils who made good.

Robert, George's son, was appointed as the other main assistant. He was just eighteen but was withdrawn from his apprenticeship to Nicholas Wood, George's old friend and the manager at Killingworth, to join the survey. He had done two of his three years and was apparently very glad to give up having to go underground and escape from colliery life generally. George had wanted him to get the sort of professional engineering training he himself had never had – which meant colliery engineering. Although by this time George's main concern was locomotives, there was still no such person as a railway engineer to whom Robert could have been apprenticed. However, now was a chance for him to widen his experience, to help his father and to get out into the fresh air. George was always worried that Robert, like his mother, was suffering from poor health.

The weather was good and they finished the initial field work in just over two weeks, and by January 1822 George had his survey ready. He had managed to shorten Overton's route by just under four miles and had worked out ways of creating easier gradients. He was privately confident of being allowed to run locomotives on the line, though the company had still not considered such a suggestion. In a letter to William James in December 1821 he says, We fully expect to get the engines introduced on the Darlington Railway.'

James had become a national figure on railway matters, rushing round the country inspecting rails, surveying lines, holding meetings, encouraging people to set up railway committees. The motive power was to be horses plus stationary engines, but he was soon talking about locomotives. After his public encouragement of George's engines they had become family friends, exchanging many letters and affectionate greetings. In 1822 Robert, to his delight, was allowed to join William James in an initial survey for a line being proposed between Liverpool and Manchester. George obviously missed his son and wrote to James in October 1822 saying he'd like him back soon as he had so much work to do.

The work to be done was tremendous. Only four days after his survey had been presented George was appointed Engineer of the Stockton and Darlington Railway. He was still employed by the Grand Allies at Killingworth, doing the finishing off on the Hetton colliery line and he made it clear that he could spend little more than one week a month on the Darlington job. All the same, the company were willing to pay him £600 a year, including expenses, to be their engineer.

One of the most important problems still being discussed was the nature of the rails. It will be remembered that some time previously George had taken out a patent with William Losh for the manufacture of cast iron rails and had had them laid at Killingworth. Other collieries had ordered similar rails and the two of them must have been making a regular income in royalties. But in 1821 John Birkinshaw, an engineer at Bedlington iron works near Morpeth, had patented a new method of rolling wrought iron rails in fifteen feet lengths. George went to see these malleable rails and came to the conclusion that they were superior to his own invention. 'I think they will do away with the cast iron railways,' so he wrote to Robert Stevenson in Edinburgh, still an advisor to the company, though like Overton before him, George was becoming a bit disgruntled at having such a consultant in the background.

George recommended to the company that they should put down malleable rails, even though they were expensive and even though he personally would be the loser. 'To tell you the truth,' so he told the directors, 'although it would put £500 in my pockets to specify my own patent rails, I cannot do so after the experience I have had.' Smiles in his biography waxes lyrical about George's decision, seeing it as yet another shining example of George's amazing honesty and integrity. And so it was, although it could be said that at the same time he was breaking a moral obligation to Losh, his partner. All the contemporary and later reports give prominence to the same story and Michael Longridge (the owner of Bedlington works), who was given the order for the malleable rails, felt indebted to Stephenson for the rest of his life.

George was determined to have locomotives on the Darlington line. He now realised it could be the biggest project he'd ever been involved in, and he knew from his own experiments that malleable rails were by far the most suitable. A smaller man, interested in short term gain, might well have gone for the quick, easy money. But in the long term it was in his interests to have malleable rails. The canal owners, the turnpike road owners, the landowners, they were all blinded by their own interests in opposing railways. George, with his belief in the future of railways, had no doubts about choosing malleable rails and losing £500 in royalties for himself.

Both Stephenson and Pease were inspired by their belief in railways, even when it went against their own immediate interests. In his letters George is constantly plugging away at the idea of railways being the transport of the future. Judging by the company minutes, it is obvious that Pease was constantly dragging the rest of his directors with him, even at the risk of family differences. There was no unanimity from the board about George's recommendation for malleable rails. Several of them had their own vested interests in cast iron rails. It was with difficulty that Pease got them to agree to compromise, laying down two-thirds of the route in malleable (later it became four-fifths), using cast iron on the rest.

In building the railway George was truly a pioneer, facing problems that had been encountered by no engineer before, making his own rules, creating new professions, making decisions that were to stand for a hundred years – some of them to this very day. For example, the gauge he chose was 4ft 8 ½ ins, the same as it is today in Britain and in most of the world.

There is still some controversy among railway historians about where he got this odd width from, apart from it being the one he'd laid down at Killingworth. At one time it was said that all the early wagon ways were this width, taking it in turn from the width of the average cart on the ordinary roads, but recent research has shown that wagon ways varied in width in different parts of the country. On the Wylam wagon way, outside his home, the width is now thought to have been five feet. There is a nice theory that it was the Romans who first laid down 4ft 8½ ins as a standard cart width – using this width in the entrances to all their forts. As there were forts on Hadrian's Wall not far from George's birthplace, the width could have been handed down without anyone realising.

There is an added minor mystery in the fact that some contemporary documents about the Stockton and Darlington, and the Liverpool–Manchester which followed suit, state the width as being 4ft 8 ins. Yet later on, it was measured and found to be 4ft 8½ ins. No one knows where that extra half an inch crept in. However, there is no argument about the fact that it was Stephenson, in building the Stockton and Darlington, who chose what was to become the world's standard gauge.

George also had to decide about the problem of sleepers. He knew that horsedrawn traffic would still be used in part, if not all, so the rails had to be laid on blocks either side, not on transverse sleepers, allowing an open path down the middle for the horse. They naturally couldn't be expected to jump over the sleepers as if they were in a hurdle race. George did meticulous market research in his quest for the best sleeper blocks, as he did with the rails arid everything else.

He went down to London in early 1822 (his first trip to the capital as far as is known) to inspect and purchase some oak blocks which he ordered to be sent up by sea to the Tees. On the western end of the line, near the collieries, he had decided to use locally quarried stone blocks. Then he went to south Wales to order some cast iron rails which the board were still insisting must be used in part of the line. (His row with Losh over his preference for malleable rails must have been pretty serious to have made him go all the way to Wales rather than obtain them locally from Losh.)

In all the negotiations over prices and types of material to be used, in giving out the tenders and choosing the most suitable, George made all the major decisions. There are several of his letters from this period – dictated to secretaries or assistants – all very detailed, full of the latest prices and suppliers. If only he'd written just a few letters in his own hand we might have been able to see how he felt at this stage in his life. There is no letter to his beloved Robert, not even a picture post card telling him how he found London and the southerners. As for a letter to his wife, stuck at home in the old cottage at Killingworth, she appears to have been completely forgotten. They had been married only two years, after his twelve years as a widower, but in many respects she had become widowed herself, an engineer's widow, left alone as he rushed round the country. There is not one letter in existence either to his first, or his second wife. (And the second was literate, judging by her marriage signature.) The most she ever gets is a hurried reference in the last paragraph if the person George is writing to happens to be a family friend. 'Mrs Stephenson sends her best respects.' George, like so many self-made men before and since, was married to his work.

Now and again there are hints about the changes in his life, and how he felt about them, especially in the few letters written to close friends. At this time William James was a close friend and there are many letters between the two as George tells him how the Darlington railway is going and James tells him about his Liverpool and other projects.

In a letter dated early 1822 he tells James how by chance he had got on the coach at Darlington to return to Newcastle and found himself sitting beside two gentlemen who were strangers to him.

> The gents were in for N. Castle and we had not gone far till they found I belonged to the neighbourhood they were going to. They asked me if I knew one G. Stephenson. I answered that I did. They then enquired very closely after his character. I kept myself unknown till we got to near N. Castle. I soon found their knowledge of railways was very limited. It would take a volume to hold our conversation on Railway Locomotive Engines and Stephenson before I was known to them, however in the end we got very kind and I showed them our Engines and Railways which they candidly confessed were superior to anything they ever saw and far exceeded their expectations.

The letter then goes into long lists of the latest speeds and loads of his locomotives, but this opening anecdote reveals many things. Firstly that his fame is spreading south. (One of the two gentlemen turned out to be Lord Dudley's engineer, looking into the possibility of using Stephenson's locomotives.) Secondly it shows his pride in his own achievements, perhaps superiority, even arrogance. Thirdly there's a trace of cunning, keeping his identity hidden for all those hours, or perhaps it was simply an example of obtuse northern humour. Between the lines, there's also a feeling of him, G. Stephenson, man of the people, against them, the Gents, the educated professional classes, though this might be reading too much into a simple story. It certainly comes out strongly in later letters whenever any of the so-called professional classes dares to cross him. If this feeling was there in the early days, such as during the safety lamp row, it was usually kept well hidden.

In another letter to James he complains that Robert Stevenson is still hanging around, getting in his way. Stevenson had earlier been a patron of George, perhaps patronisingly so, and had patted him on the back on paper telling Edward Pease how marvellous his engines were. Now George has definitely turned against him.

> The knowledge of machinery has not yet entered his head, at least I have not seen any remarks of it when in his company. I have heard him make some remarks on Railways which I hardly

could have expected from a child. He has collected news like other book makers and setting it off for his own.

One of the roots of the trouble, apart from the obviously impossible position for George of having a consultant in the background, was that Mr Stevenson, the educated and famous gentleman engineer from Edinburgh, apparently thought that the rough, uncultured Geordies were beyond the pale. There is a letter from Robert Stephenson (George's son) to James confirming that he too has gone off Robert Stevenson whom he'd heard remarking that 'the Northumbrians were only emerging out of the darkness'. He warns James to make sure that Stevenson doesn't muscle into the Liverpool project.

These letters between George and William James show that George has not only become confident enough to run down his enemies but confident enough to dash off a few sentences in his own handwriting, something he rarely seems to have done until now. They are remarkable for their lack of grammar, punctuation and weird spelling. In one he talks of sitting in his 'wet close' and worrying about 'the poor of my Engines'. But they have a power (or poor) and a richness of invective which his dictated letters never have.

He was arrogant and headstrong, insisting on his opinions and in choosing his own men and materials, but with good reason. His engines were indeed far superior to anyone else's – in fact everyone else seems to have given up. And if he wanted a railway fit to accommodate them he had to do it himself. No one else could do it for him, Organising such a vast, multidisciplined project needed someone with determination and arrogance. Where Trevithick had failed was in giving up when the ancillary problems seemed insoluble. George was creating his own problems and he made himself responsible for solving them, even at the expense of becoming possessive and accusing others of interfering.

The first rail was ceremonially laid in place on 23 May 1822 at Stockton by the chairman of the company, Thomas Meynell. Stockton seems to have wholeheartedly taken to the project by now and all their civic dignitaries turned out, bells were rung and ships on the river sounded their sirens. There was a procession through the streets and a royal salute was fired as Mr Meynell laid the first stretch of malleable rail. We haven't the benefit of his few chosen words on this great occasion for the simple reason that he didn't choose any. Jeans, in his Jubilee account of the railway, published in 1875, relates that soon after the opening ceremony a boy was heard shouting in the streets of Stockton 'Speech of Mr Meynell, one penny'. Those who spent a penny found that all the sheets were blank.

At the head of this opening procession were between two and three hundred workmen carrying spades and axes, a species of the human race that was to become familiar, not to say notorious, throughout the industrial world for the rest of the nineteenth century – the railway navvies. Many of these first navvies had probably worked on the canals, drawn to Stockton by the new sort of construction. A lot of their leaders had been hand picked by Stephenson himself, men he'd known personally back on Tyneside, people he could trust and could talk to in their own language. The specialist workmen came from Killingworth, like two of his own brothers James and John. When these workmen left Tyneside they weren't to know that they would probably never go back, that Darlington wasn't simply a one-off job. For decades afterwards Geordie navvies who had worked on the Darlington line turned up all over Europe, following one line after another. The skilled men, Stephenson's assistants, like John Dixon, became eminent railway engineers in their own right. The engineers got the credit and the glory but it was the nameless navvies who did all the work. Navvies, not machines, built the railways. All they had were picks and shovels and horses plus a little gunpowder. While Mr Meynell, exhausted by his formal duties, went off with the other dignitaries to a mayor's reception, the navvies adjourned to the local pub for ale and bread.

There are no tales of drunken orgies amongst the navvies on the Darlington line. No doubt Mr Pease saw to that. The Quaker line, as it became known to the rest of the country, couldn't very well be party to any sort of intemperance. Mr Pease went through the contracts of the outside undertakers (as contractors were called in those days) and made sure that no one was a 'friend of publicans'. In the contract of a carrier called Thomas Close appear the words, 'The first time he is seen intoxicated he will be dismissed and the sum due to him as wages shall be forfeited.'

George Stephenson had neither the time nor inclination for drinking, either with the promoters or the workmen. He was too busy. Having got the first rails laid he had to decide how to fence them in. In the old colliery line days there had been no need to fence in the railway – which was why George's first job as a young boy had been to keep the children and the cattle off the line. They were private concerns on private property. The Darlington line was going to be enormous by comparison and would go through towns and villages and through public and private properties. He advertised for undertakers to put up stone walls or in some cases to have lines of 'quicks' planted (quicks were quick-set hedges).

George himself is credited with designing the first iron railway bridge. This went across the river Gaunless and remains of it are preserved to this day. It was fifty feet long and had four spans. For the bridge which had to be built in Darlington itself, across the river Skerne, he was persuaded to bring in a proper architect, Ignatius Bonomi of Durham. The directors wanted it to be made of stone and look as impressive and imposing as possible, which it did. This is the bridge which is seen in Dobbin's well-known painting of the opening of the railway.

While they were pressing on with the construction of the railway line, for which they had been given permission by their act of parliament, they were at the same time applying for an amended bill to allow them to make some changes suggested in Stephenson's survey. Most of all, they wanted the act changed to allow them to use locomotives. The first act had made no mention of any sort of engine, referring only to wagons being drawn by 'men or horses'. Pease and Richardson had been suitably impressed by George's work at Killingworth, where he'd demonstrated his locomotives, and by now the Hetton locomotives were successfully working for all to see. The board were therefore persuaded to ask this time for power to use 'locomotives or movable engines'.

George went down to London with Francis Mewburn, the solicitor, and other officials to see the act through and was there for eight weeks, gaining his first experience of parliamentary lobbying. According to Mewburn, they had some trouble explaining to people the nature of a 'locomotive'. 'Lord Shaftesbury's secretary could not comprehend what it meant; he thought it was some strange, unheard of animal and he struck the clause out of his copy of the Act.' Mr Brandling, the MP for

Northumberland, and George were sent to explain what a locomotive was.

George never had a high opinion of the aristocracy and definitely didn't think much of Lord Shaftesbury even though he was a highly important person and chairman of many committees in the House of Lords. Mewburn later wrote to him in Darlington when it looked as if he might have to come back to London once again and George's reply is rather tart and to the point – one of the few letters where George's personality shines, or perhaps glowers, through.

> Your letter by this day post has cut me most sadly. How to set off to London at short notice I do not know as I am hemmed in with so much business and indeed I am not in a state of health for such a journey however I suppose I must go. Lord Shaftesbury must be an old fool. I always said he had been a spoilt child but he is a great deal worse than I expected. I have not seen Mr Edward Pase nor yet Joseph and I suppose I shall not see them till tomorrow night. If you get this in time to give me a line back by the same coach saying whether there is any possibility of postponing my journey I will have some one at the Coach office at night to receive it from the guard.

Apart from the revealing remarks about Lord Shaftesbury (father of the factory reformer) it is interesting to note how a high-powered engineer of the day managed to speed up the postal system.

Lord Shaftesbury's ignorance in the end didn't matter. Their new act became law on 23 May 1823, making the Stockton and Darlington Railway the first public railway in the world able to employ locomotives. The unheard of animal was about to become known.

# 6

# THE OPENING

Railways, as the public know them, began with the Stockton and Darlington Railway, but railway historians get very cross unless you define your terms exactly. All 'firsts' in connection with railways have to be very carefully worded.

There were railway acts before the Stockton and Darlington Railway got its railway act, but they referred to railways in their strict, literal sense, meaning a way laid out with rails. No mention was ever made of locomotives because, as Lord Shaftesbury's secretary well knew, it was horses who provided the pulling power.

Strictly speaking, you can't call the Stockton and Darlington the first public railway because the Surrey Iron Railway, opened in 1803, has that honour. It was a railway and was open to the public, but it was with horses pulling the wagons. You can't even say that the Stockton and Darlington was the first steam railway. George had been using steam on rails at Killingworth and at Hetton long before the Darlington opening. It takes quite a mouthful to give the Stockton and Darlington its true and correct niche in history. You must include the three vital elements. It was a railway. It was public. It was going to use steam locomotives.

After the act had been passed allowing locomotives, they had to decide who was going to make them. The company kept everything above board by looking around at the market, even though their engineer appeared to be the only person building locomotives. The Leeds manufacturers of the Blenkinsop locomotive, the ones with cogged wheels, were approached but were unable to help, replying that they hadn't made any locomotive engines for eight years.

In June 1823 the two Stephensons, Edward Pease and Michael Longridge (whose works were making the malleable rails) decided to open their own locomotive works. Once again, Stephenson and

Pease between them had shown their faith in the future of steam locomotion. They were later accused of having carved up the locomotive business, establishing their own monopoly, but the truth was that they had no alternative. The history of the first hundred years of this firm was published in 1923 by J.G.H. Warren and it shows clearly that most of the money was put up by Pease. The initial capital was £4,000 with Pease putting up £1,600 and the other three £800 each. It later came out that Pease had loaned young Robert £500 towards his share.

George knew that his engines were good, even though he had only been making them on a small scale at his colliery workshops, but it shows great faith on the part of Edward Pease to have put up so much money. He had no technical understanding of the machines, his railway had yet to open and there was still a majority of engineers convinced that locomotives would never work. Perhaps the most surprising thing about their brave new locomotive works was that they were to be called Robert Stephenson and Company. Robert, George's nineteen-year-old son, was appointed managing partner. We might suspect such an arrangement today, looking for some tax device, believing that an inexperienced lad of nineteen must be a front. His father, as engineer of the railway company, perhaps didn't want to be seen ordering engines from himself. The very fact that Pease was a Quaker is enough to put a stop to any cynicism. And yet, were they all absolutely convinced that a slip of a boy could run such a firm? Or was perhaps old George pushing them a bit?

Robert had certainly had a lot more experience than his age might suggest. He'd assisted in two railway surveys, at Darlington and at Liverpool, and after his father had called him back from helping William James he'd been sent for six months to Edinburgh university where he'd been studying natural philosophy, chemistry and natural history. He was coming almost straight from the academic world of Edinburgh to the practical job of setting up a factory and turning out locomotives, but there is not the slightest suggestion of any of the partners thinking he was perhaps a bit young for such a job. We know their confidence was not misplaced from Robert's subsequent career but it was a brave gesture all the same.

A site was bought at Forth Street in Newcastle, men were hired and the Stockton and Darlington Company ordered two locomotives at a cost of £500 each, *Locomotion* and *Hope*. George and his wife moved from their cottage home at Killingworth into Newcastle to Eldon Street to be near the works and keep an eye on progress. Though Robert was in charge of the works George was providing the plans for the new engines as well as pushing on with the completion of the railway itself.

During 1824 progress was slowed down by bad weather, by several cuttings and gradients being more difficult than expected and by a few little local legal problems. Two gentlemen who were trustees of the road between Stockton and Darlington objected to the way in which the railway was going to cross their road. They issued a summons against some of the company's workmen for trespassing. The workmen were fined forty shillings each by the magistrates – who turned out to be the same two gentlemen who'd objected.

The legal case which kept County Durham agog for quite some time was the one brought by a Mr Rowntree, a shareholder of the company, who refused to accept the price offered for his land. It was only just over an acre, and eight independent land surveyors put its value at between £200 and £320. He wanted £700. The case went to the sessions in Durham and lasted seven hours during which his counsel argued that the 'locomotives, or as they had been called, infernal machines, would go so near to Mr Rowntree's house as to render the premises useless'. The judge awarded him £500.

The anti-locomotive lobby were filling the newspapers, and the courts, with scare stories about the highly dangerous speeds of the locomotives, alleging they would go at ten or even twelve miles an hour, which the Company denied. Even Nicholas Wood, that great railway advocate, scolded the speculators who were talking of twelve miles an hour calling it 'ridiculous expectation'. Mr Lambton (later the Earl of Durham) admitted that the railway would not be seen even from the highest point of his house 'but that the noise would be heard in every room of it'. Lord George Cavendish wrote that he would 'not have the country harassed and torn up by these infernal machines'. Lord Eldon wrote, 'As to railways, and all the other schemes which speculation, running wild, is introducing, I think Englishmen who were wont to be sober, are grown mad.'

The protest was being raised in many counties, not just in County Durham, because for the first time there was a genuine wave of national interest in locomotives. Now that the Stockton–Darlington line was nearing completion deputations – such as Lord Dudley's – were catching the coach up to the north east to find out what all the fuss was about. Promoters who'd been planning a horsedrawn line were being forced at least to consider locomotion. The Liverpool–Manchester promoters sent across a party to look at Stephenson's infernal machines and so did groups from Birmingham, Sheffield and Gloucester. One of the reasons why progress was relatively slow in 1824 was that the company's engineer was suddenly being besieged by offers from elsewhere. George brought in Timothy Hackworth from Wylam, who had also been doing pioneer work on locomotives, to help at Forth Street and then to be locomotive superintendent for the Darlington company. Many of the railway projects being discussed never came to anything, or at least they decided to wait and see what happened at Darlington, but it meant a great deal of travelling and discussions for George, who could never resist any railway venture.

George made constant trips to Birmingham, Liverpool and elsewhere, looking at proposed lines, and also went further afield on behalf of Robert Stephenson and Company seeking possible buyers for their locomotives. In late 1823 he went with Robert to London and Bristol to sell their boilers and stationary locomotives. They then crossed to Dublin, going by road to Cork. Robert was pleased to see new parts of the country but for George, with so many projects on his plate, it was extremely time consuming. He managed to write a few letters back to Michael Longridge at the Forth Street works, all very hurried, dashed off to catch the coach, all of which show his hectic life:

> Swann Inn, Birmingham, 8 August 1824
> I shall leave this place tomorrow for Newport, where I may be a couple of days. From thence I will go to Stourbridge where I will remain also two days: from the latter place to Newcastle under Lyne where I may spend the remainder of the week. I will endeavour to be at Liverpool on the Sunday where letters will find me, I have an invitation from Boulton and Watt to dine with them today.

As a piece of name dropping his last remark couldn't have been smarter. By this date both James Watt and Matthew Boulton had died, but their Birmingham engineering works were still the most famous in the land.

In a letter from Liverpool on 11 July 1824, George gives an example of the problems of contemporary travelling.

> I expected to have set off with the mail this night but was detained by my horse breaking down on the road in passing from the Birmingham line to this quarter. This disaster put me too late for the Mail. The poor horse's knees were broken in such a desperate manner that I did not know how to venture home with him. I had a fine kick up with the inn-keeper when I did get home. The only apology I could make was by proposing to buy the horse at its value.

Stephenson had by this time been commissioned to do some work for the Liverpool line and was spending more and more of his time travelling, but he was desperate to get the Darlington line finished and opened and let the whole world see what he could do.

Given the nature of the times, it is surprising to realise how much of the world had already been to see Stephenson at work. A notable American visitor, William Strickland, was in England in early 1825 on a fact-finding mission on canals and railways sent by the 'Pennsylvania Society for the Promotion of Internal Improvement', a very fine sounding body indeed. He watched Stephenson's locomotives at Hetton and noted how Stephenson recommended the use of six wheels not four to distribute the weight better. He watched very carefully, notebook in hand, as the Darlington rails were being fixed, jotting down details of the workmen's tools, all of which he later published in his report.

This was the first American visitor to look at English railways as far as can be gathered, but French, German and Russian visitors have already been mentioned. Newspapers at the time were writing very little about locomotives so it must point to the wide circulation of the technical magazines and pamphlets which were now being brought out.

Despite all the attention, Pease was finding it necessary once again to call up more money to complete the line on time. The books show that they were running up considerable debts, such as £9,342 to the treasurer (Jonathan Backhouse) who had personally paid off some troublesome landowner. Several promoters were worried that they might not now get their 5 per cent which Pease had promised. Pease was continually issuing announcements to keep everyone happy. 'No circumstances have arisen to induce the board to alter their opinion of the great public benefit to be derived by all classes of the community from this undertaking and that a fair and reasonable return will be made to the proprietors for the capital invested.'

It was the Quakers, once again, who ensured that the line opened on time, though they kept their help quiet at the time. Gurney's in Norwich advanced another £40,000 and Richardson's London banking firm (Richardson, Overend and Company) loaned £20,000. The chief extras had been £25,000 for buying up more land (when they had estimated to spend £7,000) and a completely unexpected expenditure of £32,241 in opposing a rival railway, the Tees and Weardale, which had arisen when the success of the Darlington line began to look assured. (The Darlington company were not against obstructing others, just as they'd been obstructed in the past.)

These extra expenses were admitted in a shareholders' report of 9 September 1825, but the board were obviously full of hope. They announced that the grand opening ceremony would be on 27 September 1825, and assured shareholders that 'Your committee beg to repeat their conviction that your concern will soon obtain that rank and credit in the kingdom to which it is entitled.'

The following week the public were made aware of the arrangements for the opening with broadsheets and announcements in the local papers. The ordinary public were told where they could watch the procedures while the nobs were informed that an 'elegant dinner will be provided at the Town Hall, Stockton to which the proprietors have resolved to invite the neighbouring nobility and gentry who have taken an interest in this very important undertaking. A Superior locomotive, of the most improved construction, will be employed, with a train of convenient carriages for the conveyance of the proprietors and strangers.'

One of the handbills carried a stern warning in true Quaker fashion to any friends of inn keepers who might contemplate enjoying themselves. 'The company takes this opportunity of enjoining on all their work people that attention to Sobriety and Decorum which they have hitherto had the pleasure of observing.'

The day before the opening, George Stephenson gave a test

ride on *Locomotion* for the benefit of Edward Pease and three of his sons, Joseph, Edward and Henry, plus Thomas Richardson, the London Quaker banker. *Locomotion* had been brought down by road from Newcastle drawn by a team of horses. Its engine had been started for the first time earlier that morning by an engineman who got the fire going by the simple device of using an hour glass (which he normally used to start his pipe) on an old piece of waste material left in the engine by one of the Forth Street fitters. His workmate had gone for a lantern to light the fire, leaving him sitting in the sun, lighting his pipe, when he thought he would try to get the fire going on his own. It's nice to know that nature had a hand in man's first attempts at locomotion.

Along with *Locomotion* came the company's first passenger coach, the *Experiment*. This too had been built by Robert Stephenson and Company. It had cost £80 and looked very much like a grander version of a stage coach of the times. It was cushioned and carpeted, though without springs, and sat eighteen passengers with a table down the middle. For the trial run it was linked to *Locomotion* and off they went with George's brother James doing the driving while George pointed out the finer details to the Pease family.

They were lucky with the weather for the grand opening next day – propitious, so the local papers called it – and crowds were gathering from as early as 5.30 at Brussleton Bank near Shildon at the collieries end of the line. At 8 o'clock a stationary engine fixed beside the hill drew the VIPs in their coach up the incline then let it down the other side where they were met by the waiting, panting, giant *Locomotion*, driven by George Stephenson. The grand procession then headed east for Darlington, some nine miles away, and after that, a further nine miles on to Stockton for the elegant banquet which was waiting for the chosen gentry.

You only have to look at the smallness and simpleness of *Locomotion*, which stands to this day on Darlington station, to wonder all over again that such a fragile machine ever managed to get to Stockton. Behind it, when it started off, were thirty-three wagons and three hundred passengers. By the time it eventually got to Stockton the passengers were estimated at being nearer 650, as so many spectators had clambered on board, making the total load almost ninety tons. George Stephenson must have been highly apprehensive when they started off, wondering about the strength of his untried locomotive, which had just come from the works, wondering about the safety of the rails, the bridges and embankments, about the lives of the people on board and of those watching, and wondering whether the whole procession might result in tragedy and the end, not the beginning, of locomotion.

The total train, some four hundred feet long, consisted firstly of *Locomotion* with its tender. Next came six wagons, five containing coal and one with flour, followed by *Experiment*, the company's passenger coach which contained the directors and leading proprietors. Then came six wagons full of 'strangers' (presumably the more important guests), fourteen wagons full of workmen and finally six more wagons laden with coals. Following *Locomotion* and its train came twenty-four horsedrawn wagons filled with workmen.

At the head of the procession went several men on horse-back. 'These heralds held flags in their hands,' says Jeans, 'and gave notice to all whom it concerned that the locomotive was approaching.' Scattered throughout the train were four other large flags, especially made by the company for the occasion. They were more like banners than flags, of the kind which used to be seen at the Durham Miners Gala, emblazoned with stirring words. One displayed the company's Latin motto over a landscape of an engine drawing several coal wagons. One flag announced simply, 'May the Stockton and Darlington Railway give public satisfaction and reward its liberal promoters'.

Thousands of spectators had come for miles around, in carts and donkeys and on foot, to see the procession depart. The *Durham County Advertiser*, in its long, glowing description of the opening, reported that when *Locomotion* got up steam some of the more simple country folk, the Johnny Raws, were terrified.

About this time the locomotive engine, or steam horse, as it was more generally termed, gave 'note of preparation' by some heavy aspirations which seemed to excite astonishment and alarm among the 'Johnny Raws' who had been led by curiosity to the spot and who, when a portion of the steam was let off, fled in fright, accompanied by the old women and young children who surrounded them, under the idea, we supposed, that some horrible explosion was about to take place; they afterwards, however, found courage sufficient to return to their posts but only to fly again when the safety valve was opened. Everything being now arranged, the welcome cry of 'all ready' was heard and the engine and its appendages moved forward in beautiful style.

Some spectators, according to Jeans, had expected *Locomotion* to literally be an iron horse. 'Excitement in many minds took the form of disappointment when it was found that the locomotive was not built after the fashion of a veritable four footed quadruped, some of the older folks expecting to see the strange phenomenon of an automatical semblance of a horse stalking along on four legs.'

There were several moments of worry on the way to Darlington, once when a coach came off the line and again when the engine stopped because some waste had blocked a valve, but each time the faults were soon rectified and they managed to continue without anyone being hurt. As they went through the fields some hunting gentlemen on horseback tried to race the train, riding alongside the track, but failed. A stage coach pulled by four horses tried in vain to do the same, much to the amusement of a reporter from the *Scotsman*.

The passengers by the engine had the pleasure of accompanying and cheering their brother passengers by the stage coach which passed alongside and observing the striking contrast exhibited by the power of the engine and the horse – the engine with her 600 passengers and load and the coach with four horse and only 16 passengers.

There was a crowd of twelve thousand to greet the train's arrival at Darlington 'who gave vent to their feelings by loud and reiterated cheers'. Six of the coal wagons were uncoupled and the coal distributed to the poor of the town. Two wagons full of passengers, one containing the Yarm town band, were then joined on. They'd lost almost an hour in stoppages since leaving Shildon colliery but *Locomotion*, despite its ever increasing load, had averaged eight miles per hour. In their eagerness to join the train, spectators were now clambering on top of the coal wagons, hanging on to the sides, even hanging on to the original passengers.

Downhill, on the way into Stockton, a speed of fifteen miles per hour was reached. One workman who was clinging to the side of a coal wagon fell off and had his leg crushed. Apart from that there were, surprisingly, no other accidents. At Stockton the crowd was estimated at being nearly forty thousand. Guns were fired in salute. The band struck up 'God Save the King' and the vast crowd joined in giving 'three times three stentorian cheers'.

The very elegant banquet in the evening was attended by 102 gentlemen, including representatives from the proposed Liverpool and Manchester, Leeds and Hull railways, and went on till midnight. Mr Meynell, the chairman, took the chair and once again doesn't appear to have distinguished himself by either the brilliance or the length of his speech. (Not a word of it is recorded in any contemporary account.) No doubt they were too busy praising each other to have much time for speechifying. But every contemporary account records the fact that twenty-three toasts were drunk, the first to the King and finishing with great gusto, as was only fitting, to George Stephenson, their esteemed Engineer.

Edward Pease, alas, missed the opening day celebrations, though he might well have felt a trifle discomfited during those twenty-three toasts. The previous night his son Isaac had died and no member of the Pease family attended the opening. At least he'd had the pleasure of being given a private preview the day before and had experienced for himself the fruits of his long labours.

There was someone else of importance missing, someone else whom everyone would have liked to have been there. As managing partner of the Forth Street works Robert Stephenson would certainly have had a place of honour. As George's dearly beloved only son, as his instrument of education in those early dark days, as his professional support during the building of the Darlington line, one would have expected young Robert to have been at his father's right hand. Instead, Robert had gone off on his own to South America.

# 7

# ROBERT

Our friend Samuel Smiles would have us believe that Robert Stephenson left his father and the north east to go to South America for health reasons. 'His health had been very delicate for some time, partly occasioned by his rapid growth, but principally because of his close application to work and study.' According to Smiles, it was decided that a 'temporary residence in a warm climate was the very thing likely to be most beneficial to him'.

As a child, Robert was never robust, but he was by now almost twenty-two and had surely got over the worst effects of all that rapid growing. There are no reports of him being ill during those two open air surveys, on the Darlington line and then the Liverpool line. If anything they must have been good for his health. His years of working in a colliery, which certainly can't have been good for anyone's health, were now well behind him. If in 1824 he was feeling a bit peaky, a bit off colour with too much studying, a few weeks at Brighton might have done the trick, or at the most a trip to the south of France. Going off to South America sounds on the face of it patently ridiculous. Even today, one wouldn't think of rushing to South America for its beneficial climate. But in 1824 it was a hazardous, lengthy and most certainly an unhealthy expedition. So what made him go? Mr Smiles, alas, furnishes no further clues as to his real motives.

Mr Smiles' book first came out in 1857, while Robert was still alive, and Smiles acknowledged (in later editions) that Robert had assisted him. We have to assume, then, Robert preferred it to be thought that he was going for health reasons. When Jeaffreson's biography of Robert himself came out in 1864, after Robert's death, poor health is still given as the main motivation.

The threatening symptoms of pulmonary disease, which had from childhood made his friends anxious for him, seemed decidedly on the increase; and in his secret heart he believed that the harsh winds of Newcastle would, before many years, lay him in a premature grave. In the warm luxurious atmosphere of Columbia, surrounded by the gorgeous beauties of animal and vegetable life, he anticipated renewed vigour of mind and body.

For almost a hundred years after this all commentators on the Stephensons have accepted health as the explanation for Robert's departure. It was only with the late L.T.C. Rolt, in his book about the two Stephensons, that it was put forward that there might have been a row between them, a rift in the partnership, as he called it. Robert himself never talked or wrote about any row, but the whole incident does suggest a mystery which has never been properly explained. The basic facts about his departure for South America are known, but not his underlying motives, which was why Rolt's book in 1960 created something of a stir in railway circles and why he made his 'Rift in the Partnership' chapter such an important part of his book.

Firstly, some of the known facts. There was of course a specific reason why Robert chose to go to South America, as opposed to any other part of the globe, and it all started through the Pease connection.

We first encountered Thomas Richardson, Edward Pease's cousin, when he became a major subscriber in the Stockton and Darlington Railway. He was the founder of the important London banking house of Overend, Gurney, and took a keen personal interest in the progress of the railway. It was he who went with Pease to look at the Killingworth engines when they were making up their mind about locomotion. Like his cousin, he saw great possibilities in railways and it appears from Warren's history of Robert Stephenson and Company that Richardson put up half of Pease's original stake in the capital. Soon afterwards he loaned the company more money and became officially a partner. Naturally he became a friend of both George and Robert.

Around 1823, certain normally staid and sensible firms in the City of London got themselves very worked up about the possibilities of great fortunes to be made in South America. The idea was admittedly very exciting. Everybody knew the old stories, even if many of them were legendary, about the Inca gold mines, about the Spanish conquistadores and the undreamt of mineral wealth which they had found. These mines had been worked by hand, without machines, and long since left abandoned. Think what can now be done, suggested some bright speculator, using all our new and marvellous steam engines! As the Tyneside coal fields had been made deeper and longer through having steam winding engines and steam pumps, so the South American mines could now be opened up and all that gold and silver would be there for the taking. To this day the City of London goes slightly mad every ten years or so and it's very often at the prospect of unlimited mineral wealth. A hill made of gold in the outback of Australia can still get everyone very excited. In 1823 'a mania of speculation', as Nicholas Wood called it, became centred on South America.

There had been a similar stampede about ten years previously which everybody seems to have forgotten. In the excitement Richard Trevithick, that brilliant but impressionable engineer, had found himself with his bags and engines packed and on the way to Peru. He'd hardly been heard of since. It transpired later that he'd got caught up in Simon Bolivar's revolution against the Spanish dictators, and other adventures, but at the time no one had yet heard whether he'd made his fortune or not, or even if he were still alive.

This time, said the speculators, things are different. We're not going to Peru looking for Inca mines. We're going much further north, to Mexico, where things are peaceful and this time, thanks to the wonderful developments of the last ten years, we really have got excellent engines, made by the very wonderful engineers in our Tyneside collieries.

Thomas Richardson, in his wisdom, despite being a sobersided Quaker, was one of the City men getting together an expedition to Mexico. He turned naturally to George Stephenson, probably trying to get him to go out there, but George wasn't so gullible. He had too much to do at home, what with the Stockton and Darlington and other railway ventures, but he agreed to give his considered advice on which sort of machines and equipment should be sent out.

Young Robert was much more excited. He jumped at the idea of leading an exploratory mining expedition to Mexico. Michael

Longridge, his partner in the newly founded locomotive works, where Robert was supposed to be managing partner, wasn't at all pleased. Robert argued that it would just be for a short visit and Longridge could easily hold the fort while he was away. His father was even more against it,

> Let me beg of you not to say anything against my going out to America [so Robert wrote to his father]. I have already ordered so many instruments that it would make me look extremely foolish to call off. Even if I had not ordered any instruments, it seems as if we were all working one against one another. Only consider what an opening it is for me as an entry into business. I am informed by all who have been there that it is a very healthy country. I must close this letter, expressing my hope that you will not go against me this time.

George doesn't appear at this stage to have said yes or no but Robert nonetheless went ahead with his Mexican plans. In February 1824 he went down to Cornwall to look at likely men and machines to be taken to Mexico. He was accompanied on this trip by his Uncle Robert, George's brother, who was also involved in the Mexican scheme.

From Devon on 5 March Robert wrote to his father, keeping up his efforts to persuade him, slipping in extra reasons for going, working them in as subtly as possible.

> As far as I have proceeded on my journey to the Cornish mines, I have every reason to think it will not be misspent time; for when one is travelling about, something new generally presents itself, and though it is perhaps not superior to some schemes of our own for the same purpose, it seldom fails to open a new channel of ideas, which may not infrequently prove advantageous in the end. This I think is one of the chief benefits of leaving the fireside where the young imagination received its first impression.

However, the Mexican trip was called off around late March 1824. There were problems with land concessions out in Mexico and it looks as if Robert himself decided it wasn't such a good venture. But a month later, Robert accepts another South American venture which has suddenly come up, this time to Colombia. Once again, Thomas Richardson is one of the promoters. On this occasion there appears to be very little preparation. On an impulse, or so it would seem, Robert has decided that this time he is definitely going, whatever happens. And off he goes.

Rolt's theory about the motivation for this impulse rests on a very interesting letter, first discovered in 1930, which Robert Stephenson wrote to William James. The letter is dated 18 April 1824 – the very, time when the Mexican trip is called off. In this letter Robert says he has relinquished the Mexican trip and then, most surprisingly, asks James for employment. As Rolt says, young Robert is known to have enjoyed his work with James on the Liverpool–Manchester survey, and was a great admirer of James, but it seems very strange that he should now contemplate going to work with James instead of going back to the factory in Newcastle. He would appear not to want to go back to his father at any cost, but to be with William James.

When James received this letter, he himself was running into financial troubles, which makes Robert's request all the more surprising, unless he was doing it deliberately to help James who had taken on too many ventures, financing many of them out of his own pocket. James' health was poor and he'd been very slow to produce the necessary survey and plans for the Liverpool promoters. Robert had already heard about James' problems the previous year and had written him a very revealing letter in August 1823, just before he had set off with his father on the Irish trip.

It gives rise to feelings of true regret when I reflect on your situation; but yet a consolation springs up when I consider your persevering spirit will for ever bear you up in the arms of triumph, instances of which I have witnessed of too forcible a character to be easily effaced from my memory. It is these thoughts, and these alone, that could banish from my thoughts feelings of despair. . . . Can I ever forget the advice you have offered me in your last letters? and what a heavenly inducement you pointed before me at the close, when you said that attention and obedience to my dear father would afford me music at midnight. Ah, and so it has already. My father and I set off for London on Monday next, the 1st, on our way to

Cork. Our return will probably be about the time you wish me to be at Liverpool. If all be right, we may possibly call and see what is going on. That line is the finest project in England.

It would appear from this letter that Robert must have been moaning about his father to James, saying he was fed up, in despair, and wanting to get away but had decided to follow James' advice and stick it out. Certainly James wasn't encouraging any rebellious feelings, despite what George may have thought.

When James eventually gets the letter from Robert Stephenson asking for a job he is unable to give one because of his own dire situation which has now led to bankruptcy. But the worst blow for James comes just a month after Robert's letter about a job. In May 1824, George Stephenson is given the job of surveying the Liverpool line, displacing poor old James.

For many years the James family kept up a bombardment on George, accusing him of bringing about James' downfall and his bankruptcy, intriguing to get the Liverpool job from him. As late as 1861 a book was published called *The Two James and the Two Stephensons* by someone simply signed E.M.S.P. – later revealed to be Mrs Ellen Paine, William James' daughter. She attacks George for pinching James' glory. 'He has taken the credit for so many inventions from a cucumber to a lady's frilled petticoat.'

There now seems to be not the slightest doubt that George acted fairly in getting the Liverpool job, but the relationship between him and James is certainly rather clouded in mystery. According to Rolt, Robert was very upset, seeing the James affair as a matter of principle. James had been an early supporter of George and had helped him a great deal, publicising his name and his engines, introducing him to the right contacts. They had been business partners, taking out a patent together, though nothing much seems to have happened to it, and intimate friends, addressing long letters to each other. Then of course the business of James taking young Robert under his wing at Liverpool, originally with George's full support, shows their confidence in each other.

But when times turn bad for James, not only does George do nothing to help him, he takes the bread from under his nose by accepting the job which James desperately needed. Even if it was James' own fault that he lost the Liverpool job, Robert might well have thought that his father should have at least refused. This then is Rolt's theory – that it was the treatment of William James, the usurping of his Liverpool job by George Stephenson, that finally turned Robert against his father, convincing him he had to get away. When James couldn't give him a job, he took the next one which came along, which happened to be in Colombia.

There is no evidence in any letters to show or even suggest that Robert and his father had an argument over James, but what we know of Robert's character indicates he was a young man of high principle and what we know of George's character indicates that he wasn't a man to feel himself eternally grateful to those who'd helped him in the past. Many years later when James died, Robert put his name to a testimonial to him and got the Liverpool Manchester board to grant his widow £300. George did nothing, and is supposed not to have been pleased with Robert's actions. In none of his speeches in later life did George give James any credit.

The time scale fits in neatly – Robert leaving for Colombia almost straight after the news that George has got the James job. We know that Robert had been very close to James. Surprisingly, there is no reference in Jeaffreson or the 1857 edition of Smiles to Robert working with James on the Liverpool line. Had Robert forgotten or did he not want his friendship with James to be mentioned? It would certainly appear that George was jealous of James' influence on Robert.

However, there is one mistake in the evidence which Rolt mustered in support of his thesis that it was George taking James' job which made Robert leave. The only known connecting link at this stage between Robert and James, in fact the vital connecting link on which Rolt bases his whole supposition, is the surprising letter of 18 April 1824, the one in which Robert Stephenson asks William James for a job. This letter, so it has now been agreed, was written by Robert Stephenson, George's brother, not Robert Stephenson, George's son. Young Robert never asked James for a job nor had he any known connection with James after he lost the Liverpool position.

The confusion between Robert Stephenson and his uncle Robert is easily made. Both were involved in the Mexican scheme so the reference in the letter to Mexico no doubt convinced Rolt he had the right Robert – especially if he was already looking for a connection between young Robert and William James. The letter, which was bought by the Liverpool Library from Sotherbys, 'the property of a lady', in 1973 has now been recatalogued – under Robert the brother, not Robert the son. (For a fuller explanation of the background to the letter see Appendix.)

Rolt's theory might still be right – that young Robert was upset by the treatment of James – but the most important element in his proof now collapses. All the same, whether or not there was a row about James, Rolt was the first to suggest that Robert went off to South America not for his health but because for some reason he wanted to get away from his father.

I don't personally believe there was any row, or even a specific difference of opinion over James or over any other subject. It was simply that young Robert, to put it in its simplest terms, was fed up with his father. He didn't need a pretext. He just wanted to get away. And the reasons why he wanted to get away are surely archetypal. The symptoms of an intense, claustrophobic father–son relationship can be traced back many years and, as so often happens, the son finally decides to make a break. The strong, domineering father has brought up his only son to take over the family business (in this case to help him make the family business) till the equally strong minded son, having doted on his father as a youngster, starts to rebel as a teenager. The son feels he's been used and bossed around, and decides at length to cut free and for once to be himself.

The picture we've always been given of Robert as a schoolboy is very endearing, the two of them together in the evening lamplight, the son testing the father's knowledge. It was a story beloved by the later Victorians. In Jeaffreson's biography he relates that Robert's earliest memory is of sitting on his father's knee 'watching his brows knit over the difficult points of a page'. How Robert felt throughout these years can only be guessed at but there are several anecdotes in Jeaffreson where Robert is being forced to stay indoors and study when he clearly wants to go outside. Spurred on no doubt by all the physical hardships that George endured as a boy, and later boasted about, in fact quite soon boasted about, Robert himself wanted to be out doing robust things with the other lads in the mining village. He wants to go out, for example, and help his aunt Nelly at harvest time and then again to help take the men's picks to be sharpened (a job George himself did as a boy) but George tells him to 'mind his buiks' instead. The neighbours thought George was too strict, forever saying that his son must 'wark, wark, wark'.

George was very pleased with himself when Robert was sent to Dr Bruce's Academy but Robert doesn't appear to have been all that happy, perhaps beginning to revolt against his father's insistence on endless study. None of Robert's contemporaries interviewed later by Jeaffreson remember Robert as being anything special academically. 'Goading him to work harder,' says Jeaffreson, 'gave him a transient distaste for subjects to which he was naturally inclined.'

As in many father–son sagas, George naturally wanted Robert to have all the advantages he'd never had, especially the education. He wanted his son to be a skilled, trained, professional engineer, a profession for which Robert had definite talents, but was against him studying anything on the arts side. He wasn't concerned with him getting the Latin, which George also had missed, or being a cultured gentleman.

George probably made Robert even more aware of his poor health than was necessary, using it as one of the arguments why he shouldn't be out playing in the street or helping the men, but inside studying his books. The nature of Robert's ill health isn't clear, though it was assumed he had inherited his mother's consumptive tendencies. Having lost his wife so early – and having had her an invalid for two years earlier – it's not surprising George should be so worried about his only son's health. According to Jeaffreson, Robert as a boy was 'afflicted with profuse nightly perspirations to obviate which the doctors made him sleep on a hay mattress. He was liable to catch cold and the tendency it had to strike at his lungs made his father apprehensive that tubercular consumption might attack him.' Could the nightly perspirations have been psychological?

Robert always had a strong liking for the outdoor life, perhaps to counter this closeted childhood, perhaps to prove he was as strong and healthy as his father. Bearing this in mind, it could be that Robert's insistence in one of his letters that South America would be good for his health was a half-joke, turning George's old argument back at him. Having been forced to live with decisions supposedly good for his health, he was now turning his health to his own advantage.

As for examples of teenage revolt, there is admittedly no

evidence, but some of George's actions would indicate that George was deliberately keeping him happy, perhaps to counter signs of unrest if not open revolt. In a contemporary situation the father lavishes fast cars and other material presents on the son to keep him at home. The attractions which George put Robert's way were much worthier, as befitted a worthy father who wanted the best training for his worthy son, and would certainly please a son who was genuinely studious at heart, but they nonetheless smack of paternal peace offerings.

It is noticeable how many interesting jobs and visits George regularly contrived for Robert. There are omissions and confusions in both Smiles and Jeaffreson, which have obscured for many years the sequence of events in Robert's early life, but it is now clear from his letters that he was receiving treats since his early teenage days. For example, during his apprenticeship years with Nicholas Wood, George paid for him to have a holiday in London on his own. He went to see the usual sights, like St Paul's, plus some others which show his scientific bent, such as the London Water Works and one which was the talk of the town at the time – a model of an Egyptian tomb which had been sent to London by Belzoni – which with hindsight would indicate Robert's early interest in foreign places.

As we have already seen, he was taken away prematurely from his apprenticeship in October 1821 to help his father with the Stockton–Darlington survey. George even put Robert's name on the plans as engineer, though it was only on a later branch line that he was in charge. From a tender age he took a leading part in the London parliamentary lobbying for the Darlington railway. Exactly a year later, in October 1822, he's off on another survey, this time with James on the Liverpool line. He then went directly, if briefly, to Edinburgh university which, according to his letters, he was attending from November 1822. (Smiles wrongly says that Robert went to Edinburgh in 1820, straight from his apprenticeship.) Next of course came the founding of the loco works in his name and then the numerous exciting trips round the country, to Ireland with his father in September 1823 and with his uncle Robert to Cornwall and Devon in February and March, 1824.

Unlike his father, Robert was educated and literate and wrote amusing and informative letters, all in his own hand, describing the places he was visiting, These letters provide some of the best insights into the character of Robert and of the relationship with his father. Naturally, they tend mainly to be technical, as that was the reason for the trips, reporting back on locomotive possibilities, and in the past it has been mainly the technical side which has been deemed of interest. Even Rolt, for all his good work on the James affair, wrote as a trained engineer and his interests were obviously on the mechanical side.

From letters written during his six months or so at Edinburgh, Robert emerges as a self-assured young man, rather critical of his lecturers. He appears much older and more worldly than his years – at the time he had just turned nineteen – but perhaps his practical experience in the coal mines and on railway surveys made him feel superior to those students who'd come straight from school. Should it be true that George had pushed him up to Edinburgh to free him from James, then this could explain some of the cynicism.

This early letter from Edinburgh was written to Michael Longridge back in Newcastle, his father's business partner and a lifelong friend of both Robert and George.

Edinbro' 4, 1822

SIR, – I would have sent my Lectures ere now had they contained anything new. Mr. Jameson's Lectures have hitherto been confined chiefly to Zoology, a part of Natural History which I cannot say I am enraptured with; nor can I infer from many of his Lectures any ultimate benefit, unless to satisfy the curiosity of man. Natural historians spend a great deal of time in enquiring whether Adam was a black or white man. Now I really cannot see what better we should be, if we could even determine this with satisfaction; but our limited knowledge will always place this question in the shade of darkness. The Professor puzzles me sadly with his Latin appellations of the various divisions, species, genera, &c., of the animal kingdom. He lectures two days a week on Meteorology and three on Zoology. This makes the course very unconnected.

I have taken notes on Natural Philosophy, but have not written them out, as there has been nothing but the simplest parts, and which I was perfectly acquainted with. Therefore I thought I might spend my time better in reading. I shall send you them when he comes to the most difficult parts. Leslie intends giving a Lecture on Saturdays to those who wish to pursue the most abstruse parts of Natural Philosophy. I have put my name down for one of those: he gives questions out every Friday to answer on the Saturday. I have been highly delighted with Dr. Hope's Lectures. He is so plain and familiar in all his elucidations. I have received the books all safe.

There's a rather curt letter several months later, on 11 April 1823, again to Longridge, asking for some money which his father hasn't yet sent.

Edinburgh: April 11, 1823

SIR, – I wrote home. on the 5th, but from yours it appears my father would be set off for London before the arrival of my letter, in which I desired him to send me a bill for £26. I should feel obliged if you will send me it at your first convenience, as I am rather in want of it at present.

The Natural History finishes next Tuesday. The Natural Philosophy on Friday the 18th. Chemistry finishes on the 27th or 28th.

I have been fortunate in winning a prize in the Natural Philosophy class, for some mathematical questions given by Professor Leslie relative to various branches of Natural Philosophy.

I remain, Sir,
Yours very sincerely,
Mich. Longridge, Esq.                ROB. STEPHENSON

At the end of his term at Edinburgh, Robert went on a geological expedition led by Professor Jamieson round the north of Scotland. He enjoyed this enormously and in later life often talked about it. The students went with knapsacks on their backs and as Jeaffreson observes, 'led the same sort of vagrant life which Robert had more than a year before enjoyed during the railway survey'.

George was no doubt delighted to have a son at university – though that prize Robert mentions was apparently not a competitive prize open to all students but a book award given by his professor to the student who had done the best work. It was an award, nonetheless, and George must have been pleased with Robert's progress.

In one of George's rare personal letters he can be clearly seen to be boasting about his son. This letter is quoted by Jeaffreson in his 1864 book, though I have been unable to trace its whereabouts today, nor is it in Skeat's 1973 collected letters of George Stephenson. From the poor spelling it would seem that George wrote it himself. (Some punctuation has been added to make it easier to read.) He is writing to an old friend, William Locke, who has left Killingworth colliery to work in the south:

March 31, 1823

DEAR SIR, – From the great elapse of time since I seed you, you will hardly know that such a man is in the land of the living. I fully expected to have seen you about two years ago, as I passed throw Barnsley on my way to south Wales but being informed you was not at home I did not call. I expect to be in London in the course of a fortnight or three weeks, when I shall do my self the pleasure of calling, either in going or coming. This will be handed to you by Mr. Wilson a friend of mine who is by profession an Atorney at law and intends to settle in your neighbourhood, you will greatley oblidge me by throughing any Businness in his way you can conveniently can. I think you will find him an active man in his profession. There has been many upes and downs in this neighbourhood since you left. you would no doubt have heard that Charles Nixon was throughing out at Walbottle Collery by his partners some years ago. he has little to depend on now but the profets of the ballast machine at Willington Quey wich I darsay is verey small. many of his Familey has turned out verey badley. he has been verey unfortunate in Famaley affairs. If, I have the pleasure of seeing you I shall give you a long list of occurences since you and I worked together at Newburn. Hawthorn is still at Walbattle. I darsay you will well remember he was a great enamy to me but much more so after you left. I left Walbattle Collery soon also after you and has been verey prosperous in my concerns ever since. I am now far above Hawthorn's reach. I am now concerned as Civil Engineer in different parts of the Kingdom. I have onley one son who I have brought up in my own profesion he is now near 20 years of age. I have had him

educated in the first Schools and is now at Colledge in Edinbro'
I have found a great want of education myself but fortune has
made a mends for that want.

> I am dear sir yours truly
> GEO. STEPHENSON.

The reference to Hawthorn, George's 'great enamy', is interesting
because Robert Hawthorn was the successful colliery engineer
who had personally recommended George for the job as
brakesman at Willington Quay. George owed a lot to him, but
they'd obviously fallen out, as George was wont to do with people
who'd helped him. Once he was beyond their reach he forgot
their past help. He does admit that 'fortune' has made amends for
his lack of education but there is no mention of anyone but
himself making his good fortune happen.

After Edinburgh, Robert's letters from his numerous other trips
and treats are full of local colour and excitement. In this one,
during an Irish business tour with his father, he is once again
writing to Longridge:

> Dublin: Sept. 10, 1823

DEAR SIR, – We have just arrived at Paddy's Lane 'in far Dublin
city.' We left London on Monday, at half-past one o'clock,
travelled all night, and reached Bristol the next morning, and
expected to have got the steam packet to Cork, but we were
disappointed on being informed that the Cork packet had
broken her machinery a few days before, and was laid up for
repair. We were therefore obliged to come on to Dublin,
upwards of two hundred miles out of our way. We leave here
this evening in the mail, and shall arrive at Cork tomorrow
evening, where we shall probably remain a few days, and then
make the best of our way into Shropshire. The concern we are
going to at Cork was set fire to by the mob, where the
disturbance has been for some time. . . .

We have some hopes of some orders for steam engines for
South America, in the Colombian States. *This, however,
depends on the success of Perkins's new engine.* My father and he
have had a severe scold. Indeed the most of the birkies were
embittered at my father's opinion of the engine. He one day
stopped the engine by his hand, and when we called the next

day Perkins had previously got the steam to such a pitch (equal 15 atmosphere) that it was impossible for one man to stop it, but by a little of my assistance, we succeeded in stopping it by laying hold of the fly-wheel. This engine he formerly called an 8 or 10 horse-power, but now only a 4. I am convinced, as well as my father, that Perkins knows nothing about the principle of steam engines.

> I remain, dear Sir,
> Yours sincerely,
> ROBERT STEPHENSON.

The Perkins incident, in which George triumphs, shows that Robert was impressed by his father and the way he put the 'birkies' in their place. (Birkies was a northern expression used contemptuously of any smart young fellow. Robert Burns used it to imply conceit. The present day slang word 'birk', meaning simpleton, might have the same derivation.) The new high pressure engine devised by Perkins was looked upon as a serious threat and George had gone especially to see it in London. Jacob Perkins was an American who had impressed many experts in Europe. Our friend Mr Richardson, the banker, was one of those interested in its possibilities, having heard glowing reports. With his dramatic action George demonstrated its flaws.

Later the same month Robert writes from Cork about their further experiences, though this time he has a feeling that his father hadn't been as brave as he'd appeared.

> Cork, Sept. 16, 1823

DEAR SIR, – We left Dublin on the evening of the day we wrote out last, for Cork, in the mail, and we were not a little alarmed, when it stopped at the post office, to see four large cavalry pistols and two blunderbusses handed up to the guard, who had also a sword hung by his side. I can assure you, my father's courage was daunted, though I don't suppose he will confess with it. We proceeded on, however, without being in the least disturbed, except, now and then having our feelings excited by the driver, or some of our fellow passengers, relating, and at the same time pointing towards the situation, where some most barbarous murder had recently been committed. In one instance, a father, mother, and son had been murdered one evening or two before. As we passed along, everywhere distress seemed to be the prevailing feature of the country, and this to an incredible degree among the poor. Indeed, numbers of them appeared literally starving. We frequently have read accounts in the English newspapers of the distressed state of Ireland, but how far they fall short of conveying a just idea of it. With regard to the appearance of the cities Dublin and Cork, I must say the former falls far short of the description given of it by some Irishman in the steam packet, as we came over from England. I asked some of them if it was equal to Edinburgh, and they seemed insulted at the comparison, but I can now say they ought to have felt highly honoured. Dublin excels certainly in size and business, but as to scenery and beauty of building, it shrinks into insignificance.

When Robert arrived in London during early 1824, to do some parliamentary work for the Darlington railway but spinning out his stay as long as possible, he was also making his departure plans for South America, though from a letter to Longridge written in March he is obviously trying to keep his latest plans secret from his father. This is the first mention of Colombia and Robert is clearly very excited.

> Imperial Hotel, Covent Garden:
> March 9, 1824
>
> DEAR SIR, – Your letter the other day gave me pleasure in hearing you were going on (I suppose, of course, at Forth Street) pretty regularly. I wrote to my father this morning, but positively I durst not mention how long it would be before I should be able to reach once more the North. Indeed, I scarcely dare give it a thought myself. I saw Mr. Newburn yesterday, and he informed me it would at least be fourteen days before I could get my liberty. For heaven's sake don't mention this to my father. Joseph Pease will perhaps give him the information: it will, I know, make him extremely dissatisfied, but you know I cannot by any means avoid it. There are some new prospects here in agitation, which I look forward to with great satisfaction. It is the making of a road in Colombia. What a place London is for prospects! This new scheme of the road or railway is also connected with four silver mines at Mariquita.

The road is projected between La Guayra and the city of Caracas. You may find La Guayra on the coast, I believe, of the Gulf of Mexico. The climate, from Humboldt, is not quite so salubrious as that of Mexico. Mr. Powles is the head of the concern, and he assures me there is no one to meddle with us. We are to have all the machinery to make, and we are to construct the road in the most advisable way we may think, after making surveys and levellings.

The date of this letter, 9 March 1824, shows that Robert was making plans for Colombia long *before* George got the Liverpool job (in May 1824), which should disprove once and for all that he rushed to Colombia out of pique for the displacement of James. He also admits in this letter that the Colombian climate cannot be described as an attraction. The big attraction of South America must simply have been to do something new and exciting well away from his father.

Apart from a need to create his own identity, having been well and truly trained and educated and, indeed, used by his father for so long, emotionally and practically, Robert felt that at twenty the last thing he wanted to do was to join a family firm up in Newcastle, in however important a position. He must have felt that he was being forced into a corner. This was it, for ever, a lifetime's occupation. And he'd better be duly grateful for what his father and his father's friends were doing for him.

For all his integrity and high principles, Robert pulled a slight fast one over his father and business partners. He did eventually get permission, however reluctantly it was given, from his father and partner to have leave of absence from the Newcastle locomotive works, telling them that he'd signed a contract for only one year. It was only after his departure that they discovered that in fact he'd signed on for three years. It was no doubt fear that he would never get away, rather than deceit, which made him mislead them. A slight feeling of fear of his father, mixed with awe, comes through in many of his letters.

George finally realised that his son wanted to go off and stretch his wings in a new country and there was nothing more he could do about it, no further inducements he could offer. As it was to be only for a year, so he thought, he might as well make the best of it, though it couldn't have come at a worse time – with the Darlington and Liverpool lines now both under way – and though he had personally been very hurt and saddened by his son's decision.

In a letter written to Longridge on 7 June, eleven days before Robert's departure, George sounds distinctly miserable, even bitter, though trying hard to hide it, at the prospect of travelling to Liverpool in time to see Robert off. 'I am a little more cheerful to night as I have quite come to a conclusion that there is nothing for me but hard work in this world therefore I may as well be cheerful as not.'

After he arrived in Liverpool and met up with Robert to bid him farewell, George wrote to Longridge, this time on 15 June, saying what a pleasure it has been to see Robert again. He describes the smart dinner parties that he and Robert have been to together.

Liverpool: June 15, 1824

DEAR SIR,– I arrived here on Saturday afternoon, and found Mr. Sanders, Robert, and Charles, waiting for me at the coach office. It gave me great pleasure to see Robert again before he sails. He expects to leave the country on Thursday next. We dined with Mr. Sanders on Saturday, and with Mr. Ellis yesterday. He had three men servants waiting in the entrance hall to show us to the drawing-room. There was a party to meet us, and kindly we were received. The dinner was very sumptuous, and the wine costly. We had claret, hock, champagne, and madeira, and all in great plenty; but no one took more than was proper. It is a good custom not to press people to take so much as does them harm. We dined at seven and left at twelve o'clock. Sanders and Ellis are magnificent fellows, and are very kind; Mrs. Sanders is a fine woman, and Mrs. Ellis very elegant. I believe she is niece to Sir James Graham, M.P.; I must say that we have been very kindly received by all parties. I am teased with invitations to dine with them, but each indulgence cannot be attended by me. What changes one sees! – this day in the highest life, and the next in a cottage – one day turtle soup and champagne, and the next bread and milk, or anything that one can catch. Liverpool is a splendid place – some of the streets are equal to London. The merchants are clever chaps, and perseverance is stamped upon every brow. There is a Doctor Trail, a clever mineralogist, and some famous mathematicians that we have dined with. I was much satisfied to find that Robert could acquit himself so well amongst them. He was much improved in expressing himself since I had seen him before; the poor fellow is in good spirits about going abroad, and I must make the best of it. It was singular good fortune that brought us together at this time, but the weather is very bad; it has poured with rain for the last three days. Today I am going over part of the line, but have not been able to commence yet. Robert will endeavour to write to you before he sails, and desires his kindest remembrance.

God bless you, Sir!
Believe me to remain
Yours sincerely,
G.S.

There is not the slightest hint in this letter of any row between George and Robert. According to George, they were both enjoying their farewell dinner parties. They appear the best of friends, if George a rather sad one.

As for Robert himself, he was probably not at all pleased to be hanging around Liverpool. He had had every intention of going straight to South America without having to come north and wishing any sort of farewell to his father. The main baggage party for Colombia had already left England, sailing from Falmouth. Robert himself had earlier left London in a coach for Falmouth and South America, complete with all his luggage and instruments, when he received orders to turn around and start from Liverpool instead. This was George's singular good fortune, but not Robert's.

On his log during his first day at sea, Robert betrays neither sadness nor relief. He busies himself with recording the winds and the temperatures.

June 18, 1824. – Set sail from Liverpool in the 'Sir William Congreve,' at three o'clock in the afternoon: wind from the south-east, sea smooth, day beautiful; temperature of the air towards evening in the shade, 58°. Made some experiments with 'Register Thermometer' to ascertain the temperature of the sea at various depths, but failed on account of the velocity of the vessel through the water not allowing the instrument to sink. The temperature of the surface water appeared to be 54° at seven o'clock in the evening – this ascertained by lifting a bucket of water on board and immediately immersing the thermometer. This was considered as sufficiently accurate, as the temperature could not sensibly change in the time occupied by the experiment.

Meanwhile, George was left behind on his own, having bravely waved goodbye at Liverpool's Pier head, a spot from which many hundreds of thousands have set sail for the New World before and since, most of them never to return. Then he went sadly home. Liverpool was now his home. He had moved there a few days previously, as Liverpool had become the centre of his activities. The Darlington line was yet to open but the Liverpool job was obviously on a much bigger scale and was much more important. The problems and the disasters to come were also on a much bigger scale, the worst he would ever face in his career. He certainly needed to be cheerful, having to face them all without his beloved Robert.

# 8

# LIVERPOOL: THE STORY SO FAR

The Stockton–Darlington Railway, for all its achievements, was in many ways the pinnacle of the centuries old colliery railways. It was the most highly developed line of its time, using steam locomotives as the main power (though horses were used for passenger coaches until 1833) and in being open to the public, but it had been planned essentially to be a colliery line, and a little local one at that. The opening banquet at Stockton had been suitably jolly but the dignitaries were simply County Durham dignitaries plus representatives of other railways then being planned. We realise now, looking back, that it marked the beginning of a new era, but at the time the Stockton and Darlington Railway was not greeted as a national event.

The Liverpool–Manchester Railway was something different. From the beginning of its construction the eyes of the world were upon it. In every way, it was a gigantic venture, arguably the greatest feat of engineering which had ever been attempted. It was in every way bigger, more expensive and more dangerous an undertaking than the Darlington line. The locomotives, when they came to be unveiled, were four times as fast as the primitive engines on the Darlington line and from the very beginning passengers were a vital element. It set the pattern for almost a hundred years of railway. Not the least of its problems was the size and power of the opposition. George Stephenson couldn't possibly have known what he'd let himself in for.

The growth of the cities of Liverpool and Manchester in the first two decades of the nineteenth century can only be described as phenomenal. The population of Liverpool increased from 55,000 in 1790, to 119,000 in 1821 and that of Manchester from 57,000 to 133,000. Until the 1780s, cotton for the water-powered Lancashire mills had come from Turkey, plus some from the West

Indies, all of it arriving at the port of London which meant a laborious and expensive road journey on pack horses up to Lancashire. When steam power came in with the industrial revolution, new and bigger supplies were needed and they turned to the USA, bringing it direct to the port of Liverpool. In 1792, 503 bags of raw cotton from the USA were landed at Liverpool. In 1823 the number was 412,020, another phenomenal increase for those interested in phenomenal increases. The *Liverpool Mercury* certainly was. In an article in July 1824, looking at the increase in shipping in the port of Liverpool where the tonnage had gone up from 450,000 in 1800 to 1,224,000 in 1824, a *Liverpool Mercury* correspondent said that in his opinion 'so rapid an advance is unexampled in the history of the world'. Perhaps an overstatement but his excitement was certainly understandable.

The big problem was transport – how to get all that raw cotton quickly from Liverpool inland to Manchester and the surrounding cotton mills. The big answer was water. The long established Mersey and Irwell Navigation Company was making a fortune by shipping the cotton by river upstream. In 1825 shares in the company, originally purchased at £70, were selling at £1,250 and paying an annual dividend of £35.

They had naturally not been very pleased when James Brindley, on behalf of the Duke of Bridgwater, had come along in 1759 and started to build a canal. The Bridgwater canal opened the canal age in Britain and the Duke himself made a fortune from the Liverpool–Manchester trade. Unlike his rival, the Mersey and Irwell Navigation Company, which had thirty-nine different proprietors, the duke was the sole owner of his canal. In 1822 it was estimated that his family were still making an annual profit from the canal of £100,000 – a canal that had cost only £250,000 to build.

There were such rich pickings for both the river and the canal operators that they'd learned happily to live with each other. They had their own monopolies and made sure the prices were kept up even if the industrialists waiting for the cotton and other materials had to suffer. There was so much trade that raw cotton was left for weeks in Liverpool before being transported inland. Samuel Smiles reckoned that it was common for cotton to take longer to travel the thirty miles or so from Liverpool to Manchester than it took for it to cross the Atlantic in the first place. Liverpool was of course the home of transatlantic steamships, which was why Robert Stephenson had been sent up to Liverpool to get a better, faster boat to South America. It took until 1825 and the Darlington line for steam power to be successfully harnessed to railways, but steam had been at work on the high seas for at least a decade. (The first steam boat to cross the Atlantic, the *Savannah*, arrived in Liverpool in 1819, another landmark in the rise of Liverpool.)

The Darlington line had been in some ways a stab in the dark. They weren't quite sure of the trade that would be available or the profits to be made, which was why Edward Pease had always insisted on a modest 5 per cent. But in Liverpool, everyone was more than aware of the enormous amount of trade crying out to be transported. It was a pleasant situation for the canal men to be in. In the 1820s they were still relatively new and were sure their best days were to come. The river men were equally confident, in fact they'd recently spent £250,000 on deepening and widening the Mersey and Irwell. Both the river and canal interests, having invested a million or so pounds and made themselves several millions in return, were certainly not going to welcome any newcomers.

The idea of a horsedrawn railway from Liverpool to Manchester had been around for many years. In 1797 William Jessop did a survey but could find no backers. In 1798 an engineer called Benjamin Outram, who'd perfected his own iron plateway, made a similar suggestion but fell out with his Manchester partners. (There's a nice theory that the word tram came from Outram – after his patent Outram way – but the origin of the word dates back much earlier, to 1,500, and came from the low German *traam*, meaning wooden beam.)

Thomas Gray, the writer on railways (the one who locked himself up in his room with his vision telling his wife he was going to change the world), suggested that the first locomotive railway should be built between Liverpool and Manchester because of the extensive trade, though he was thinking of using Blenkinsop's cogged wheels. This was in 1820 and it is reasonable to suppose that William James, who must be given the major credit for the original work on the Liverpool railway, had read or heard of Gray's suggestions. James arrived in 1821 in Liverpool and began talks with Joseph Sandars, a wealthy Liverpool corn merchant and a noted critic of the canal and river monopolies.

Since 1815 William James, as we know, had been the country's leading advocate of railways. His money came from his London-based land agency business, said to be the biggest in the country, which in 1812, was bringing him around £10,000 a year. According to the apologia written later by his daughter E.M.S.P., the one in which she attacks George Stephenson, James was worth at that time around £150,000.

It is relatively easy to see why Robert Stephenson found William James so attractive. He was big and fat and jolly, a great talker, full of enthusiasm and ideas. Most of all, he was a brilliant persuader, being as fluent on paper as in speech, so unlike poor old George. Many of his letters, published later by his daughter, show some nice turns of phrase. 'By the speed and cheapness of steam carriage on railroad, space is nearly destroyed.' Talking, as he always was, about the great benefits which railways would bring, he said that a railway 'tends to bless the land through which it passeth'. At the time, which was 1822, everyone thought precisely the opposite, but his words came true.

William James was indeed a friend of the rich and the famous – and even when he didn't know someone rich and famous, he was a master at introducing himself by some incredible feats of name dropping. This is a letter James wrote to Lord Stanley, one of the landowners along the route of the Liverpool railway, whom he wanted to impress.

Prescott, Nov. 13th, 1822

MY LORD, – The plans and sections of the proposed Liverpool and Manchester railroad being completed, I have applied to your noble father to allow me to submit the same to his lordship's consideration tomorrow morning. I am not so fortunate to possess a letter of introduction to the noble earl or your lordship, though from my long experience in parliamentary and other business, as land agent and engineer for his present Majesty, the land revenue, the late Dukes of Northumberland and Norfolk, the Duchess of Dorset, Earls Whitworth and Warwick, the Archbishop of Canterbury, Lord Holland, and other noble personages, I believe I must be personally known to your lordship.

Unfortunately for William James, he was so busy impressing people with his own fame and his own schemes that he gave little time to his London office and the more routine job of being a land agent. He preferred to speculate in ideas not land. He neglected his office to bustle round the country throwing out ideas for canals, bridges and railways, forming partnerships, financing surveys, then moving on just as quickly to the next town and the next wonderful scheme.

He had been thinking originally of horsedrawn railways until, as we have seen, he heard about locomotives. He came across George Stephenson at Killingworth in the summer of 1821 and exclaimed in wonder at the efficiency of his locomotive engine: 'An engine that will before long effect a complete revolution in society.' George was described, in a letter from James to Losh, as the 'greatest practical genius of the age.'

It is not clear if he saw George's machines before meeting Sandars – both events happened around the summer of 1821 – but he was continually rushing between the two, feeding and fuelling enthusiasm at the two sources. Having got Sandars excited by the prospect of a Liverpool railway to put the water barons in their place, he managed to take a look at a possible route. He did what he euphemistically called an 'oculine survey' (probably hanging out of the window of a fast coach on the turnpike, judging by the speed at which he moved), and reported that it would be a very easy job. 'The geological difficulties are very few and unimportant.' He was soon sending technical letters across to Stephenson, already convinced that not only was he going to officially survey and build the line but have steam locomotives running on it. It's hard not to find his enthusiasm attractive. (The Darlington line, remember, was still thinking of horses at this stage.)

By September 1821 James had become a partner with Stephenson and Losh on some locomotive designs and tried, but failed, to get them adopted on one of the many other railway projects (at Moreton-in-Marsh) he was currently promoting. Meanwhile Mr Sandars was busily drumming up support amongst the merchants of Liverpool. As the Stockton–Darlington Railway was very much a Darlington affair, so the Liverpool–Manchester line was born and bred in Liverpool.

The following year James was officially commissioned by Sandars and his partners to survey the line. He was to be paid £300 for the job (£10 a mile), which by now was very welcome as his land agency business was running deep into financial troubles. One at least of his many schemes looked like coming to fruition, perhaps saving him from disaster. The previous year's oculine survey, plus the plans and designs and travelling expenses, had all been paid for out of his own pocket.

This was the stage when young Robert Stephenson, the son of his new and brilliant friend, came across to be one of his assistants, plus his own son William, his brother-in-law Paul Padley and three others. Robert later talked about the great times they had but it was a much harder job than the Darlington survey. Men, women and children threw stones at them, probably encouraged by the canal lobby. At St Helens a gang of miners attacked them and threatened to throw them down the pit. The man carrying the theodolite was always singled out for the worst attacks, inspiring in the locals a Luddite rage, till James hired a prize fighter to protect him, though it didn't stop the theodolite on one occasion from being smashed.

James was spurred on rather than perturbed by this opposition and his cheerfulness and resourcefulness must have inspired his young assistant. Writing back to Sandars, James sounds almost messianic in his fervour:

At Manchester the subject encourages all men's thoughts and it is curious and amusing to hear their conjectures. The canal companies are alive to the danger. I am the object of their persecution and hate; they would immolate me if they could; but if I can die the death of Samson, by pulling away the pillars, I am content to die with these Philistines. Be assured, my dear sir, that not a moment shall be lost, nor shall my attention for a day be diverted from this concern which increases in importance every hour, as well as in the certainty of ultimate success.

His words, as usual, were more fluent and flowery than his deeds. His attention was indeed being seriously diverted, as he tried to keep other projects, and himself, afloat but his prose was certainly convincing. It probably appealed to Sandars, who was also an enthusiast and propagandist, much more so than the rather dour, solid, careful Peases and the other Quakers behind the Darlington line.

Not much is known personally about Sandars except that he was a Liverpool businessman, a Whig and a parliamentary reformer. He was said to be a better promoter than a businessman and one of his first objects was to get the local press and politicians interested in the scheme. There were some local Quakers behind his scheme, such as James Cropper, but his main Liverpool supporters were the more liberal, radical merchants, bankers and professional men. They were active in the great national causes of the day, such as the antislavery movement, and determined locally to reduce the unfair powers of the canal and river companies. Over in Manchester, where his embryo committees were much smaller in numbers, they were almost to a man cotton manufacturers.

All the Liverpool railway promoters were reasonable, solid, well respected citizens and one of the earliest moves they made, when their committee was formed in 1822, was to inform the canal people of their plans and grievances, suggesting to the Bridgwater trustees that they should reduce their exorbitant rates. Informal talks took place and the canal people, had they been foresighted, could have delayed the building of the railway for a decade at least if only they'd agreed to open up their monopoly. Alternatively they could have joined forces and together exploited the enormous transport possibilities that were so obviously available. The canal people refused point blank. They themselves had formerly been the upstarts, complaining about the river board's monopoly, but as so often happens, once in power they wanted to hold on. The result was that the railway committee was even more determined to succeed.

William James, for all his purple prose, was now patently beginning to hold them up. The committee constantly wrote to him about the survey but he was proving exceedingly slow. He wrote to George Stephenson in November 1822 saying he was now finalising the survey, asking for the latest details on what loads George's locomotives could haul.

There's a letter that same month back from Stephenson, rather elliptical and one vital word can't be read, nor is it clear what subject they are discussing, but it shows the first sign that the two of them have had some difference of opinion.

To William James, Horse and Jockey Inn,
Newton, Nr Warrington, Lancs
My dear Sir,
     You try my conscience very . . . [word missing]. I assure you I am quite inclined to do all the good I possibly can, but you will

excuse me saying more than I think I can perform. I hope you have had a safe and pleasant journey home. I have no doubt but I shall please you and the Company with the Engines in the end.

> I am Dear Sir, Yours truly, Geo Stephenson.
> Killingworth Colly.
> Nov 4, 1822.

From the look of it, William James must have been encouraging Stephenson to boost the power of his machines, perhaps exaggerating or even lying about their performance which George, being an honourable if uneducated man, is unwilling to do. However, they keep exchanging letters. In another, George says he has some improved wagons which travel with less friction and hopes James might put in a good word for them with the Stratford on Avon Railway, yet another of James' current schemes.

Sandars, meanwhile, had been very busy establishing good parliamentary contacts, getting ready for the battles ahead. Through one of the more influential members of his committee, John Gladstone, a former MP, two local MPs, both national figures, became supporters of the railway – George Canning and William Huskisson. Another of their influential supporters was Charles Lawrence who in 1823 became mayor of Liverpool. But through James' slowness in providing the survey they missed the coming session of parliament.

James had had the canal opposition to contend with, bad weather and objections from the turnpike trusts, forcing him to keep away from their roads, but the main problem was his own financial position.

'The surveys and plans can't be completed, I see, till the end of the week,' so he wrote to Sandars. 'With illness, anguish of mind and inexpressible distress, I perceive I must sink if I wait any longer; and in short I have so neglected the suit in Chancery I named to you, that if I do not put in an answer I shall be outlawed.'

The suit in Chancery, brought by his brother-in-law, went through and in 1823 James was declared bankrupt and went to prison for seven months – the first of several actions against him from his former partners. He still had the nearly completed survey which he carefully kept hold of, making sure the committee wouldn't completely forget him.

The committee at length decided they'd had enough, having had their plans put back over a year because of all the James troubles. Sandars and four others went to see Stephenson's engines at Killingworth and Hetton, inspected the progress of the Darlington line and were very impressed. On 19 May 1824, Sandars wrote to Edward Pease in Darlington telling him that they'd decided to appoint George as engineer. This letter, hitherto unpublished, is one of the letters Liverpool Library bought at Sothebys in 1973.

Dear Sir,

Tho' am aware you are not in town, I take the liberty of addressing this to you to state that the Liverpool Manchester Rail Road Compy have appointed Mr Geo Stephenson as their Engineer and if he be on your line we request you will send a special messenger to inform him that a letter has been sent to him at Newcastle advising the same. The Deputation had previously engaged him and that engagement has been confirmed by the subscribers at large.

The expense of the special messenger we shall be glad to defray. I beg the messenger be sent immediately to prevent him contracting any other engagement.

I shall feel obliged by any person in your absence acting on this.

I am, dear sir, very truly yours,
J. SANDARS.

To Edwd Pease, Esq,
Or to the Clerk of the Rail Road Office in his absence.

It would seem from this that Mr Sandars was in a slight panic, desperate to contact George. It was by now well over a year since James' downfall and they obviously thought that in the meantime George might well have taken on other jobs and be unable to work for them. It would be hard to believe from this letter that George had been in any way scheming with the committee to get James' job, which was what the James faction later claimed.

A week later, presumably having heard in the affirmative from George, Sandars wrote to James telling him the news.

May 25, 1824

Dear Sir,

I think it right to inform you that the Committee have engaged your friend Mr. G. Stephenson. We expect him here in a few days.

The subscription list for £30,000 is filled, and the Manchester gentlemen have conceded us the entire management. I very much regret that by delay and promises you have forfeited the confidence of the subscribers. I cannot help it. I fear now that you will only have the fame of being connected with the commencement of this undertaking. If you will send me down your plans and estimates I will do everything for you I can, and I believe I possess as much influence as any person. I am quite certain that the appointment of Stephenson will, under all circumstances, be agreeable to you. I believe you have recommended him yourself. If you consent to put your plaits &c under my control and management your name shall be prominent in the proceedings and this, in such a mighty affair, will be of importance to you. You may rely upon my zeal for you in every point connected with your reputation.

James kept tight hold of the plans and still had some vague hopes of keeping contact with the Liverpool company. He wrote to his brother-in-law Paul Padley, who'd been his second in command on the survey, asking him to go to Liverpool and do a fresh survey. But George had beaten him to it. He had stepped in quickly and engaged Padley himself to work with him on the new survey.

'He knows my plans,' wrote James to his son, 'of which he and S. will now avail themselves. I confess I did not calculate upon such duplicity in either.'

The James camp have always seen this as a very nasty tactic by George. Certainly it was a smart move – but on the other hand it was eminently sensible. George knew by this time that he was losing Robert, and his first hand knowledge of the terrain, to South America, so it was as well to get any other experienced help he could.

William James now fades from the scene for ever. He did get out of prison and tried for a few years to start other railway schemes but each time something went wrong. He retired in the end to Cornwall where he lived very frugally. His family always staunchly defended him and it is hard not to feel a certain sympathy. He was an early advocate of railways and was generous in the praise and help he gave George. While other railway pioneers went on to fame and fortune he received nothing. There is no evidence that George or anyone else caused his downfall, though George might have been a bit more helpful when he did hit hard times. The flaws were obviously in James' own character. There was an exciting, honeymoon period each time he started work on a scheme – but each time it ended in tears, for reasons very similar to those at Liverpool, with James being dispensed with. In the end, William James never built a railway.

# 9

# GEORGE'S DARKEST HOUR

George was soon to find how very different the Liverpool folk were from his dear North Easterners. Having seen Robert off on his boat he started immediately on the survey, living rough in lodging houses and farmhouses, 'rising at 3.30,' so he said in a letter back to Longridge in Newcastle, 'some days working fourteen hours without bread or water.' But it was the strength and violence of the opposition which alarmed him.

> We have sad work with Lord Derby, Lord Sefton and Bradshaw the great Canal Proprietor, whose grounds we go through with the projected railway. Their ground is blockaded on every side to prevent us getting on with the Survey. Bradshaw fires guns through his ground in the course of the night to prevent the Surveyors coming in the dark. We are to have a grand field day next week. The Liverpool Railway Company are determined to force a survey through if possible. Lord Sefton says he will have a hundred men against us. The Company thinks those Great men have no right to stop a Survey. It was the Farmers only who have a right to complain and by charging damages for trespass is all they can do.

The canal company, with Bradshaw representing the duke's trustees, had by now realised that the railway committee was in earnest and could become a serious rival. They reduced their rates by twenty-five per cent for freight between Liverpool and Manchester. The Mersey and Irwell Navigation people followed suit, but it was too late to impress the uncommitted or to halt the railway committee. Their propaganda campaign nonetheless helped to whip up the antagonism of many ordinary people along George's route. They issued pamphlets which claimed that steam locomotives would cause women to miscarry, stop cows grazing, cause hens to cease laying, country inns to close, kill birds in the air, destroy farm land, burn down farmers' houses, pollute the air, remove foxes and pheasants, extinguish horses as a species and make oats and hay unmarketable. In Manchester, posters appeared in shop windows showing poor, half-starved horses looking over a fence at the monstrous passing trains. In the captions they were telling each other that their lives had finished. To avoid being attacked by the mob or shot at by the gentry, George was frequently forced to take levels in the moonlight, sending men to some other spot to set off guns in an effort to confuse the landowners.

In May 1824, the month that George was appointed engineer, the committee formally registered itself and became a company with a young man of thirty-five called Henry Booth as its treasurer. His father had been on the provisional committee two years previously and he too was a corn merchant, like Sandars. Henry Booth much preferred the excitement of the new railway company and threw himself into every aspect of railway work. Not only did he show a flair for organising support and raising the initial capital of £300,000 but he also wrote all the prospectuses and most of the reports issued by the company from 1824 to 1830. He became the company's official historian, but, even more surprising, he turned out to have an inventive and mechanical turn of mind. He was a strong and knowledgeable supporter of Stephenson's engineering and in the end proved to be the source of one vital engineering development.

The progress of the Liverpool line, now that it was moving forward once again, was creating a lot of national interest. With the Stockton and Darlington well on the way to its opening, there was a spate of railway projects up and down the country, though they were mainly colliery lines. It was nothing like the railway rush that was to follow some years later but at the time the handful of schemes that were being floated seemed a lot to George. He was involved with many of the schemes – scheme being the word, judging by the amount of scheming that was going on. He wrote in November 1824, from Chester to Longridge at the loco works in Newcastle, telling him about the busy time he was having. He sounds rather bossy and, despite his apparent moans, obviously enjoying being so much in demand, perhaps even being carried away slightly by his new found success.

Michael Longridge, Esq.                  Chester, November 16, 1824
Dear Sir,

There are nothing but railways and rumours of Railways in this country. I am desired to examine Lord Crew's Coalworks in the neighbourhood of Newcastle under line and give a report thereon; as I can make it convenient to do so. Several other Coal owners in this neighbourhood desire me to give similar reports. How I shall get all ends to meet I do not know. I think your words will come true. I shall have to work until I am an old man. I have a bag full of news to tell you on the defects of your rails. You have got your friends in the north as well as myself. The indirect secrets are getting out. It is astonishing the deep schemes that men contrive for the overthrow of their neighbour: and how often does it fall upon their own heads. I assure you I have been twisted backwards and forwards as I think few poor fellows ever were. Notwithstanding all those difficulties my spirits are still up, and I think I have got four times as much face as I had when I inhabited the north. I am sometimes obliged to use my tongue like a scolding wife.

My kind respects to Mrs. Longridge and your family: also to Mr. and Mrs. Birkinshaw: not forgetting my friend Mr. Gooch. It is now eleven O'Clock and a great deal of work yet to do. I cannot get to bed at your time.

I am Dear Sir,
Yours very sincerely
GEO. STEPHENSON

In a letter to Joseph Sandars in December 1824, George comes back to the same theme. 'The rage for railroads is so great that many will be laid in parts where they will not pay.' The rage turned out to be very small scale – only one railway act was passed by parliament in 1825 – but George's prediction eventually came true.

George completed his Liverpool–Manchester survey by the end of 1824 and in February 1825 produced an estimate of all costs – construction and rolling stock – of £400,000. This was £100,000 more than anticipated during the James survey but the company was pleased to have hard facts and costs at last and immediately announced they were going for a parliamentary bill. They launched a publicity campaign in the local papers, to which the rivals answered back, and for months the letters columns were full of 'Yours Disgusted' letters with 'Veritas' arguing with 'Liverpoolian'. To keep it all as scientific as possible the company organised some public demonstrations at Killingworth showing off the strength and speed of George's engines. The Mersey and Irwell Navigation Company, not to be outdone, did river tests, loading two horsedrawn barges at Liverpool, sending them up to Manchester where they were unloaded and sent back, doing the round trip in twenty-four hours. They did the test again the next day to prove it wasn't a fluke or a fiddle. The railway company, unimpressed, steamed on.

When the company's parliamentary application was announced it was seen by all how much progress they had made in acquiring support in London. Of the potential shareholders (who had to be listed under parliamentary law) most came from Liverpool, with 164; but London wasn't far behind with 126. The Manchester shareholders numbered fifty-four. It augured well for a safe passage at Westminster,

First there was some opposition in Liverpool which had to be settled. A strong element on Liverpool Council was against the company bringing the nasty steam locomotives into the boundary of the city. 'The vilest nuisance that ever the town had experienced,' so it was said at a council meeting. Despite the arguments of Charles Lawrence, who'd been mayor the previous year and had become the company's first chairman, the railway lobby had to agree that they would use stationary engines, not locomotives, at the Liverpool end. The local papers examined the hundred-page draft bill in great detail. The *Liverpool Mercury* was worried by the 'vomiting forth of long and black smoke at the places of rendezvous for the engines'. The use of the word rendezvous makes them sound very suspicious, as if locomotive engines – which of course people in Lancashire had yet to see – were in the habit of congregating secretly together and then ganging up on unsuspecting humans. But the *Mercury* on the whole still seemed to be in favour of the railway, though the arguments continued to rage in its correspondence column. The editor finally announced that because some letters were so obviously personal and biased they would in future be regarded as advertisements and the writers would be charged for their insertion. (A novel idea which would no doubt appeal to many of today's correspondence column editors.)

The debate on the bill started in parliament in March 1825. During the preliminary speeches William Huskisson, president of the Board of Trade, who spoke as a Liverpool MP and not as a member of the government, came out in its favour. He said if he listened only to all the private individuals who had approached him and to those with their fortunes tied up in the canal then he should oppose the bill. He personally had no interests in either the canal or the railway company but for the sake of the public good he was convinced that the railway promoters had aims above the mere accumulation of profit. The whole trade of the area, he said, would prosper with the railway. William Peel, brother of Sir Robert Peel, also supported the bill.

For several months the opposition had had expert engineers analysing every comma in Stephenson's survey. Once the bill entered its committee stage one hundred and fifty different petitions suddenly appeared, ranging from poor spinsters, impoverished reverends to the trustees of the Bridgwater canal, all with detailed and lengthy objections to the railway. The committee examination of all of the relevant papers and witnesses began on 21 March and sat for thirty-seven sessions in all, ending on 31 May.

The opponents of the bill had hired a total of eight counsel to present their case and it was the cross-examining of George Stephenson by Edward Alderson, their leading counsel, that was to prove the most vital.

George himself wasn't called for some time. The first eleven days were taken up with the proposers of the bill taking their own local witnesses through their grievances against the canal and river boards. Three corn merchants testified that it took them from eighteen to twenty-four days to get their goods dispatched from Liverpool to Manchester. Others described queues of forty merchants waiting at the canal office to be served. The frequency of bad weather – ice, frost, high tides – was gone into and the ensuing delays on traffic. For six days, expert engineers were called, such as Nicholas Wood, all of whom were handled rather gently by Alderson and his colleagues, though he did permit himself a bit of sarcasm when one engineer couldn't answer a question: 'Read a little upon it.'

George was called on Monday 25 April and started off confidently enough, being examined quite mildly, on the general feasibility of railways and locomotives. This was his home ground and no one knew more about it than he, after all his experiences at Killingworth and Hettan. Since 1813, he stated, he had built fifty-five steam engines, sixteen of them locomotives. He'd been briefed by one of the railway counsel, Henry Brougham, on no account to overstate his case. Beforehand, George had wanted to mention a speed of twenty miles per hour, which was no more than the truth, but Brougham said he must mention a much lower speed 'or he would be regarded as a maniac fit for Bedlam and damn the whole thing'. When Alderson put the question in the committee Stephenson committed himself very soberly to a speed of between four and eight miles per hour – then he damned himself by blurting out, 'I am confident that much more might be done.'

This enabled Alderson from then on to cleverly and continually refer to the proposed locomotives as going at twelve mph, thus confirming everyone's worst suspicions and fears. It has to be remembered that the bulk of even intelligent opinion in 1825 could not believe that any machine could travel at over ten miles an hour without disintegrating and killing everyone in sight. Even supporters of locomotives were worried about speeds. A writer in the *Quarterly Review* of March 1825 (which came out during the hearings) admitted that he was in favour of the Liverpool–Manchester Railway but only if the speeds were kept within reason.

> What can be more palpably absurd than the prospect held out of locomotives travelling *twice* as fast as stage-coaches! We trust that Parliament will, in all railways it may sanction, limit the speed to eight or nine miles an hour.

In May 1825, again during the hearings, Nicholas Wood's great *Treatise on Rail-Roads* appeared, and he too warned against excessive claims.

> It is far from my wish to promulgate to the world that the ridiculous expectations, or rather professions, of the enthusiastic speculists be realised, and that we shall see them travelling at the rate of 12, 16, 18 or 20 miles an hour; nothing could do more harm towards their adoption, or general improvement, than the promulgation of such nonsense.

Alderson, by encouraging George in the committee to predict speeds much higher than eight mph, had therefore done great psychological damage on a national scale to the railway case. He went on next to ask George about the rate of accidents and if at twelve mph and other high speeds a locomotive could cope with smooth rails, (An old chestnut which had worried even locomotive engineers for years until Killingworth had proved them wrong.) George was able at least to answer such a technical question with care and confidence. He even provoked a smile when one member of the committee broke in to ask what would happen if a cow strayed on the line in the way of an engine doing ten mph. 'Would not that, think you, be a very awkward circumstance?' 'Very awkward,' replied George. 'For the coo.'

Alderson at length moved on to the survey itself, for which George as engineer was responsible. Almost at once George's credibility and confidence collapsed. In managing to complete the survey on time he had allowed subordinates to take vital measurements, many of which were soon proved in the committee to be completely wrong.

Worse than that, George didn't even have any figures at all for many vital parts of his proposed railways.

Q: What is the width of the Irwell there?
A: I cannot say exactly at present.
Q: How many arches is your bridge to have?
A: It is not determined upon.
Q: How could you make an estimate for it then?
A: I have given a sufficient sum for it.

As a sample of his answers, that was fairly typical. Alderson went on and George was reduced more and more to answers like 'I do not recollect', 'I did, but I do not recollect', 'It may, I cannot speak of it', or 'It was a mistake'.

To call Alderson's questions a cross-examination is putting it politely. Poor George was annihilated. Alderson, who'd at one time been a law reporter, later to become a judge and a baron, won his fame by his handling of George Stephenson.

It need hardly be said that George was out of his depth, untrained and ungifted in presenting himself verbally, unable to master his thoughts or arguments and for most of the time unable to make himself understood through the thickness and incoherence of his Geordie accent. His remark about the coo became a society dinner table joke for months. Notwithstanding, and trying hard to avoid too much sob stuff or easy sympathy, it has to be said that George had rather left himself wide open to attack.

George was forced to admit error after error. It was stipulated, for example, that the railway should cross the Irwell at a height which would provide a minimum headroom of 16 ft 6 ins for navigation, yet the plans showed a rail level only ten feet above the water and three feet below maximum flood level. Having established this damning fact, Alderson's relentless cross-examination continued by proving that Stephenson had estimated the cost of this Irwell bridge at £5,000 without any idea as to its dimensions or form. 'So,' he concluded scathingly, 'you make a bridge, perhaps 14 ft high, perhaps 20 ft high, perhaps with 3 arches and perhaps with one, and then you boldly say that £5,000 is a proper estimate for it?' 'I think so,' answered Stephenson lamely, and, turning to the committee, 'I merely set out the line for other surveyors to follow.' 'Did you not survey the line of the road?' asked Alderson. 'My Assistant did,' replied Stephenson.

As Alderson had by now established that there were numerous errors in the levels of anything up to ten feet, he next put the obvious question. 'What,' he asked, 'was the original base line on which all your levels are calculated as marked on the section?' 'Near the Vauxhall Road in Liverpool,' came the reply. 'Whereabout?' pressed Alderson. 'I think,' answered the unhappy Stephenson, 'about 150 yards from it, but I am not quite sure.' Pursued further, it became obvious that George had no idea how the base line had been determined.

The final confrontation went like this:

Q: Then it is possible you may be out at other parts?
A: It may be, but I do not think so.
Q: You do not believe you are out on your levels?
A: I have made my estimate from the levels which I believe are correct.
Q: Do you believe, aye or no, that your levels are correct?
A: I have heard it reported that they are not.
Q: Did you take the levels yourself?
A: They were taken for me.

Q: Other people have taken them for you and upon their estimate you have made your estimate?
A: Yes.

An eminent engineer, William Cubitt, who had been employed by the railway company to check certain levels, was forced to admit Stephenson's mistakes. You have not found Mr Stephenson's level correct at any one point?' 'I have not found them correct in any point that I have taken.'

Stephenson's counsel, Mr Spankie, tried to defend him, explaining how the landowners had refused many levels to be taken, but he too was forced to admit mistakes. 'It will be said on the other side that Mr Stephenson, having been guilty of one error, the whole credit of his estimate is shaken. But the truth is that Mr Stephenson, on a datum given by others, calculated it would cost so much to make the Railway.'

The opposition, having revealed countless flaws in the survey methods, went on to take the estimate itself to pieces. One of their experts, the engineer Francis Giles, said that Stephenson's proposal to take his railway across Chat Moss, a large marshland wilderness, was ridiculous. He personally would never attempt it, but if it were tried, the railway should estimate not £400,000 but a figure closer to £1,500,000.

Harrison, one of the opposition's other leading counsel, didn't score direct hits like Alderson, but he poked endless fun at Stephenson's idea of 'floating' his railway line across Chat Moss.

It is ignorance almost inconceivable. It is perfect madness in a person called upon to speak on a scientific subject to propose such a plan. . . . Every part of this scheme shows that this man has applied himself to a subject of which he has no knowledge, and to which he has no science to apply.

Turning to the proposal to work the intended line by means of locomotives, Harrison proceeded:

When we set out with the original prospectus, we were to gallop, I know not at what rate; I believe it was at the rate of 12 miles an hour. My learned friend, Mr Adam . . . says that they would go at the rate of 12 miles an hour with the aid of the devil in the form of a locomotive, sitting as postilion on the fore horse, and an honourable member sitting behind him to stir up the fire, and keep it at full speed. But the speed at which the locomotive engines are to go has slackened: Mr. Adam does not go faster now than 5 miles an hour. The learned serjeant (Spankie) says he should like to have 7, but he would be content to go 6. I will show he cannot go 6; and probably, for any practical purposes, I may be able to show that I can keep up with him *by the canal*. . . . Locomotive engines are liable to be operated upon by the weather. You are told they are affected by rain, and an attempt has been made to cover them; but the wind will affect them; and any gale of wind which would affect the traffic on the Mersey would render it *impossible* to set off a locomotive engine, either by poking of the fire, or keeping up the pressure of the steam till the boiler was ready to burst.

It was Alderson's final summing up which completed Stephenson's humiliation.

This is the most absurd scheme that ever entered into the head of man to conceive. I think I may put it to them fairly whether they ever before saw such an estimate. My learned friends almost endeavoured to stop my examination. They wished me to put in the plan, but I had rather have the exhibition of Mr. Stephenson in that box. I say he never had a plan – I believe he never had one – I do not believe he is capable of making one. . . . He is either ignorant or something else which I will not mention. . . . His is a mind perpetually fluctuating between opposite difficulties: he neither knows whether he is to make bridges over roads or rivers, or of one size or another; or to make embankments, or cuttings, or inclined planes, or in what way the thing is to be carried into effect. When you put a question to him upon a difficult point, he resorts to two or three hypotheses, and never comes to a decided conclusion.

Moving to the subject of the Irwell bridge, and all George's mistakes about it, Alderson kept up his stream of invective.

It was the most ridiculous thing I ever heard stated by any man. I am astonished that any man standing in that box would make such a statement without shrinking to nothing. . . . Did any ignorance ever arrive at such a pitch as this? Was there ever any ignorance exhibited like this? Is Mr. Stephenson to be the person upon whose faith this Committee is to pass this Bill involving property to the extent of £400/500,000 when he is so ignorant of his profession as to propose to build a bridge not sufficient to carry off the flood water of the river or to permit any of the vessels to pass which of necessity must pass under it, and leave his own Railroad liable to be several feet under water?

He makes schemes without seeing the difficulties, and when the difficulties are pointed out, then he starts other schemes. He has produced five schemes all resulting in one estimate. . .

And when did Mr. Cubitt make his survey to detect his mistakes? Long before; and Mr. Stephenson has the face to say that he only *heard* that his levels were not correct. Why, at that time he knew they were incorrect and that Mr. Cubitt had been sent down to ascertain to what extent they were so.

I never knew a person draw so much upon human credulity as Mr. Stephenson has proposed to do in the evidence he has given.

I am told they are going to throw Mr. Stephenson and his estimate overboard and to call upon Hon. Members to decide without his evidence. Now if they attempt that it will be the strangest thing that was ever attempted in the House of Commons. . . . Upon Chat Moss, I care not whether Mr. Giles is right or wrong in his estimate, for whether it be effected by means of piers raised up all the way for four miles through Chat Moss, whether they are to support it on beams of wood or by erecting masonry, or whether Mr. Giles shall put a solid bank of earth through it, – in all these schemes there is not one found like that of Mr. Stephenson's, namely, to cut impossible drains on the side of this road; and it is sufficient for me to suggest and to show, that this scheme of Mr. Stephenson's is impossible or impracticable, and that no other scheme, if they proceed upon this line, can be suggested which will not produce enormous expense. I think that has been irrefragably made out. Everyone knows Chat Moss – everyone knows that the iron sinks immediately on its being put upon the surface. I have heard of culverts, which have been put upon the Moss, which, after having been surveyed the day before, have the next morning disappeared; and that a house (a poet's house, who may be supposed in the habit of building castles even in the air), story after story, as fast as one is added, the lower one sinks! There is nothing, it appears, except long sedgy grass, and a little soil to prevent its sinking into the shades of eternal night. I have now done, sir, with Chat Moss, and there I leave this railroad.

The bill had little chance after all that. The turning point had been George Stephenson's evidence. He'd been completely flattened and his defenders could offer no real reply. The first clause of the bill was beaten by 19–13 and the second clause by 23–14, and the bill was withdrawn.

George afterwards confessed that from the first day of Alderson's attack he had wilted. 'I began to wish for a hole to creep into. Some members of the committee asked if I was a foreigner, and another hinted I was mad.'

The Times slightly softened the immense blow felt by the railway lobby by accusing four members of the committee of having voted against the bill without having been present during the thirty-seven days of evidence. This was denied, naturally, and The Times was unable to furnish any proof.

The opposition was ecstatic. Thomas Creevey, an MP who'd been at the forefront of their case, famous afterwards for his Creevey Papers, gives a fine picture of their rejoicing.

Well – this devil of a railway is strangled at last. I was sure that yesterday's division had put him on his last legs, and today we had a clear majority in the Committee in our favour, and the promoters of the Bill withdrew it, and took their leave of us. . . . We had to fight this long battle against an almost universal prejudice to start with – interested shareholders and perfidious Whigs, several of whom affected to oppose us upon conscientious scruples. Sefton's ecstasies are beyond, and he is pleased to say it has been all my doing; so it's all mighty well.

Having been completely humiliated in parliament and in the public reports, there was worse to come: the Liverpool–Manchester board decided to dispense with George Stephenson's services. They were determined to call for a fresh survey, but this time from another engineer, one more distinguished, properly educated and trained, who wouldn't let them down. If only young Robert, with his parliamentary experience, had been in England he could have been invaluable to George in his hour of need. George was left alone, dismissed, abandoned and rejected.

# 10

# ROBERT RETURNS

Robert Stephenson arrived in South America on 23 July 1824, thirty-five days after leaving Liverpool. He landed at the port of La Guaira in Venezuela, eight miles from Caracas. According to his diary, his initial impression of South America was poor. 'Observed with silence the miserable appearance of the town.' His first job was to look into the possibility of building a railway between the two towns, one of the schemes which the London backers were very interested in, but he finally reported that it would cost £160,000 and would never pay its way.

In October he set off inland on mule-back for Bogota, the capital of Colombia, a journey of some twelve hundred miles, through equatorial forests into the foothills of the Andes. He managed to avoid the many ruffians and cutthroats, says Jeaffreson, and was truly amazed by the wonderful vegetation and manners of the natives he met on the way. They must have been quite intrigued by him. He wore a large hat made of plaited grass, a white cotton suit and a blue and crimson cloak. 'My cloak is admirably adapted for the purpose, amply covering the rider and mule, and at night answered the purpose of a blanket in the net hammock which every traveller carries and suspends to the trees or in the house, as occasion may require.' Robert Stephenson sounds very much like one of nature's boy scouts, though it was eighty years before Baden-Powell got round to christening the species. (Lord Baden-Powell's christian names, by a coincidence, were Robert Stephenson.)

It was just as well that Robert had not been telling the truth when he said he was going for only a year. If he had, he would have reached the mines just in time to turn round and come back again. As it was, he didn't start mining till a year and a half after leaving Liverpool. His destination was Mariquita, up the valley of the river Magdalena beyond Bogota, which the London office had led him to believe was a thriving mining town. It had been, under the Spaniards, but revolution, earthquakes and assorted acts of god had reduced its population from 20,000 to 450 and had destroyed almost every building and left every mine deserted and overgrown. Robert decided not to mine in the ghost town and moved to a village called Santa Ana, higher in the mountains, and therefore not so hot, where he built himself a hut of bamboo and palm trees and waited for the miners to arrive. On his way from Bogota he'd kept coming across piles of abandoned mining equipment left by the river side. Mules were the only form of land transport and they had obviously been unable to carry the huge steam engines. He wrote back frantic letters to London, saying there were no roads and therefore no carts, only mule-back, and that in future all machinery should be sent in pieces. The letters either never arrived or arrived too late, for huge chunks of machinery kept appearing to be left to rust by the riverside where no doubt they lie to this day.

The miners finally arrived in October 1825, which was when his troubles really began. They were all Cornishmen and most of them were drunk when they arrived – and stayed that way. They have already commenced to drink in the most outrageous manner,' wrote Robert in a letter to his firm's agent in Bogota. 'I dread the management of them. Their behaviour in Honda has, I am afraid, incurred for ever the displeasure of the Governor.' He needed the governor's help in opening up the mines and also for the chance of any social life, hence the white suit. It's strange to think of the social occasions which Robert did eventually attend, despite being stuck out in the jungle. There were many smart balls, dinners and parties in Bogota, given by rather eccentric but terribly upper class émigré Englishmen who'd gone off to the depths of South America to investigate the flora and fauna, to act as engineers or as the representatives of the many London mining expeditions. It was in South America, meeting so many well-bred Englishmen, that Robert finally lost his Geordie accent.

The biggest trouble with the Cornishmen turned out not to be their 'detestable vice of drunkenness' but the fact that to a man they hated young Robert. He was a slip of a boy, just twenty-two, and they refused to believe that he could possibly know anything about mining. 'They plainly tell me that I am obnoxious to them because I was not born in Cornwall, and although they are perfectly aware that I have visited some of the principal mines in that county and examined the various processes on the spot, yet they tell me that it is impossible for a North-Countryman to know anything about mining.'

One night, when almost all of them were drunk, they surrounded his hut, chanting and singing and jeering, saying they were going to come in and beat him up. In the best tradition of the brave lone Englishman surrounded by unruly natives (in this case, unruly Cornish natives) Robert rose from his bed and came out to face them, half dressed. According to Jeaffreson, Robert stood calmly in the midst of them, drawing himself to his full height and said: 'It won't do for us to fight tonight. It wouldn't be fair, for you are drunk and I am sober. We had better wait till tomorrow, So you better break up this meeting and go away quietly.'

They turned their eyes to the ground, says Jeaffreson, cowed by his coolness, and started slinking slowly away while Robert, with great dignity, went back inside. 'Robert lit a cigar, and, sitting down in the room, allowed the tipsy scoundrels to see him through the open door calmly smoking.' Bravo.

Robert did finally gain the confidence of some of them by organising sports, such as hammer throwing and lifting weights, taking part himself to show he might be a northerner but he wasn't a softie, but he never managed to discipline them completely. Their leaders continually addressed him as the company clerk, sent to pay their wages, refusing to acknowledge that he really was in charge. He later estimated that at any one time at least one third of the hundred and sixty miners in his control were dead drunk. Even the sober ones never managed more than half a day's work.

The full horror of his situation, which he was perfectly aware of, never seemed to make him want to pack up, though others encouraged him to break his contract. By this time his letters were arriving home in England and he told them about the deplorable conditions. 'I have my health just now very well,' he wrote to Longridge in Newcastle. 'Though I cannot say I am so strong as when I left England. The tropical climates are far from being so unhealthy as is generally supposed by those in northern latitudes. The rainy season is the only objectionable part. It occurs twice in one year.' In a postscript to this letter he added: 'May I beg the favour of your attending to the payment of my yearly subscription to the Lit. and Phil. Society? I rather suspect it has been neglected.'

Longridge, in his turn, kept Robert up to date with the latest development in the Old Country, some of which rather perplexed Robert when he wrote back.

> In the close of your last letter you mention that the calisthenic exercises have just come into fashion. This puzzled me not a little. I could not find for the life of me any significance for the new-coined word, and therefore I am as ignorant of the kind of exercise which has become fashionable amongst the ladies as I was before I left England and I suppose I must remain so until I return.

But there was soon more serious news from England. The locomotive works at Forth Street were doing badly in the absence of Robert. Longridge had got his own iron works to look after and couldn't manage to run two businesses. Edward Pease wrote to Robert telling him about the difficulties.

> I can assure thee that thy business at Newcastle, as well as thy father's engineering, have suffered very much from thy absence and, unless thou soon return, the former will be given up, as Mr Longridge is not able to give it that attention it requires: and what is done is not done with credit to the house.

Longridge himself wrote in a similar vein.

> I feel anxious for your return and I think you will find your Father and your Friend *considerable* older than when you left us. Pray take care of your own [health] and let us see you able as well mentally and physically to fill up our stations.

Robert did at last begin to think of coming home early, but he was laid low with a fever and reported that he was 'completely wearied and worn down with vexations'. Mr Richardson, the Quaker, told him he must stay to see out his contract.

Robert had written to his father and to his step-mother at regular intervals since his arrival in South America, which shows there was no family split. One of his first letters was to his stepmother telling her he was having three-fifths of his South American salary sent direct to his father. Was he now feeling guilty at having gone off leaving the new firm in the lurch?

The worst news of all must have been that of his father's dismissal by the Liverpool railway company. On 15 December 1825, Robert wrote to Longridge.

> The failure of the Liverpool and Manchester Act, I fear, will retard much this kind of speculation; but it is clear that they will eventually succeed, and I still anticipate with confidence the arrival of a time we shall see some of the celebrated canals filled up. It is to be regretted that my father placed the conducting of the levelling under the care of young men without experience. Simple as the process of levelling may appear, it is one of those things that requires care and dexterity in its performance.

In a letter to his stepmother, in June the following year, trying to comfort them in their difficult times, he shows the affection which rarely disappeared for any length of time.

> My dear father's letter, which I received a few days ago, was an affectionate one, and when he spoke of his head getting grey and finding himself descending the hill of life, I could not refrain from giving way to feelings which overpowered me, and prevented me from reading on. Some, had they seen me, would perhaps call me childish: but I would tell them such feelings and reflections as crossed me at that moment are unknown to them. They are unacquainted with the love and affection due to attentive parents, which in me seems to have become more acute, as the distance and period of my absence have increased.

Meanwhile, the Liverpool board, after George's failure in parliament and subsequent dismissal, decided this time they must have a national figure and accordingly hired the Rennie brothers, George and John, two of the most respected engineers of the day, sons of John Rennie the Scottish engineer who built the old Waterloo and Southwark bridges in London. Under their direction a young and talented engineer called Charles Vignoles started a new survey. He slightly altered the line, avoiding the estates of the more vociferous opponents. At the same time, the board came to terms with the majority of the previous obstructionists, paying them huge amounts in compensation and in some cases giving them railway shares. The Rennies' estimate was £500,000, £100,000 more than George's, but they got their survey and plans carried successfully through parliament. Vignoles was very smooth, cultivated and confident under cross-examination and Alderson failed to find any flaws or inconsistencies in the survey. William Huskisson made a strong speech in favour of the bill but perhaps the most important thing in its favour this time, apart from the absence of George, was the fact that the use of locomotives was played down. Out of two hundred clauses in the new bill, only one contained a reference to locomotives. The railway board well knew that the bogey must be well hidden from the public. The bill was carried by forty-five votes on 5 May 1826.

The board was naturally delighted and approached the Rennies, grateful for their excellent survey and their parliamentary expertise, about becoming the engineers in charge of the construction of the line. They took their time giving an answer, saying they were very busy, they were going away. The board had to wait very patiently. In the end they suggested that perhaps the Rennies would agree if they were given the help of a couple of secondary engineers, someone like George Stephenson for example. When the Rennies finally replied their conditions were long and complicated. They wanted £600 per annum, for which one of them guaranteed to make six visits a year to the railway, which was very decent of them. They said they would like some assistant engineers, but it would have to be someone like Thomas Telford. On no account would they have George Stephenson.

The directors decided, after a lot of discussion, to refuse the Rennies' conditions. Another engineer was considered but after Sandars had investigated his work and his conditions for doing the job he too was deemed to be unsuitable. Almost by default they turned once more to George Stephenson, asking if he would be engineer for the Liverpool–Manchester Railway.

By this time the Stockton and Darlington had successfully opened, which put George in a better light, making up slightly for his parliamentary debacle. Sandars, and Booth, the treasurer, had both remained his supporters but they'd been in a minority ever since George's parliamentary failure. However, they were not sending begging letters or messengers to Stephenson, worrying if perhaps he'd got something better. They were doing him the favour this time and laid down conditions accordingly. He was to devote at least nine months in every year to full time work on the line and during its construction he was to take on no new work for any other railway company. His salary was to be £800 a year. Vignoles was to be his chief assistant, which didn't please Stephenson, nor did it please Vignoles, having done the parliamentary survey. However, Vignoles looked on himself as 'co-engineer', not assistant to George, a situation which was bound to lead to trouble.

They were soon arguing over the work, with George blaming Vignoles for everything that went wrong, saying it should be done his way. George realised he was in the stronger position and eventually managed to ease out Vignoles, getting him paid off by the board. Vignoles, unlike William James, went on to greater things becoming president of the Institution of Civil Engineers. In later life he described what working with George had been like.

> I acknowledge having on many occasions differed with him (and that in common with almost all other engineers), because it appeared to me he did not look on the concern with a liberal and expanded view but with a microscopic eye; magnifying details and pursuing a petty system of parsimony very proper in a private colliery line or in a small undertaking but wholly inappliable to this national work. I also plead guilty to having neglected to court Mr. Stephenson's favours by crying down all other engineers, especially those in London for, though I highly respect his great natural talents, I would not shut my eyes to certain deficiencies.

Even before Vignoles had gone, George called in all his old assistants, his tried and true assistants and colleagues from the north east, such as John Dixon and Joseph Locke. He hired navvies who had worked on the Darlington line and set about personally designing all the bridges, machinery and engines. There were to be sixty-three bridges on the thirty-mile double track railway line, the most difficult being the Sankey Viaduct with nine arches. The biggest tunnel was the Edgehill tunnel at the Liverpool end, a monument of engineering to this day. They had to cut deep into the sandstone for over two miles, excavating half a million tons of rock. The tunnel itself was to be 2,240 yards long. But the biggest obstacle of all was the dreaded Chat Moss, the one that the opposition had said in parliament would only be attempted by a fool or a madman.

On John Dixon's arrival from Darlington in July 1826 he was taken on his first day, as a fearful initiation rite, to watch progress on Chat Moss. He fell off some planks into the Moss and was up to his knees, fast disappearing, before they managed to drag him out. George was failing completely to make any impression on the Moss. The more he tipped in ballast, the more it disappeared. Instead he ordered his workmen to strap wood to their feet, like snow shoes, and to attempt to lay blankets of heather and wood across the worst of the twelve square miles of the Moss. Once again, the heather and wood just disappeared, swallowed up by the bog. His ultimate idea was to make a raft strong enough to take the railway, an idea which was ridiculed by every expert and worried over by every member of the board. The board was continually having urgent meetings, sending out delegations to inspect the works, trying to talk George into having advisory engineers in an effort to keep his madness in check. Drivers of stage coaches, driving past the Moss, were always bringing back alarming intelligence to Liverpool and Manchester which kept the public and the local papers agog. 'Hundreds of men and horses sunk! The work completely abandoned. The Engineer swallowed alive! Railways at an end for ever!'

George was working round the clock, rising at five and going off on his favourite horse Bobby, brought with him from the north east, to inspect a tunnel or a viaduct or the latest attempt to grapple with the Moss. At breakfast time he'd return to the pub or farm house where he was staying and make his own breakfast of 'crowdie', which according to Smiles was a porridge made by pouring hot water over a handful of oats. (In Scotland crowdie is a cream cheese made out of sour milk, popular with workmen, who leave it to drain overnight in an old handkerchief.) That was his meal for the day before going off on further inspections of the works. When home, at his new house in Liverpool, in Upper Parliament Street, he would work late into the night with his pupils and assistants on drawings and designs, dictating letters and reports to his secretaries.

At the frequent board meetings, where he had to explain yet further delays in conquering Chat Moss, he would argue his point by sticking his right thumb through the button of his coat lapel and vehemently hitching his right shoulder, 'as was his habit,' says Smiles, 'when labouring under any considerable excitement'.

He might have been excited, nay agitated, but he was never nervous, unlike his son Robert. For all Robert's daring adventures and expeditions he was a worrier by nature, rarely optimistic about the future, facing everything carefully and humbly, never really happy until the end or a result had been achieved. George was always confident in his powers, dismissing the cautious as weak and the critics as fools, completely convinced he would win through in the end. Years later (at a speech in Birmingham in 1837) he described his eventual triumph at Chat Moss. By then he was speaking with the confidence of hindsight, but all contemporaries confirm that he had always been convinced of success, right from the beginning.

> After working for weeks and weeks . . . we went on filling in without the slightest apparent effect. Even my assistants began to feel uneasy and to doubt the success of the scheme. The directors, too, spoke of it as a hopeless task, and at length they became seriously alarmed. . . . There was no help, however, but to go on. An immense outlay had been incurred and a great loss would have been occasioned had the scheme been then abandoned, and the line taken by another route. So the directors were compelled to allow me to proceed with my plans, of the ultimate success of which I myself never for one moment doubted.

To make sure he was giving them his best, in early 1827 the board increased his salary to £1,000 a year, on condition that he gave his complete, full-time attention to the works. Though he'd agreed to take on no new schemes since being made engineer, he already had an existing contract with the Canterbury and Whitstable Railway, and a couple of small ones at Bolton and in Wales, plus the loco works and other interests in Newcastle.

In February 1827 George wrote a letter to Robert in South America, the longest letter in his own hand which survives to this day – probably the longest he himself ever wrote. It now resides in the records office in Liverpool, which acquired it in 1968. It is difficult to read, having no punctuation, no paragraphs and very little grammar. To make matters worse George had written extra sentences down the margins, trying to cram in as much as possible.

It is of importance to railway historians interested in George's technical development because it gives in great detail, plus little sketches, his latest thinking on the many engineering problems he was facing at the time on the Liverpool line, and the progress of many of the more important works. There is, for example, a detailed description of an experimental locomotive which has foxed engineers for generations, having seen references to it elsewhere but never knowing the details.

But as a personal look at George, his thoughts, his attitudes, his literary skill – or lack of it – it is of unique interest. There is no other primary source which has the same freshness or immediacy.

It has been brilliantly analysed by Professor Jack Simmons of Leicester University, who published his observations in the *Journal of Transport History* (Volume 2, September 1971, pages 108–15) under the title 'A Holograph Letter from George Stephenson'. As he points out, it is an exceedingly rare example of George's hand. (The only other one of note is the letter referred to earlier, to the old Walbottle Colliery friends about his great enemy Hawthorn.) In both letters, if the punctuation is once inserted, it can be seen that George has in fact a natural flow, a genuine command of words and phrases. One can see what Samuel Smiles meant when he said that George had a great capacity for dictating and could sit for hours giving lengthy yet coherent and technical letters straight to his secretaries. But here, for once, is George himself. Punctuation and paragraphs have been added where possible, to make it easier to read, but the spelling has been left unchanged.

Leverpool feb. 23rd 1827

My Dear

Robert your very welcom letter dated Oct 26 1826 we duly received and was glad to here such good newes from Colombia respecting the mines – but at the same time greatly disapointed at you not geting home so soon as was expected. however I hope all will be for the best, and I must waddle on as well as I can until you get to joine me. There has been a florishing a count of your men in the English pappers and great creadit is given to Robert Stephenson for his good management of them.*

I must now let you know how we are geting on in this quarter. Yore mother is geting her tea beside me while I am riting this and in good spirits. she has been in Leverpool a bout a fortnight. We have got a very comfortable home, and a Roume set a side for Robert and Charels when they arive in England.[†]

We are getting rapitly on with the tunnal under Liverpool it is 22 feet width & 16 feet high we have 6 shafts and driving right & left we have also got a great deal done on chat moss and on the same plans that I prepared befor parlament 2 years a go which plans was condemed by almost all the Engineers in England. these plans is by cuting & imbanking with the moss some of the laths 12 feet high and stand remarkably well—it was said that Renney[‡] had some of the best surveyors in England with hire here and one of the best was left with me which I supposed was expected by menny of our directors to be a guid[e] to me.[§] I set him to surveye the tunnval and mark out the different shafts after which I found a meathat of cheking his work and found eny shaft out of the line. this was after we had spent about woof., in that part. this was a finishing blay [blow] to Renny & his . . . My asstance is now all of my own chosen.

The Bolton line which was clandistanly got from me when we were in parlament with the Liverpool bill has been given to me – a welsh line 9 miles long has been put into my hands. a line at Canterbury is in my hands likewise – we have a most magnificent Bridge to build a cross the sankey valley near newton it will be 70 feet high so as to cross the masts of ships that navigate that canal. I have drawen a plan on the gothick

---

*Prof. Simmons searched the contemporary press and could find only one small report, in *The Times*, which contains a reference, but no praise, of Robert. George was obviously trying to flatter his son.
[†] Robert's great friend in South America was Charles Empson, another young engineer, and they made plans to travel home together.
[‡] George Rennie, who'd been in charge of the previous survey.
[§] Presumably Charles Vignoles, one of Rennie's engineers, whom George disliked and eventually helped to sack.

principal. there will be 20 arches of 40 feet span. it will be quite a novel in England as there will be a flat arch sprung between the centre of the tops of the gothick and so on. it has a fine a pearance in the plans. we have also 2 bridges in hand at present, one at the river adjoining chat moss and the other crossing the duckes (Duke's) cannai near manchester the one 30 feet span and the other 25.

we have just advertised for 400 waggon wheels & 200 axels and strange to say Robert Stephenson & Co. offer was lower than any other house and we have had offers from almost all the best houses in England –my plan of wheels is now put up like the maile Coach axels but still fast so that one greaseing per day is a nough – the locomotive engine is working very well at Darlington– and a great many Coaches on the line I think a' bout 6 and each drawen (by) one horse which take a bout 30 passengers and run to Stockton in 1½ hours and many come from a great distance to ride in those Coaches. it is expected that a line will be made from Darlington to York and I have been asked to take the survey – but hope it will be cept back untill you come to England–this line will sute Mr Charels.

I think the projected tunnat under the thames was talked of befor you left – it is now got a good way under the river but will cost a great deal more money than was expected. This is however a very common case with engineers – the estimate for this concern is 500000£, and I daresay it will require it all.[*]

the line passes Rainhill very near the same place where Dameses line passed. we shall want one steam engine at that place and a nother at near parr moss also one at the top of the tunnat. I want these engines to be constantly moveing with an endless Rope so that the locomotive engines can take hold of the Rope and go on with out stoping. the Incline plane will only be ¾ of an inch per yard. so that the poor (power) of the locomotive assisted by the perment (permanent) ones will get the traffict on in grand stile. we most (must) go at to miles per hour. I think I told you about my new plan of locomotive it will be a huge job the Cylinder[s?] is intirely within the Bolior and

---

[*] The tunnel at Rotherhithe was built by Sir Marc Isambard Brunel, assisted by his son Isambard Kingdom Brunel, and cost £468,000.

neaither Cranks nor cham will be wanted. I have no fire door(?) and I will not use more than the coals that has heather (hither) to been used. you will think I have mistaken some ideas about this but I think not.

you may depend upon it that if you do not get home soon every thing will be at prefecttion and then there will be nothing for you to do or invent–however we will hope that some usfull Ideas will be brought from the western world. – the coal trade has been very bad in Newcastle last year. you cannot immagine how kindly Mr. Lambert inquires after you. Mr. Charels Weatherly is now a father – I think I told you of his marriage last year–Mr. Wood* is expected to he maried very soon of a young lady with a great posithen. she be long to Alnwick. he got a quainted with her at the election –†

your mother expects you will not forget the presents. you must bring more than one as Mrs Robert Stephenson will want one by & by – and we expect Mr. Charels will bring plenty of amarica plants seeds for our (garden). cannot you bring your favorate mule with you. I trust (this?) letter will just catch you befor living (leaving) the country. my kindest love to Charels I am my Dear Dear Robert your affectionate father Geo: Stephenson

George's spelling was largely phonetic, based on what he heard, which explains his fondness for a plural subject followed by a singular verb. He's also fond of splitting words in two, words which when spoken do sound as if they could be two – such as a go, be long, a cross, and even a-nough (enough). No doubt his secretaries were well aware of his peculiarities and could easily polish up his grammar and correct the verbal agreements when writing out his business letters.

George comes across strongly as being rather sharp and sardonic, getting in dry asides at his enemies whenever he has a chance, such as the reference to the Rennies and to his parliamentary battle. He

---

* Nicholas Wood (1795–1865), George's friend who was manager at Killingworth Colliery.
† This election, in June 1826, was famous in Northumberland as it led to a duel on Bamburgh Sands involving John Lambton, later Earl of Durham.

is also dogmatic and opinionated, convinced he's right and people like Vignoles are wrong. (Though he must have changed his plans for the Sankey viaduct as he ended up building it with nine arches, not twenty as mentioned in this letter.) His phrase 'must waddle on' is attractive. For a supposedly illiterate man he could be a fluent and interesting writer.

The letter also shows a good relationship between the father and son which will perhaps dispel for ever the idea that there had been a serious row between them. It is obvious from the last paragraph that Robert has sent a long chatty letter to his father. In turn George's homely details, with his wife getting the tea beside him, are endearing. George is cheerful and it is obvious that life and the Liverpool works are going well, though he is patently missing his son.

In March of 1827 Joseph Locke, George's assistant, wrote to Robert telling him the latest progress, confirming that George was now well and truly back in favour. 'The shade which was unfortunately cast on the fame of your father has disappeared; and the place which he must often have reflected on with pain is now such a scene of operations as sheds lustre on his character and will, no doubt, immortalise his name.'

Robert's operations in South America were at last being organised into some sort of order, though it's hard to find out if the mines he opened ever made much of a profit. In the three years he was there, 1824–7, he spent a total of £200,000 on behalf of the Colombian Mining Association, a large sum for a young man. They wanted him to renew his contract, which indicates they were pleased with his work. By the summer 1827 he finally felt able to make plans to return home. In a letter to Longridge at the end of July he said he was leaving 'with all convenient dispatch because of the parlous state of the locomotive works'. However, he appears to have been in no hurry to rush back to the bosom of his family, despite his protestations of affection, or to rescue the locomotive works in Newcastle. He spent some time planning an expedition to the nearby Isthmus of Panama as he wanted to have a look at the route of a canal that had been the talk of engineers for some time, a canal Iinking the Atlantic with the Pacific. A group of British financiers had got the money ready for its construction but the Colombian government were showing little interest. 'How it would influence commerce in every quarter of the world! ' wrote Robert in a letter to Longridge. 'One would have thought with a young country that this proposal would have met with immediate sanction.' (It wasn't until 1903 that the Panama Canal was begun, this time with American money.)

His Panama trip fell through and in August 1827 he finally packed his bags, his specimens and the diaries he'd kept during the three years, and travelled up the Magdalena river to the Colombian port of Carthagena where he waited for a boat to New York. He wasn't going directly back to Liverpool but the long way round, planning to have a look at the brave new United States of America, though his official reason for not going back the way he'd come, direct to England, was that the boats were faster from New York.

While hanging around a quayside inn in Carthagena, waiting for a New York boat, there occurred one of those chance encounters which are the stuff of history. He fell into conversation one day with a down-and-out Cornishman, not normally his favourite sort of Englishman, and discovered it was Richard Trevithick, *the* Trevithick, the builder of the first locomotive. He'd last been heard of some ten years earlier when he'd been greeted like a king on his arrival in Peru. He'd become a friend of Simon Bolivar and his horse had been shod with silver by a grateful people. Now he was in rags and destitute, having trailed on foot across half of South America.

Trevithick boasted to Robert that he'd bounced him on his knee when he'd been at the height of his English fame and on a grand tour of Tyneside some twenty years previously. It sounds unlikely as George at the time was still an obscure engine-wright, but Robert was sufficiently touched by Trevithick and his stories to give him £50 for his passage home to England. They compared notes about mining in South America, then they parted, Trevithick on a boat back to Falmouth and to the last ignoble stages of a once brilliant career. Robert set sail for New York and England and what was eventually to prove a series of brilliant engineering successes.

Robert was lucky to reach New York. His ship came across the trail of some boats which had been shipwrecked ahead of them. Firstly they picked up some half dead survivors, down to their last rations, then a second lot who had eaten all their supplies and had been reduced to eating each other. (Years later, when Robert told

London dinner parties about the incident, people refused to believe that in the year of grace, 1827, humanity would ever be reduced to cannibalism.) Then Robert's own boat hit the worst of the storm and they too were shipwrecked, though luckily everyone reached shore without loss of life. But most of Robert's precious specimens and diaries, plus his baggage and three years' savings, were all lost. 'Had I not been on the American side of the Atlantic,' he wrote, 'I "guess" I would not have gone to sea again.' (His use of quotation marks round 'guess' shows how old this Americanism must be.)

In New York he managed to obtain some more money (though Jeaffreson doesn't explain where it came from – presumably his firm's New York agent) and decided to spend some time looking at the natives, putting off even longer his return to England. He didn't think much of them.

On entering New York we felt ourselves quite at home. All outward appearances of things and persons were indicative of English manners and customs; but on closer investigation we soon discovered the characteristic impudence of the people. In many cases it was nothing short of disgusting. We stayed but a short time in the city, and pushed into the interior for about 500 miles, and were much delighted with the face of the country, which in every direction is populated to a great extent, and affords to an attentive observer a wonderful example of human industry; and it is gratifying to a liberal-minded Englishman to observe how far the sons of his own country have outstripped the other European powers which have transatlantic possessions.

We visited the Falls of Niagara, which did not surprise me so much as the Tequindama. Their magnitude is certainly prodigious; but there is not so much minute beauty about them as the Salta.

After seeing all that our time would permit in the States we passed over into Canada, which is far behind the States in everything. The people want industry and enterprise. Every Englishman, however partial he may be, is obliged to confess the disadvantageous contrast. Whether the cause exists in the people or the system of government I cannot say – perhaps it rests with both.

Robert journeyed by foot and horse, with his friend Charles, once again living a vagrant life, still wearing his cloak-cum-poncho which he'd affected in Colombia. By the sound of his letter he must have covered at least a thousand miles. When he got to Montreal, so he wrote in a letter, he changed into 'the ordinary costume of an English gentleman' (surely not that white suit) and attended a few balls before returning to New York, where he caught the steam packet, *Pacific*, to Liverpool.

It must have been an interesting meeting when George greeted his long lost son at Liverpool at the end of November 1827. Robert's friend Charles was with him, to take up the 'Roume' Mrs Stephenson had set aside for them. They spent a long evening telling their travellers' tales and the next morning, by their bedside, they each found a handsome watch, left for them by George to help make up for their loss at sea.

George had been through a lot while Robert had been away and his hair had indeed turned white and his face had become heavily lined. He was now forty-six, still healthy but a man past his physical peak. Robert, on the other hand, had become a man. He was now twenty-four, a man of the world, a man who'd had experiences and seen sights far beyond his years, who'd faced dangers, controlled men; a man who'd overcome his self-imposed tests. From now on he could never be in any sense George's tool. He had proved himself, on his own. They were no longer father and son, but partners.

# 11

# RAINHILL AND THE *ROCKET*

Robert Stephenson returned to Newcastle in January 1828 to run the locomotive works and made them his headquarters and primary concern for the next five years, five of the most important years in the history of locomotives. Each technical development during these years has been exhaustingly written about by scores of engineering experts, all trying to agree on who invented which valve, which blast, which boiler. We need not over-concern ourselves here with such arguments.

During this period of intense engineering activity, Robert somehow found time to get married. From March onwards he was continually popping down to Broad Street in the City of London to see a certain Miss Fanny Sanderson, the daughter of John Sanderson, a gentleman of good repute, in the City. 'Robert Stephenson had been introduced to the young lady before leaving England for South America,' wrote Jeaffreson, 'and even at that date he had entertained for her sentiments which, if not those of love, closely resembled them.' It just needs one single letter to turn up showing that there had been a row between Robert and Fanny before he went off to South America and everybody's theories about Robert's departure will have to be rethought. However, no one has ever suggested such a possibility. So far.

'I plainly perceive a man can only be a man,' wrote Robert to a friend in August, 1828. 'As soon as he ever aspires to be anything else he becomes ridiculous. Come, come away with moralising thus gloomily. Affairs go on smoothly in London, at least, the last time I heard from thence, they cannot have undergone any material change.'

Fanny doesn't appear to have been much of a beauty, but everyone spoke highly of her intelligence. In October, Robert introduced her to his father and the meeting went off successfully,

145

to Robert's relief. 'I took him to the house without her having the most distant idea of his coming. He likes her appearance and thinks she looks intelligent. She did not appear confused and the visit passed off extremely well.' They were married the following June at the parish church in Bishopsgate. Robert took her back to Newcastle at a house he'd taken at 5, Greenfield Place.

While he'd been away in America not only had the locomotive works been in financial troubles but the state of locomotives generally had been at a low ebb. George had been too busy with the Liverpool line and all its problems. Timothy Hackworth, who'd been recommended as engineer at Darlington by George, was about the only engineer actively working on the problem, improving and developing the Stockton and Darlington engines. But they were still very primitive. Brakes, for example, were little more than a matter of the driver bringing pressure on the wheels with his foot.

For all the local excitement of its opening, the Darlington line still had many critics. Rumours swept the north about the number of accidents, all exaggerated, and even its fans had to admit that the locomotives were slow and cumbersome. They were going so slowly, rarely more than four mph, that small boys were running after them, jumping on and travelling free. It was realised that many engine drivers were turning a blind eye to such tricks so the company issued a public notice warning drivers and illegal passengers of the serious consequences. A handsome reward was promised for information about offenders.

Local estate owners were still complaining about their lands, claiming now that plantations were being set alight by hot cinders from the engines. Any engineman who allowed this to happen, so the company announced, would be dismissed. Hackworth was told to have large numbers painted on the chimneys of each engine so that two company spies, who were to be hidden in the plantations on hot summer nights, would be able to write down the numbers of the guilty men. From the very beginning railway companies were always very tough on any offenders. (Just a few years later the Newcastle and Carlisle Railway was warning that trespassers on the line would be transported for seven years.)

Horses were still being used until 1833 for passenger traffic on the Stockton and Darlington, though they weren't attracting many customers. Up to 1832 the average number didn't rise above

520 a week. Horses generally were still considered as a vital source of power in most of the railways being planned. In 1829, which was when the Newcastle and Carlisle Railway Bill was passed, it was on condition that horses, not locomotives, should be used.

There was one interesting development in the horsedrawn wagons on these early railways, a system known as the dandy. When a horse had finished pulling its load up a hill it was trained to stand aside, then jump onto the open end of the last wagon, where some hay would be waiting for it. It would then ride in comfort down the hill, getting out at the next hill to start pulling again. George Stephenson maintained he'd first suggested the idea of these dandy carts. In a letter to Hackworth from Liverpool in 1828 he wrote, 'Brandreth has got my plan introduced for the horses to ride which I suppose he will set off as his own invention.' (The term dandy cart later referred to any railway wagon pulled by a horse. One of the last ceased operation on a line near Carlisle, from Drumburgh to Port Carlisle, in 1914.)

One of the most serious rumours in circulation about the time of Robert's return was that locomotives were to be withdrawn as too expensive. Financially the Darlington line was certainly not proving a gold mine, confirming what Edward Pease had always said. At the end of their second year in operation the annual revenue was just £18,304, only £2,000 more than Pease had estimated. Until 1830, when the revenue was still only £23,727, they were paying dividends of 5 per cent. (It was only after 1830 that traffic and profits started booming, especially when the iron trade began.)

Locomotives, from every point of view, still had to prove themselves, as Robert soon realised on his journeys round the country. From 1 January 1828, which was when he wrote the following letter to Longridge, he decided to make them his first priority.

Liverpool, Jan 1, 1828

My Dear Sir,

I had hoped my father would accompany me to the North this time, but he finds that all his attention must be devoted to this road alone.

I have just returned from a ride along the line for seven miles, in which distance I have not been a little surprised to find excavations of such magnitude. Since I came down from London, I have been talking a great deal to my father about endeavouring to reduce the size and ugliness of our travelling-engines, by applying the engine either on the side of the boiler or beneath it entirely, somewhat similarly to Gurney's steam-coach. He has agreed to an alteration which I think will considerably reduce the quantity of machinery as well as the liability to mismanagement. Mr. Jos. Pease writes my father that in their present complicated state they cannot be managed by 'fools,' therefore they must undergo some alteration or amendment. It is very true that the locomotive engine, or any other kind of engine, may be shaken to pieces; but such accidents are in a great measure under the control of enginemen, which are, by the by, not the most manageable class of beings. They perhaps want improvement as much as the engines.

While Robert moved back up to Newcastle, George remained in Liverpool, struggling to complete the construction of the line, but he was in regular correspondence with Robert about the progress of new engines, passing on information about likely customers for the locomotive works.

Liverpool, March 3, 1828

Dear Robert,

I wish you could contrive to come here to stay a week or a fortnight. . . . There is an American Engineer here and I think he will also want four Loco motive engines. There is also a neighbour of mine who will want a Steam Mill Engine, and I think it will be better for you to be here to close the bargains yourself in case we can agree for prices – I expect now in a few weeks to receive orders to proceed with the Canterbury Engines. The Bill is now in Parliament and is expected to pass shortly, to enable Mr. Ellis to take the lease of that concern and I suppose as soon as it goes forward I must deliver my profits up to Robert Stephenson & Co. I think it is likely the Chester Line will go forward which I was speaking to Mr. Longridge about – I only returned last night from examining the ground – I send in my report tomorrow of the practicability and expense of the Line – I am glad to hear you have got a Horse to suit you,

George Stephenson, engraving after Moses Haughton
(Institute of Mechanical Engineers)

The cottage at Wylam, Northumberland, where George Stephenson was born. George's family, all eight of them, lived in one room. His first job, at the age of eight, was to keep cows off the line (from Samuel Smiles's biography).

George Stephenson's cottage at Killingworth Colliery, Newcastle. He started in one room but as he progressed as a colliery engineer he gradually took over most of the cottage (from Samuel Smiles's biography).

Bedlington Iron Works, Northumberland. A typical early industrial revolution scene set in rural surroundings. Michael Longridge, owner of the works, became a lifelong friend of George Stephenson and produced the malleable iron rails for George's early colliery lines (from a lithograph of 1827).

Hetton Colliery Railway, the first entirely new line laid out by George Stephenson. It was eight miles long and used stationary steam engines – which were fixed beside the track and hauled the wagons by chains – as well as locomotives. It was begun in 1819 and engineers from Europe came to see it (from a lithograph by J.D. Harding).

Richard Trevithick, the Cornish engineer who built the first locomotive (portrait by Linnell/ Science and Society Picture Library).

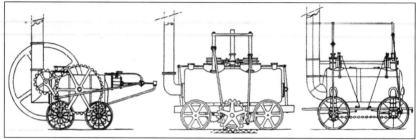

(Above left) Trevithick's Gateshead Locomotive, 1805. It never left the factory. (Above centre) Blenkinsop's Rack Locomotive, 1812. It worked but was clumsy and uneconomic. (Above right) Early Stephenson locomotive which ran successfully at Killingworth Colliery from 1816.

Trevithick's *Catch Me Who Can* which he exhibited in London (near the site of the present Euston Station) in 1808, charging one shilling to those who dared ride it. It tore the tracks and afterwards Trevithick gave up locomotive inventing (Science and Society Picture Library).

Edward Pease, the Quaker merchant who created the Stockton and Darlington Railway and commissioned George Stephenson to be its engineer.

Nicholas Wood, manager of Killingworth Colliery (Science and Society Picture Library).

William James, early railway promoter.

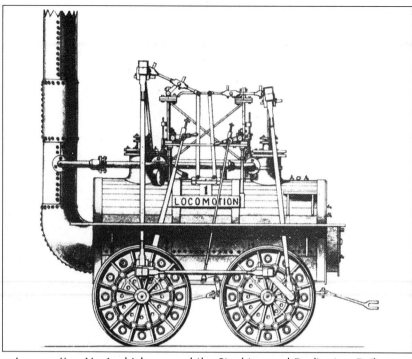

*Locomotion No 1* which opened the Stockton and Darlington Railway, 1825, the world's first public railway (Science and Society Picture Library).

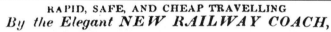

Stockton and Darlington's trains were for goods only for the first few years, with passengers using horsedrawn coaches (from the *Durham County Advertiser*, 14 October 1826).

Robert Stephenson, George's only son, as a young man. He came back from South America in time to help his father prepare for the Rainhill Trials (engraving after George Richmond).

# THE LOCOMOTIVE STEAM ENGINES

*which competed for the Prize of £500 offered by the Directors of the Liverpool and Manchester Railway Comp.? – drawn to a Scale ¼ inch to a foot*

### The ROCKET of M.ʳ Rob.ᵗ Stephenson of Newcastle

*which drawing a load equivalent to three times its weight, travelled at the rate of 12¼ miles an hour, & with a carriage & passengers at the rate of 24 miles Cost per mile for fuel about three halfpence*

### The NOVELTY of Mess.ʳˢ Braithwaite & Erricsson of London.

*which drawing a load equivalent to three times its weight, travelled at the rate of 20¼ miles an hour, & with a Carriage & Passengers at the rate of 30 miles. Cost per mile for fuel about one halfpenny*

C Bush del.ᵗ on Stone

### The SANS PAREIL of M.ʳ Hackworth of Darlington

*which drawing a load equivalent to three times its weight, travelled at the rate of 12¼ miles an hour — Cost for fuel per mile about two-pence.*

Three of the locomotives which competed at the Rainhill Trials in 1829
(from the *Mechanics Magazine*).

Stephenson's *Northumbrian* which opened the Liverpool–Manchester Railway in 1830, the world's first passenger railway (from an etching by I.Shaw, Jr.).

*(Left)* Fanny Kemble, the actress, one of the VIP visitors at the Liverpool opening, who wrote that she was 'most horribly in love' with George . Purely platonic of course! (Portrait by Sir Thomas Lawrence/Royal Academy of Arts).
*(Bottom left)* William Huskisson, MP and Cabinet Minister, who met his death at the Liverpool opening after being run over by the *Rocket* (Science and Society Picture Library).
*(Bottom right)* A Liverpool–Manchester souvenir.

Two views of the Liverpool–Manchester Railway drawn and engraved by I. Shaw, Jr. (Science and Society Picture Library)

George Hudson, the draper's assistant from York who used his friendship with Stephenson to build a railway empire worth thirty million (painted by Francis Grant).

Isambard Kingdom Brunel who fought Stephenson over the battle of the gauges (Brunel University Library).

Railway Mania provided endless material for cartoons (Victoria and Albert Museum, by permission of Mr and Mrs M.G. Powell).

The speculators made the money out of Railway Mania, but the navvies did the work. Early photographs taken near Crystal Palace, 1853 (Hulton Archive).

Spectacular section cut through the rocks on the Liverpool–Manchester (drawn and engraved by I. Shaw, Jr./ Science and Society Picture Library)

Central Station, Newcastle-upon-Tyne, opened in 1850, scene of a railway banquet held in honour of Robert Stephenson (engraving after J. Dobson).

The Stephenson family: a popular Victorian painting, showing George Stephenson's family as they never were. Fanny, George's daughter (left) who died aged three weeks, is held by George's first wife who also died young. The others represent his parents, his second wife and son Robert. George holds the miners' safety lamp, very symbolically. (Stephenson and his Family, 19th century, Anonymous/Science Museum, London, UK/Bridgeman Art Library).

Robert Stephenson in middle age, became one of the greatest Victorian engineers and was buried in Westminster Abbey (engraving by Henry Adlard from a photograph).

Tapton House, Chesterfield, George Stephenson's last home. He is buried in Chesterfield church (photograph by Professor Pearson, and reproduced by his kind permission).

A fancy one-off locomotive built by Robert Stephenson and Co. for the Viceroy of Egypt.

George Stephenson never went to school and learned to read and write with difficulty, in later life. This is one of the few letters in his own hand, written to his son Robert in South America in 1827 (reproduced by kind permission of the Liverpool Record Office).

but if it is a cheap one I think it is very likely to be a shabby one and very unfit to come by the side of mine; the whole of which are as fat as pigs –

I am
Dear Robert
Your Afft. Father
GEO. STEPHENSON

Despite George's promises to the Liverpool board, it is obvious from this letter that he was still involved in other lines, though when it came to an official engagement, he usually passed over the job of engineer to other people – usually to someone in his own family or to his assistants. Robert, the most talented of his three brothers, had been telling the truth when he wrote to James that time about a job, extolling his own virtues. He'd laid down the rails for George at Hetton and was now appointed to construct the Bolton and Leigh Railway, one of the lines George had helped to survey. Young Robert had got the job of engineer to the Canterbury and Whitstable line, which was useful to him when he was courting Fanny, giving him a good excuse, as well as paying his expenses, to go down to London.

It's hard to decide whether George was power mad, greedy or simply a genius, managing to be involved in so many jobs. His critics certainly accused him of the first two, and he'd already made many enemies, but from his point of view, believing implicitly in the future of locomotion, he felt he had to take on everything offered because he alone knew what had to be done. The more railways he built, the more locomotives would be needed. But his mono-mania led to many rows with the board and on several occasions almost led to his downfall.

In 1828, work on the Liverpool line was proving so difficult and so expensive, in construction and in keeping the opposition quiet, that the board ran out of money and was forced to apply to the government for an exchequer loan of £100,000. One of the government's conditions was that an outside expert should be sent to find out what on earth was going on at Liverpool and advise if a loan of £100,000 was really justified. Their expert turned out to be none other than Thomas Telford, the greatest engineer of the day, famed throughout Europe for his roads, bridges and canals. He was by now seventy-two, but still the most distinguished man in his profession. He had been the first president of the Institution of Civil Engineers, a body of gentlemen whom George, with some justification, thought were against him. He was in the middle of the construction of the Birmingham and Liverpool Junction Canal (a project begun in 1827, the same year as the Liverpool earthworks, and not finished till 1835) and sent an assistant at first to check up on George. George refused to see him, being always out or unavailable. Telford finally came in person and toured the line with George, not at all happy with what he saw. He was highly critical of George's method of fixing prices (paying different contractors different prices for the same job, depending on how George felt about them) and of George's insistence on supervising and deciding everything himself. He felt that a sum nearer £200,000 would be needed to finish the job, if it was ever finished.

The board had to insist that George made some of the changes Telford recommended, and that he signed an agreement promising to get the line completed by 1830, before they were allowed their £100,000 loan. George must have been furious, but he had no alternative.

One of the many matters that puzzled Telford was the haulage. He couldn't really see locomotives doing the job the line was being built for. Nor could many other people, including some of the most influential members of the Liverpool board, notably Cropper the Quaker. Though an early plan to use horses had long since been abandoned, there was still a strong lobby in favour of stationary engines. George certainly planned to use several of them, fixed beside the incline planes, hauling the wagons and coaches up by ropes, but he was determined that his main power was going to be locomotives. The successful parliamentary act had played down locomotives, not just for fear of bad publicity but because the board as a whole preferred stationary engines. George and Robert, however, had been going ahead with their locomotive plans. They wanted the Liverpool line to be different from all the little local colliery lines, including the Darlington line, with few stationary engines, using instead the new and improved locomotives which Robert was now working on, capable of going at much faster speeds. But the board, apart from Sandars and Booth, wasn't convinced.

A deputation was sent over to Darlington to investigate both types of engine, stationary and locomotive. Edward Pease instructed Hackworth to 'have the engines and men as neat and clean as can, and be ready with the calculations, not only showing the saving, but how much more work they do in a given time'. The deputation reported in favour of fixed haulage.

George tried to keep his fury within bounds, but there is little doubt he flew into a rage, judging by the careful euphemisms used by Smiles to describe George's nature, long after the problem had been settled. 'Though naturally most cheerful and kind hearted in his disposition, the anxiety and pressure which weighed upon his mind during the construction of the railway had the effect of making him occasionally impatient and irritable, like a spirited horse touched by the spur; though his original good nature *from time to time* shone through it all.' (My italics.) On this occasion, he recovered quickly from his irritability and composed a powerful 4000-word thesis on why the deputation was wrong and why locomotives were better in terms of haulage, speed, economy and price. His arguments were brilliantly constructed, with all facts and figures clearly marshalled. It was a triumph of sustained reasoning, not least because it came from an uneducated mechanic. (It is quoted in its entirety in chapter eleven of Warren's *A Century of Locomotive Building*, 1923.)

The upshot was that two outside engineering experts, Messrs Walker and Rastrick, were asked by the board to conduct an independent report. A second party arrived at Darlington, where the engines and men were clean and at attention once again, to inspect the books and put the machines through their paces. Their report was presented in March 1829. Once again it was in favour of fixed engines. They outdid George in the length and detail of their thesis. One of their many damning statistics was that moving a ton of goods for thirty miles by fixed engines cost 6.4 pennies a mile, while the cost of moving by locomotives was 8.36.

'We are preparing for the counter-report in favour of locomotives,' wrote Robert to a friend, 'which I believe will ultimately get the day, but, from present appearances nothing decisive can be said: rely upon it, locomotives shall not be cowardly given up. *I will fight for them until the last.* (His italics.) 'They are worthy of a conflict.'

The only slight hope in the Walker–Rastrick report was a sentence which admitted there were grounds 'for expecting improvements in the construction and work of locomotives'. In

April 1829 the board, deciding to settle the matter once and for all, announced that they would award a prize for the best locomotive, depending on its speed, weight, power, consumption and smoke. The prize would be £500 and the competition would take place at a completed stretch of the company's line at Rainhill in October 1829. It was exactly what George and Robert wanted. An open, public performance of their new locomotive engine, a chance to prove it to the world.

They weren't the only ones convinced they were going to show the world what they could do. By the date of the trials, so Henry Booth, the company treasurer, wrote, the company had received suggestions from every mad inventor in the known world. Booth's description of the ideas which flooded in is one of the nicest bits of writing to come from the early years of locomotion:

> Multifarious were the schemes proposed to the Directors, for facilitating Locomotion. Communications were received from all classes of persons, each recommending an improved carriage; from professors of philosophy, down to the humblest mechanic, all were zealous in their proffers of assistance; England, America, and Continental Europe were alike tributary. Every element and almost every substance were brought into requisition, and made subservient to the great work. The friction of the carriages was to be reduced so low that a silk thread would draw them, and the power to be applied was to be so vast as to render a cable asunder. Hydrogen gas and high-pressure steam – columns of water and columns of mercury – a hundred atmospheres and a perfect vacuum – machines working in a circle without fire or steam, generating power at one end of the process and giving it out at the other – carriages that conveyed, every one to its own Railway – wheels within wheels, to multiply speed without diminishing power – with every complication of balancing and countervailing forces, to the *ne plus ultra* of perpetual motion. Every scheme which the restless ingenuity or prolific imagination of man could devise was liberally offered to the Company: the difficulty was to choose and to decide.

George and Robert Stephenson's entry was called *Rocket*. They started work on it immediately the prize was announced. A long correspondence took place between George in Liverpool and

Robert in Newcastle as they battled through each stage in its development, with Robert sounding depressed each time he reached a snag in construction and George cheerfully passing on new suggestions to get round each problem. The most important development in the *Rocket* was the multi-tube boiler. One of the problems with all locomotive engines had been to increase the heating surface of the boiler and therefore the power of the engine. *Rocket* had twenty-five copper tubes, each three inches in diameter, which extended from one end of the boiler to the other. The idea had, apparently, been thought of earlier but no one had ever successfully done it. This was the basis of all locomotive boilers for well over the next hundred years, in fact until the end of the steam engine era. Henry Booth, the company's remarkable treasurer, is credited with having thought of the idea with Robert being responsible for its execution, helped by George's advice.

Another important element in the *Rocket*'s construction was the use of the blast-pipe – leading the exhaust steam from the cylinders back into the chimney. This greatly increased the draught in the chimney and kept up the pressure. There has also been great argument about who first perfected this idea. Some experts say that both Trevithick and Timothy Hackworth had already tried it and that George only got to it by accident, having turned the exhaust steam into the chimney as a way of stopping it escaping, discovering by chance that it increased the pressure. In a handwritten letter to the draughtsman at Forth Street in August, George described the process. 'I may mention to you that I have put on to the coke engine a longer exarsting pipe, riching nearly to the top of the chimeney but find it dose not do so well as putting it into the chimeney lower down.'

While Robert worked on the *Rocket*, George was completing the great tunnel into Liverpool. During the summer of 1829 it opened on certain days and became a great attraction for the people of Liverpool. George had the roof whitewashed and gas lamps hung at twenty-five-yard intervals, and for one shilling the public could inspect its entire length. On 21 August, William Huskisson was one of several important visitors, watched by a crowd of three thousand, who visited the tunnel. He praised Stephenson's work, envying him for 'the honour of the direction and completion of such an undertaking'. He recommended that the public should also go and visit the great work being done across Chat Moss, at the Manchester end of the line.

George was very pleased with the compliments and described the visit in a letter to Longridge in Newcastle.

Many of the first families in the County were waiting to witness the procession which accompanied by a band of Music occupying one of the waggons descended in grand style through the Tunnel. The whole went off most pleasantly without the slightest accident attending our various movements. Mr Huskisson and the Directors dined with Mr Lawrence [the Chairman] in the evening. The Engineer was one of the party and a most splendid set out there was I assure you. The evening was spent in a very pleasing manner.

The *Rocket* was ready on 12 September, when it was taken to pieces at the Newcastle works and put in carts and sent by road to Carlisle. It went from there by barge down the canal to Bowness and thence by sea to Liverpool.

Ten locomotive engines had at one time been intending to take part in the Rainhill trials but on the official opening day, 8 October, only five were ready. It was organised like a race meeting, with the five iron horses in their own colours, each limbering up to the delight of the large crowd in the grandstand and the enclosures. They each had to go up and down the course twenty times, a distance in all of sixty miles. There was, amongst many other conditions, a weight limit of six tons. A race card gave the details of each engine.

No 1. Messrs. Braithwaite and Ericsson of London, 'The Novelty'. Copper and Blue, Weight: 2 tons 15 cwt.

No 2. Mr. Hackworth of Darlington, 'The Sans Pareil'. Green, Yellow and Black, Weight: 4 tons 8 cwt 2 qr.

No 3. Mr. Robert Stephenson of Newcastle-upon-Tyne, 'The Rocket'. Yellow and Black, White Chimney, Weight: 4 tons 3 cwt.

No 4. Mr. Brandreth of Liverpool, 'The Cyclopede'. Weight: 3 tons, worked by a horse.

No 5. Mr. Burstall of Edinburgh, 'The Perseverance'. Red Wheels, Weight: 2 tons 17 cwt.

Timothy Burstall's *Perseverance* was not powerful enough to be taken seriously and was damaged in transit from Edinburgh. It never managed to do a proper trial run and was soon withdrawn. *Cyclopede* was a joke entrant, a piece of eccentric entertainment rather than a serious contestant, made by Thomas Shaw Brandreth, one of the Liverpool company's leading shareholders and a friend of George's. The motive power was a horse, which certainly wasn't new, but its method was ingenious. It walked up and down a moving platform, like a treadmill, and so turned the wheels of the machine.

Timothy Hackworth's *Sans Pareil* was a good engine, but everything went wrong. Firstly he'd had to farm out many of its pieces, not having enough facilities at his engine sheds at Shildon, on the Darlington Line. The boiler was made for him by Longridge at Bedlington and the cylinders by Robert Stephenson at Forth Street. (His supporters said, quite wrongly, that he had been deliberately supplied with inferior parts.) Hackworth experienced endless breakdowns and in any case his engine had not complied with all the conditions.

The real threat to the *Rocket* came from *Novelty*, the London entrant, built by Braithwaite and Ericsson (a Swedish inventor) and named after a theatre. One of its supporters was Vignoles, the engineer George had quarrelled with. They'd built it in seven weeks and had been unable to try it out beforehand as there were no railways in the London area. It was considered by far the most beautiful of the entrants, the lightest and fastest looking, and the large crowd took to it immediately.

The crowd included many engineering experts, critics as well as enthusiasts for the cause of locomotion, from Britain and abroad. Americans in particular had been sending regular deputations to look at the Liverpool line for some time. The Baltimore and Ohio Railroad Company had sent its first party of engineers in 1828 and they had representatives at the Rainhill trials. They planned to publish a full report, which they did, using it as a means of whipping up support for their own railway. Horatio Allen, on behalf of the Delaware and Hudson Canal Company, a gentleman who was to become one of the greatest engineers in the history of the American railways, was present in person at the trials.

For George this was the climax of fifteen years' work on locomotives, the final test of all those engines he'd developed since *Blucher* in 1814. He was not being tested verbally, as in parliament, on his education or his knowledge as an engineer, but where it really mattered – in producing results. This was to be a straight competition and there was nothing he liked better than a contest to show his so-called betters that he was right and they were wrong. If he turned out to be wrong, well, people might, perhaps, let him build more railway lines but who would want his locomotives? Or anybody's locomotives, come to that.

For the vast majority of the crowd it was simply a gala day, a cross between Le Mans and Ascot. Comparisons with a horse race meeting were used by most observers in the newspapers. The directors encouraged the festive atmosphere, seeing it as a public relations exercise for their exciting new railway as well as a way of publicly and finally testing the value of locomotives. The reporter on the *Liverpool Courier* describing the opening day, 6 October, was highly delighted by what he saw.

Wednesday, Oct. 7 1829

The Directors of the Liverpool and Manchester Rail-Road having offered, in the month of April last, a prize of £250 for the best Locomotive Engine, the trial of the carriages which had been constructed to contend for the prize commenced yesterday. The running ground was on the Manchester side of the Rainhill Bridge, at a place called Kenrick's Cross, about ten miles from Liverpool. At this place the Rail-Road runs on a dead level, and formed, of course, a fine spot for trying the comparative speed of the carriages. The directors had made suitable preparations for this important as well as interesting experiment of the powers of Locomotive Carriages. For the accommodation of the ladies who might visit the course (to use the language of the turf), a booth was erected on the south side of the Rail-Road, equi-distant from the extremities of the trial ground. Here a band of music was stationed, and amused the company during the day by playing pleasing and favourite airs. The directors, each of whom wore a white ribbon in his buttonhole, arrived on the course shortly after ten o'clock in the forenoon, having come from Huyton in cars drawn by Mr. Stephenson's Locomotive Steam Carriage, which moved up the inclined plane from thence with considerable velocity. Meanwhile, ladies and gentlemen, in great numbers, arrived from Liverpool and Warrington, St. Helen's and

Manchester, as well as from the surrounding country, in vehicles of every description. Indeed all the roads presented, on this occasion, scenes similar to those which roads leading to race-courses usually present during the day of sport. The pedestrians were extremely numerous, and crowded all the roads which conducted to the raceground. The spectators lined both sides of the road, for the distance of a mile and a half; and, although the men employed on the line, amounting to nearly 200, acted as special constables, with orders to keep the crowd off the course, all their efforts to carry their orders into effect were rendered nugatory, by the people persisting in walking on the ground. It is difficult to form an estimate of the number of individuals who had congregated to behold the experiment; but there could not, at a moderate calculation, be less than 10,000. Some gentlemen even went so far as to compute them at 15,000.

Never, perhaps, on any previous occasion, were so many scientific gentlemen and practical engineers collected together on one spot as there were on the Rail-Road yesterday. The interesting and important nature of the experiments to be tried had drawn them from all parts of the kingdom, to be present at this contest of Locomotive Carriages, as well as to witness an exhibition whose results may alter the whole system of our existing internal communications, many and important as they are, substituting an agency whose ultimate effects can scarcely be anticipated; for although the extraordinary change in our river and coast navigation, by steam-boats, may afford some rule of comparison, still the effect of wind and waves, and a resisting medium, combine in vessels to present obstructions to the full exercise of the gigantic power which will act on a Railway unaffected by the seasons, and unlimited but by the demand for its application.

There were only one or two public-houses in the vicinity of the trial-ground. These were, of course, crowded with company as the day advanced, particularly the Rail-Road Tavern, which was literally crammed with company. The landlady had very prudently and providently reserved one room for the accommodation of the better class visitors. The good lady will, we imagine, have substantial reasons for remembering the trial of Locomotive Carriages. But there is nothing like making hay while the sun shines.

When the trials began, the tough no-nonsense journalists from the technical press came into their own, ignoring any human interest or flowery descriptions of the crowds but getting straight down to the hard facts – or what they saw as hard facts. Though one hesitates to accuse any journalist of biased reporting, it would seem that the worthy reporter from *Mechanics' Magazine* was determined from the beginning that *Novelty* was going to win.

The engine which made the first trial, was the 'Rocket' of Mr. Robert Stephenson (the son, we believe, of Mr. George Stephenson, the engineer of the railway). It is a large and strongly-built engine, and went with a velocity, which, as long as the spectators had nothing to contrast it with, they thought surprising enough. It drew a weight of twelve tons, nine cwt, at the rate of ten miles four chains in an hour, (just exceeding the stipulated maximum,) and when the weight was detached from it, went at a speed of about eighteen miles an hour. The faults most perceptible in this engine, were a great inequality in its velocity, and a very partial fulfilment of the condition that it should 'effectually consume its own smoke'.

The next engine that exhibited its powers was 'The Novelty' of Messrs. Braithwaite and Ericsson, The great lightness of this engine, (it is about one half lighter than Mr. Stephenson's,) its compactness, and its beautiful workmanship, excited universal admiration; a sentiment speedily changed into perfect wonder, by its truly marvellous performances. It was resolved to try first its speed merely; that is at what rate it would go, carrying only its complement of coke and water, with Messrs. Braithwaite and Ericsson to manage it. Almost at once, it darted off at the amazing velocity of twenty-eight miles an hour, and it actually did one mile in the incredibly short space of one minute and 53 seconds! Neither did we observe any appreciable falling off in the rate of speed; it was uniform, steady, and continuous. Had the railway been completed, the engine would, at this rate, have gone nearly the whole way from Liverpool to Manchester within the hour; and Mr. Braithwaite has, indeed, publicly offered to stake a thousand pounds, that as soon as the road is opened, he will perform the entire distance in that time.

It was now proposed to make a trial of the 'Novelty', with three times its weight attached to it; but through some inattention as to the supply of water and coke, a great delay took place in preparing it for its second trip, and by the time all was ready, the day was drawing so near to a close, that the directors thought it proper to defer the prosecution of the competition till the following day.

From other contemporaneous reports, the faults in *Novelty* were due to slightly more than 'inattention' and the directors were more than kind in allowing *Novelty*'s endless delays. It was also more than unfair of the gentleman from the *Mechanics' Magazine* to compare *Novelty*'s great speed travelling on its own with *Rocket* travelling with a train of weighted wagons behind it. A vital condition of the trials was that each engine should pull three times its own weight.

However, the *Novelty* did look exceedingly beautiful, so everyone agreed, and when it reached its amazing velocity of twenty-eight mph, the *Liverpool Mercury* representative was one of the many who fell in love with it.

It seemed, indeed, to fly, presenting one of the most sublime spectacles of human ingenuity and human daring the world has ever beheld. It actually made one giddy to look at it, and filled thousands with lively fears for the safety of the individuals who were on it, and who seemed not to run along the earth, but to fly, as it were, on the 'wings of the wind'. It is a most sublime sight; a sight, indeed, which the individuals who beheld it will not soon forget.

Alas for the *Novelty*, it was unable to show its flying feats the next day, because of various delays and faults, nor the following days, though it did finally do one round of three miles on the Saturday, the last day of the first week's trials. It couldn't manage a second round because of an accident to one of its steam pipes. During this first week, *Rocket* was the only engine to consistently go up and down the trial stretch when told to do so, carrying its full load in accordance with the rules. While it waited for the laggards who were messing around with their engines, doing little spurts then collapsing, *Rocket* did extra exhibition runs, showing off its speed, but the crowds had taken *Novelty* to its heart and still considered *Rocket* too big, too ugly, too dirty.

On Monday, 13 October, the trials began their second week and this time Hackworth had got his *Sans Pareil* in some sort of order. It ran for two hours, then a water pump failed and a crowd of spectators pushed it to the blacksmith's shop. He never got it going again and the judges finally decided that the engine was ineligible on weight grounds. *Novelty* reported again on the Wednesday, after four days and nights of constant work by its engineers, during which they'd taken it to pieces and started again. It did two round trips this time, fully loaded, but a boiler pipe gave way. Its owners, realising it would take weeks to repair, withdrew it from the trials.

In the meantime, *Rocket* did its stuff several times again, reaching even higher speeds, fully loaded, than the week before. George made it do demonstration runs up a 1 in 96 incline which it climbed easily at a speed of twelve mph, fully loaded, about twice the speed that any stationary engine could haul wagons up an incline, proving once and for all that locomotives were far superior for any work on the Liverpool line.

*Rocket* alone fulfilled all the conditions of the trials and had fulfilled them in style, proving convincingly that it was the best engine. It had done seventy miles without any hitch, any fault, whereas its nearest rival never managed even half that distance without breaking down several times. Even the man from *Mechanics' Magazine* had to admit, grudgingly, bending over backwards to pick holes in the rules, that *Rocket* had turned out to be the best.

'The Novelty' still remains at Liverpool and Messrs. Braithwaite and Ericsson have publicly announced that as soon as it is repaired, and the cement of the joints sufficiently hardened, they will (with the leave of the Directors) complete the exhibition of its powers; and show that but for the accidents which it unfortunately met with, it was more than equal to the accomplishment of the task that was last assigned to it.

The prize is not expected to be positively awarded for some little time yet to come. It appears that the gentlemen who were appointed to act as *judges*, have had only the name and not the usual powers of *judges* conferred upon them. All that they have been required and permitted to do is to make an exact report to the Directors of the performances of the competing engines; the

Directors reserving to themselves the power of deciding which is best entitled to the premium . . . but it so happens, that this competition has taken a course which makes it difficult for the Directors to go far wrong in their decision. What *all* the tests were by which the comparative merits of the competing engines were to be tried, it would be hard to say, neither the original 'Conditions and Stipulations,' nor the 'Ordeal,' which was subsequently substituted in their place, being, separately considered, sufficiently full and explicit on the subject; but this much is certain, that the performance of seventy miles, *for a continuance*, was one criterion of excellence to which all the competitors expressed a willing submission. 'The Rocket' started on this understanding; and performed the distance at a rate of speed, which, for a continuance, stands as yet unrivalled in the annals of railway-racing. 'The Sans Pareil' next made the attempt; but in consequence of part of its machinery giving way, only performed about half the distance. 'The Novelty' followed; but had scarcely started, when it was brought by a similar accident to a dead stand. Now, though we are of opinion that 'The Novelty' is the sort of engine that will be found best adapted to the purposes of the railway, and are inclined to think that 'The Sans Pareil' is at least as good an engine as 'The Rocket'; yet as neither the one nor the other has equalled 'The Rocket' in performance, which had the winning of the prize of £500 expressly for its object, we do not see how the Directors can in justice do otherwise than award that prize to Mr. Stephenson. Besides, whatever may be the merits of 'The Rocket', as contrasted with either of its rivals, it is so much superior to all the old locomotives in use, as to entitle Mr. Stephenson to the most marked and liberal consideration, for the skill and ingenuity displayed in its construction.

The judges, upon whom the *Mechanics' Magazine* was nastily trying to cast aspersions, had in fact no hesitation in awarding *Rocket* the prize. One of the three judges was Nicholas Wood, chief engineer and manager at Killingworth, George's old friend (it is surprising that the *Mechanics' Magazine* managed to refrain from any personal insinuations). To balance any suggestion that Wood might be prejudiced, there was also John Rastrick, a well-known Lancashire engineer, one of those brought in earlier by the

Liverpool company who had reported in favour of stationary engines. These two were both highly qualified civil engineers. The third judge doesn't appear to have had much effect on the technical judgements. He was John Kennedy, a Manchester cotton spinner, and was there to give the layman's view. Both Wood and Rastrick kept copious notes on the trials, many of which have survived to this day. (The Northumberland Record Office recently acquired some original notes made by Wood during the trials.)

It is ironic that the *Mechanics' Magazine* should have been so prejudiced against George Stephenson – the epitome of the mechanic made good, if ever there was one. It was a highly influential magazine, a cause and symptom of that early nineteenth-century yearning for scientific knowledge. In 1824 its circulation was sixteen thousand, but its readership must have been ten times as great as it was passed from hand to hand in the new mechanics' institutes which were springing up throughout the country. However, it was run from London and dominated by the professional engineering classes, most of whom looked upon George as a nasty upstart. Its editor and owner was J.C. Robertson, a great friend of William James (so he'd heard the James' side of the Liverpool story). Another of its powerful backers, and a frequent contributor, was Charles Vignoles, the engineer brought in by the Rennies whom George had managed to oust. He seems to have been George's strongest opponent behind the scenes. (Wood, in the third edition of his Treatise, 1838, mentions in passing that the *Mechanics' Magazine*'s glowing reports of *Novelty*'s performances in practice were based on statements by Vignoles.)

However, the rest of the world was open and honest in its praise for *Rocket* and the Stephensons. The local and national newspapers gave glowing accounts. When the news reached America there was a rush of railway plans. The Directors of the Internal Improvement of Massachussetts, who had representatives at Rainhill, greeted the reports with delight. 'We have been called to receive, in astonishment, the accounts which are given of recent experiments in England upon the capacity of Steam Carriages, as a self moving power of Rail Roads. This invention promises to produce a new era in the business and arrangement of Society.' (In January 1831, the Baltimore and Ohio Railroad

Company offered a prize of 4,000 dollars for the best locomotive that could haul 15 tons at 15 mph.)

The Stephenson camp was equally delighted, no doubt pleased that the *Mechanics' Magazine* and the London Establishment had been forced to eat their words, at least for the meantime. The best and most amusing description of their reaction comes in a letter written by John Dixon, Stephenson's young assistant from their Darlington days. He is writing to his brother James in Darlington on 16 October, the day the Rainhill trials finished. (Notice the 'thy' at the end which would indicate that John Dixon was a Quaker.)

Patricroft, Oct. 16 1829

Dear James,

We have finished the grand experiments on the Engines and G.S. or R.S. has come off triumphant and of course will take hold of the £500 so liberally offered by the Company: none of the others being able to come near them. The Rocket is by far the best Engine I have ever seen for Blood and Bone united. Story* will give you particulars besides the Newspaper accounts.

Timothy (Hackworth) has been very sadly out of temper ever since he came for he has been grobbing on day and night and nothing our men did for him was right, we could not please him with the Tender nor anything; he openly accused all G.S.'s people of conspiring to hinder him of which I do believe them innocent, however he got many trials but never got half of his 70 miles done without stopping. He burns nearly double the quantity of coke that the Rocket does and mumbles and roars and rolls about like a Empty Beer Butt on a rough Pavement and moreover weighs above 4½ Tons consequently should have had six wheels and as for being on Springs I must confess I cannot find them out either going or standing neither can I perceive any effect they have. She is very ugly and the Boiler runs out very much, he had to feed her with more Meal and Malt Sprouts than would fatten a pig. . . .

The London Engine of Braithwaite & Erickson called the

---

* Thomas Story (or Storey) was chief resident engineer at Darlington and had been assisting George at Rainhill.

'Novelty' was a light one, no chimney upright but a Boiler thus (sketch) blown by a Blast at A by Bellows and pipes carried like a Still worm along the Tube B C to the discharge C point on Chimney E. She only weighed 3. 7. 3 and did not stand 10 ft. high. Two 6 in. cylinders working a Bell Crank lever to turn the Axle which was cranked so as to be turned by the Bell and Bob lever out of sight, but a very weak form of axle, a Water Tank under the carriage close to the ground and Boiler Bellows Flues, etc., were all covered with Copper like a new Tea Urn all which tended to give her a very Parlour like appearance and when she started she seemed to dart away like a Greyhound for a bit but every trial he had some mishap, first an explosion of inflammable gas which Burst his Bellows then his feed pipe blew up and finally some internal joint of his hidden flue thro his boiler so that it was no go.

Burstall from Edinbro, upset his in bringing from L'Pool to Rainhill and spent a week in pretending to Remedy the injuries whereas he altered and amended some part every day till he was last of all to start and a sorrowful start it was; full 6 miles an hour cranking away like an old Wickerwork pair of Panniers on a cantering Cuddy Ass. Vox Populi was in favour of London from appearances but we showed them the way to do it for Messrs. Rastrig & Walker in their report as to Fixed and permt. Engines stated that the whole power of the Loco. Engines would be absorbed in taking their own bodies up Rainhill Incline 1 in 96 consequently they could take no load. Now the first thing old George did was to bring a Coach with about 20 people up at a galop and every day since he has run up and down to let them see what they could do up such an ascent and has taken 40 folks up at 20 miles an hour.

He is now going on with an extension of the Way to Derbyshire and I am to begin on Monday to survey, etc. from Manchester to meet the others. Robert is about a new line in Leicestershire. I dined with Story at Mr. S.'s and we were all as kind as cousins.

Love to all friends and believe me, Dr. James,<br>
Thy affectionate Bro. in haste,<br>
JOHN DIXON

# 12

# THE GRAND OPENING

In the summer of 1830 Fanny Kemble was young and pretty and talented and acting in Liverpool. She'd recently had her first acclaim, at the age of twenty, for her performance as Juliet at Covent Garden, thus saving her actor-manager father from financial ruin. Everyone was now saying that she might turn out to be as great an actress as her famous aunt, Sarah Siddons.

She was on a provincial tour and on her arrival in Liverpool an invitation came for her and her father to attend a sneak preview of something called the Liverpool and Manchester Railway. The railway was not to open for another three months but the directors, in the manner of directors of all new enterprises, then as well as now, were desirous of inviting any public personages, especially those who were young and pretty and talented, to come and see and marvel at their wonderful new enterprise. They didn't call it a sneak preview but a 'private view', though it was far from private, for crowds of many thousands lined the route whenever it was rumoured that one of the locomotives was taking some important visitors on a tour of inspection. Miss Kemble was lucky on her inspection. Her personal guide was none other than the engineer himself, Mr George Stephenson.

Miss Kemble did indeed go on to greatness, as an actress and as a famous beauty, having her portrait painted for posterity by Sir Thomas Lawrence, President of the Royal Academy, but when she is remembered today it is more likely to be for her account of her experiences that day. It first appeared in a book she published in 1878 about her girlhood, and has delighted generations of railway historians ever since. Amidst the lifeless locomotive statistics, or carping criticisms from mechanical magazines, her observations stand out fresh and bright, a virgin view of a sight the rest of the world had still to see, full of the gaiety and hopefulness of youth.

This is the letter she wrote to a friend from Liverpool on 26 August 1830.

And now I will give you an account of my yesterday's excursion. A party of sixteen persons was ushered into a large courtyard, where, under cover, stood several carriages of a peculiar construction, one of which was prepared for our reception. It was a long-bodied vehicle with seats placed across it back to back; the one we were in had six of these benches, and it was a sort of uncovered *char à banc*. The wheels were placed upon two iron bands, which formed the road, and to which they are fitted, being so constructed as to slide along without any danger of hitching or becoming displaced, on the same principle as a thing sliding on a concave groove. The carriage was set in motion by a mere push, and, having received this impetus, rolled with us down an inclined plane into a tunnel, which forms the entrance to the railroad. This tunnel is four hundred yards long (I believe), and will be lighted by gas. At the end of it we emerged from darkness, and, the ground becoming level, we stopped. There is another tunnel parallel with this only much wider and longer, for it extends from the place we had now reached, and where the steam carriages start, and which is quite out of Liverpool, the whole way under the town, to the docks. This tunnel is for waggons and other heavy carriages; and as the engines which are to draw the trains along the railroad do not enter these tunnels, there is a large building at this entrance which is to be inhabited by steam engines of a stationary turn of mind, and different constitution from the travelling ones, which are to propel the trains through the tunnels to the terminus in the town, without going out of their houses themselves. The length of the tunnel parallel to the one we passed through is (I believe) two thousand two hundred yards. I wonder if you are understanding one word I am saying all this while.

We were introduced to the little engine which was to drag us along the rails. She (for they make these curious little fire horses all mares) consisted of a boiler, a stove, a platform, a bench, and behind the bench a barrel containing enough water to prevent her being thirsty for fifteen miles,– the whole machine not bigger than a common fire engine. She goes upon two wheels, which are her feet, and are moved by bright steel legs called pistons; these are propelled by steam, and in proportion as more steam is applied to the upper extremities (the hip-joints, I suppose) of these pistons, the faster they move the wheels; and when it is desirable to diminish the speed, the steam, which unless suffered to escape would burst the boiler, evaporates through a safety valve into the air. The reins, bit, and bridle of this wonderful beast, is a small steel handle, which applies or withdraws the steam from its legs or pistons, so that a child might manage it. The coals, which are its oats, were under the bench, and there was a small glass tube affixed to the boiler, with water in it, which indicates by its fullness or emptiness when the creature wants water, which is immediately conveyed to it from its reservoirs. There is a chimney to the stove but as they burn coke there is none of the dreadful black smoke which accompanies the progress of a steam vessel. This snorting little animal, which I felt rather inclined to pat, was then harnessed to our carriage, and Mr. Stephenson having taken me on the bench of the engine with him, we started at about ten miles an hour.

The steam horse being ill adapted for going up and down hill, the road was kept at a certain level, and appeared sometimes to sink below the surface of the earth and sometimes to rise above it. Almost at starting it was cut through the solid rock which formed a wall on either side of it, about sixty feet high. You can't imagine how strange it was to be journeying on thus, without any visible cause of progress other than the magical machine, with its flying white breath and rhythmical, unvarying pace, between these rocky walls, which are already clothed with moss and ferns and grasses; and when I reflected that these great masses of stone had been cut asunder to allow our passage thus far below the surface of the earth, I felt as if no fairy tale was ever half so wonderful as what I saw. Bridges were thrown from side to side across the top of these cliffs, and the people looking down upon us from them seemed like pygmies standing in the sky. . . .

He [Mr Stephenson] explained to me the whole construction of the steam engine, and said he could soon make a famous engineer of me, which, considering the wonderful things he has achieved, I dare not say is impossible. His way of explaining himself is peculiar, but very striking, and I understood, without difficulty, all that he said to me. We then rejoined the rest of the party, and the engine having received its supply of water, the carriage was placed behind it, for it cannot turn, and was set off at its utmost speed, 35 miles an hour, swifter than a bird flies (for they tried the experiment with a snipe). You cannot conceive what the sensation of cutting the air was; the motion is as smooth as possible, too. I could either have read or written; and as it was I stood up, and with my bonnet off 'drank the air before me'. The wind, which was strong, or perhaps the force of our own thrusting against it absolutely weighed my eyelids down. When I closed my eyes this sensation of flying was quite delightful, and strange beyond description; yet strange as it was, I had a perfect sense of security, and not the slightest fear.

At one time, to exhibit the power of the engine, having met another steam-carriage which was unsupplied with water, Mr. Stephenson caused it to be fastened in front of ours; moreover, a waggon laden with timber was also chained to us, and thus propelling the idle steam engine and dragging the loaded waggon, which was beside it, and our own carriage full of people behind, this brave little she-dragon of ours flew on. Farther on she met three carts, which, being fastened in front of her, she pushed on before her without the slightest delay or difficulty; when I add that this pretty little creature can run with equal facility either backwards or forwards, I believe I have given you an account of all her capacities.

Four years have sufficed to bring this great undertaking to an end. The railroad will be opened upon the fifteenth of next month. The Duke of Wellington is coming down to be present on the occasion, and, I suppose, that with the thousands of spectators and the novelty of the spectacle, there will never have been a scene of more striking interest. The whole cost of the work (including the engines and carriages) will have been eight hundred and thirty thousand pounds; and it is already worth double that sum. The Directors have kindly offered us three places for the opening, which is a great favour, for people are bidding almost anything for a place, I understand.

Now for a word or two about the master of all these marvels, with whom I am most horribly in love. He is a man from fifty to fifty-five years of age; his face is fine, though careworn, and bears an expression of deep thoughtfulness; his mode of explaining his ideas is peculiar and very original, striking, and forcible; and although his accent indicates strongly his north country birth, his language has not the slightest touch of vulgarity or coarseness. He has certainly turned my head.

George must have been thrilled – and probably wouldn't have minded being taken for around fifty-five, when he was only forty-nine, as personal vanity was never one of his vices. He'd certainly been letting off steam, in every sense, showing off by touching thirty-five mph, but who wouldn't have done with such a pretty companion, so obviously enraptured. Naturally, one assumes that she was horribly in love with George in a purely theatrical sense. Even actresses on tour in Liverpool are allowed a little West End license. But what thoughts passed through George's grey, careworn head? He was in love with steam, as we well know, but memories of his own dear long departed Fanny must have crossed his mind, the mother of his beloved Robert and of the baby daughter, also called Fanny, who died in infancy.

A few months earlier George had made an impression, though a slightly different one, upon another well-known personage of the day who'd also been given a private tour of the line. He was Thomas Creevey, MP, the friend of Lord Sefton and a noted critic of the railway. Creevey had played a major part in opposing and humiliating George when the railway bill had been thrown out of parliament five years previously and had gone so far as to describe one railway supporter as 'insane'. He didn't change his mind completely, after his little trip, but he was nonetheless interested enough to take a ride, and to live, to his surprise, to tell the tale. His tale, in the form of a letter written to his daughter in November 1829, first appeared in *The Creevey Papers* in 1903, a valuable source of social insight into the Georgian period.

Today we have had a *lark* of a very high order. Lady Wilton sent over yesterday to say that the Loco Motive machine was to be upon the railway at such a place at 12 o'clock for the Knowsley party to ride in if they liked and inviting this house to be of the party. So of course we were at our post in 3 carriages and some horsemen at the hour appointed. I had the satisfaction, for I can't call it pleasure, of taking a trip of five miles in it, which we did in just a quarter of an hour – that is 20 miles an hour. As accuracy upon this subject was my great object, I held my watch in my hand at starting, and all the time; and as it has a second hand, I know I could not be deceived. But observe, during these five miles, the machine was occasionally made to put itself out or go it and then we went at the rate of 23 miles an hour, and just with the same ease as to motion or absence of friction as the other reduced pace. But the quickest motion is to me *frightful*; it is really flying, and it is impossible to divest yourself of the notion of instant death to all upon the least accident happening. It gave me a headache which has not left me yet. Sefton is convinced that some damnable thing must come of it; but he and I seem more struck with such apprehension than others. . . . The smoke is very inconsiderable, indeed, but sparks of fire are abroad and in some quantity: one burnt Miss de Ros's cheek, another a hole in Lady Maria's silk pelisse and a third a hole in someone else's gown. Altogether, I am extremely glad indeed to have seen this miracle, and to have travelled in it. Had I thought worse of it than I do I should have had the curiosity to try it; but, having done so, I am quite satisfied with my *first* achievement being my *last*.

Creevey's reaction could not be called ecstatic compared with Fanny's, but it was enough to confirm George's usual confidence, getting him in the right mood for the grand opening to come, knowing that his enemies were now highly intrigued, if nothing else.

The success of the Rainhill trials had immediately resulted in an order with Robert Stephenson and Company of a further four locomotives on the *Rocket* model. Cropper, the director who'd always been against George, also managed to get the Liverpool board to order two engines from the makers of *Novelty*, at a cost of £1,000 each, much to the delight of the *Mechanics' Magazine*. But alas for the mechanicals, the two engines failed their trial runs, for reasons never given, if ever known.

The *Manchester Guardian* came to the defence of the Stephensons with the use of some pretty sharp liberal invective, a definite cut above the language that had been used in local newspaper disputes back in the north east. They launched an attack on the *Mechanics' Magazine*, calling their persecution a 'system of petty detraction so long and insistently levelled at Mr Stephenson's engines by a little knot of pseudomechanics'. The *Mechanics' Magazine* replied by accusing the *Guardian* of treating the truth as exceedingly superfluous'. The *Guardian*, very wisely, then appealed to the public.

> What the practical difficulties are which Mr Stephenson has had to encounter with his engines we do not know; but we understand the difficulty which Messrs Braithwaite and Ericsson had, and still have to encounter (and it is 'practical' enough) is that their engines will not work – at all events, not to any useful purpose, whilst those of Mr Stephenson perform their allotted tasks in the admirable manner which most of our readers have, no doubt, witnessed.

However, George's enemies didn't all give up, despite George's success in making friends and influencing actresses. His old enemy Cropper persuaded the board to bring in William Chapman, an early locomotive pioneer, to report on the latest state of the construction of the line. This was early in 1830, the year George had said he would be finished, so in some ways it wasn't too unreasonable to have a progress report. But not in George's eyes. Fresh from his success at Rainhill, he was furious that anyone should question his work. He wrote a letter of such self-righteous passion to the board complaining about Chapman and about the many other occasions when the board had dared to doubt his capabilities that it is worth quoting several paragraphs to show how absolutely confident of his own powers he had become.

> When you engaged Mr. Chapman I understood that it was for the sole purpose of reporting to you on the progress made on the different works on the line. Whatever might be my private opinions at to the utility of such an officer I did not urge any objection to his election, especially as you informed me that his duty would in no way interfere with mine. Since his appointment I find that his attention has not merely been devoted to reporting on the progress of the works, but extended to things which I trust you will consider strictly within my department.
>
> An engineman has been discharged from one of the Locomotive Engines because he did not give a satisfactory answer to some questions put to him by Mr. Chapman. The dismissal of this man from all I can learn is certainly

injudicious. I brought him from the North where he bore a most excellent character. . . . His answers to Mr. C. may have been unsatisfactory, but it is doubtful whether he understood the import of the questions and it is still more doubtful if they were intelligible to any working Mechanic. I cannot but feel some reluctance to bringing Enginemen with their families from the North, who alone are capable of managing this class of engine . . . if they are to be interfered with by an individual unacquainted with the nature of the work.

A note also has been addressed by Mr. C. to Mr. Booth requesting him to give one of my assistants such directions as he might think fit respecting the Embankment at Newton, and that only two or three days after I had been on the spot myself. On the impropriety of such a step on the part of Mr. Chapman I shall make no comment as it is sufficiently obvious. It is a direct interference with my duty and by a person entirely ignorant of Engineering; nor can he be acquainted, when he views a piece of work on the line, what plans I intend adopting, why I am doing it, or what I intend to do afterwards.

This kind of interference with my duties as well as the doubts and suspicions which had been expressed regarding the opinions I have from time to time given on different subjects connected with this work has occasioned me much uneasiness. I have been accused of jealousy and a want of candour in the case of Mr. Brandreth's and Mr. Winan's waggons as well as in that of Mr. Erickson's engine, and even of worse than this in the case of Stationary v. Locomotive engines. In all these instances, instead of jealousy operating I confidently state that I have been only influenced by a disinterested zeal for the complete success of your work and by a laudable desire to support and establish my own credit.

May I now ask if I have supported your interests or not? Has Mr. Brandreth's carriage answered? Has Mr. Winan's saved 9/10 of the friction? Was not Walker & Rastrick's report wrong? Has the *Novelty* engine answered your expectations? Have the *Lancashire Witch* and the *Rocket* not performed more than I stated? These facts make me bold, but they also stimulate me to still further improvement. But I cannot believe that you will permit me to be thwarted in my proceedings by individuals who neither understand the work nor feel the interest which attaches me to this railway. Allow me therefore to ask if you intend Mr. C. to continue on the works.

George won his way, confirming once and for all his position of strength. Everything was now going so well for him that the board were beginning to feel guilty at ever having doubted him during the previous years. Not long after he had put Chapman in his place, and had him removed, the directors adjourned to the house of one of their members, during one of the VIP tours, and called a special board meeting in which they passed unanimously the following resolution:

> That the directors cannot allow this opportunity to pass without expressing their strong sense of the great skill and unwearied energy displayed by their engineer, Mr. George Stephenson, which have so far brought this great national work to a successful termination, and which promise to be followed by results so beneficial to the country at large and to the proprietors of this concern.

In his handling of Chapman, George had sounded in his high-flown letter as if he were playing the educated engineers at their own game, with his outraged accusations of 'impropriety' and how he'd been 'occasioned much uneasiness'. He must obviously by now have been using a higher class of secretary, judging by the well polished rhetoric. However, the few hand-written private letters which survive from this period show his own command of grammar to be just as shaky as it ever had been, but he is at least showing a certain calmness, and, most interesting of all, a capacity to make jokes. The following letter was written by George to Michael Longridge in Newcastle. The Losh referred to is George's former partner, the one he fell out with. Locke is Joseph Locke, one of George's pupils who later became a great railway builder. They too had apparently had some difference of opinion, if only temporarily. Some punctuation has been added – but George's spelling is unaltered.

Leverpool Feb. 8, 1830

My Dear Sir,

You quite alarm me with the newes contained in the times, we must have something new or we will be in the back ground. . . . do you intend to let Losh of paying any more patent right, have you not an argument with him, woent the Law compels him to fulfill his agreement – I think you have mannagered badly with the N.le [Newcastle] & Carlisle Railway to let it out of our hands, I suppose Losh & his friends has been prepared to meet you – will your frends still be subscribers to the work and if they do not will the work go on, we must have it ultimatly –

Locke has not withdrawen himself from me, I was under the nessisity of taking him from this concren to go on with the stockport bill as I could not go on with it my self on account of the marques of stafford and Robert could not get to it in time to look after the sirveying – the severe winter has pervented us geting on with our masonery so much that we can not be opened before the latter end of may or, the begining of june.

As soon as I can spare time you know you & I are to go and set the Railway out from the meditirranean to the Red Sea. & we shall send the young men to execute it. after it is done, we will take a trip to the east indes by that rute, and set them to work in that quarter after which there will be plenty of orders for boath Losh you and all the manufacturers in England. I hope you will come this way to London –

I am Dear Sir
Yours truly
GEO. STEPHENSON

The last remark is surely a pleasantry, saying that there will be plenty of work for friend and foe alike when he has taken the railway from the Mediterranean to the Red Sea. George was confident enough that railways would some day cover the whole of Britain, but in 1830 he can't seriously have been planning for Indian railways.

As 15 September, the date of opening, drew near, the invitations went out to everyone of importance in political and engineering fields in the land, from the prime minister downwards. The private views now became public views with around three hundred people being taken for short rides every Saturday afternoon, a time when construction work could be conveniently stopped and the line cleared. It was as important for the engine drivers and crew to get used to working a railway as for the public to get used to seeing one.

At Darlington there had only been *Locomotion* to worry about. Now George had to create from scratch the whole science of organising trains in the plural, arranging signals between them, coupling and uncoupling coaches, working out timetables, who would be using which bits of line at which time, where the line could be crossed and when. He issued special coloured flags to all the enginemen to that they could signal each other. White meant 'Go on', a red flag 'Go Slowly' and purple 'Stop'.

Proper signalling and safety precautions were vital because there were still great fears, in the public prints and in the public mind, about the risk of fatal accidents. Great efforts were made to spread the idea of railways being safe and smooth. The *Liverpool Mercury* did its bit to allay public fears about riding on railways by printing helpful little notes. It guaranteed that 'locomotives operated so smoothly that water would not spill from a wine glass' and that 'riders could read and write while travelling, as readily as in their arm chairs at home'. A tame medical expert was paraded, one Dr Chalmers, after rumours had spread that speeding was bad for the eyes. (It's interesting how many supposedly harmful activities have been said over the years to be bad for the eyes.) Dr Chalmers assured potential passengers that even speeds of thirty-four mph would 'cause no inconvenience or alarm nor would the eye be disturbed while viewing the scenery'.

All the big guns replied in the affirmative to their invitations, from the Iron Duke and Sir Robert Peel to Fanny Kemble and George's Newcastle friend and partner, Michael Longridge. George wrote him a personal invitation – mentioning first of all yet another trip he'd organised for the directors. It was, of course, another success for 'yours allways truly'.

Liverpool July 4th 1830

My dear Sir,

I duly received yours of the 26th of June. I am well aware that the sentiments expressed in it are sincere, and I know no one who rejoices more than you do at my welfare. The trip was a very delightful one to me, as we took the Directors and a load along with us for the first time. Mr. Dald from Scotland was with us and was I believe highly gratified. If I had slacked the Reins of our horse on that day, they would have run over the ground in less time.

Being as you know a very cautious man and desirous of doing things moderately, we were much longer than we need have been.

In coming back with the Directors not more than half the power of the engine was applied on many parts of the line. On our return home Mr. Lawrence had a splendid dinner provided for the party.

The formal opening of the Railway it is intended shall take place on the 15th of September, when I shall be glad to see you, and hope you will come a few days before, by doing which you will have an opportunity of seeing the different *horses training on the ground*. You ought I think to bring Mrs. Longridge with you, as it will I should imagine be a treat to her. I will take care to have Lodgings provided for you either at my house or elsewhere.

I am dear Sir,
Yours allways truly,
GEO. STEPHENSON

Mic: Longridge Esqr.

P.S. You shall have my opinion on the form of Rails in the course of a few days. I think the I Rails an infringement of your Patent, I have seen Foster and told him so.

G.S.

As Fanny Kemble had predicted, there was a great demand for tickets and places for the opening celebration. Guest houses suddenly started boasting about their nearness to the railway – a complete reversal of only a year or two previous when no one wanted to be thought to be anywhere near the dreadful railway line. A hotel in Wavertree Road, Liverpool, described itself as only a few hundreds from the railway tunnel, of all places, and offered 'sitting apartments and bedrooms, furnished in the completest manner', and 'wines and spirits of the choicest quality'. Another hotel owner built a grandstand outside his hotel, and a massive public one, holding one thousand people, was constructed beside the Sankey Viaduct. There is an early example of ticket touting, at least that's how it appears from a local Liverpool paper where a stock broker was offering seats in the carriages to people who bought shares through him. He must have managed to collar quite a number of tickets, none of which was meant for sale in any way but given free to directors' guests and other important people.

Two days before the opening, Liverpool was crammed with visitors, just as it is today before the Grand National, and it was difficult to find anywhere to eat or sleep. On the day itself, Wednesday, 15 September, crowds were assembling three hours before the opening at the company's engine yards at Crown Street and at least fifty thousand had gathered to watch the trains pull out of Liverpool.

There were eight locomotives, each pulling its own train, each with its own colour to assist the important passengers find their place. The tickets were printed according to the colour of the train.

| Engine | Driver | Colour |
|--------|--------|--------|
| Northumbrian | George Stephenson | Lilac |
| Phoenix | Rob. Stephenson, Jr | Green |
| North Star | Rob. Stephenson, Sr | Yellow |
| Rocket | Joseph Locke | Light Blue |
| Dart | Thos Gooch | Purple |
| Comet | Wlm Allcard | Deep red |
| Arrow | F. Swanwick | Pink |
| Meteor | Anthony Harding | Brown |

The *Northumbrian* was the newest and most developed of the *Rocket* type engines, but even as it led the triumphal procession Robert Stephenson had ready for delivery in Newcastle an even newer engine which was to replace it as a brand leader in a matter of weeks – the *Planet*.

George was in charge of *Northumbrian*, and he probably did most of the driving himself, but there were a couple of brakesmen on each engine to do the dirty work. There was also a flagman assigned to each train, travelling at the rear, acting as the first guardsman.

From the list, it will be seen that the others drivers were George's son, his brother, and his leading assistant engineers, such as Locke (now back to help), Gooch and Allcard, all known to railway historians for their later successes. Swanwick was hardly more than a boy, the son of a great friend of George's, and had only recently been taken on as one of George's apprentices (paying fifteen shillings a week for the privilege). He later became George's private secretary and assistant.

The Duke of Wellington, as prime minister, was in his own specially designed carriage, dripping with gilt and crimson drapes, which was in the middle of the leading train drawn by *Northumbrian*. The other VIPs included Lord Grey (later prime minister), Lord Melbourne (later prime minister), Sir Robert Peel (later prime minister), the Earl of Salisbury (father of a later prime minister), Prince Esterhazy (the Austrian ambassador); a host of earls and viscounts including Gower, Wilton, Glengall, Lauderdale, Belgrave, Ingestre, Cassilis, Sandon, Colville, Dacre, Delamere, Granville, Stanley, Skelmersdale and Wharncliffe; many leading MPs such as William Huskisson, Arbuthnot, Calcraft, Gascoyne; Bishops like Coventry and Lichfield; engineers such as George Rennie, Rastrick, Wood and Vignoles. It was estimated that the eight trains held 722 VIP passengers in about thirty separate coaches.

It is not recorded if the king had been invited, though the status of the monarchy at the time was not very high. George IV, who had just died in June 1830, had been known mainly for his girlfriends and good times and had been succeeded by his brother William IV, who was known for his love of the sea and nicknamed Sailor. (Without knowing it, everyone was waiting for Victoria.)

They'd been very lucky to get the Duke of Wellington and he'd been rather brave to come, considering that reports from the northern provinces had indicated that he was no longer considered the country's number one hero, saviour of the nation, but a reactionary old style Tory who was against any change, especially anything smacking of parliamentary reform. He'd already fallen out with some of his younger, more liberal Tory cabinet ministers, such as Huskisson, over his intransigence. Several moderate Tories had pushed the duke into attending the opening, hoping he might make his peace with Huskisson, bring the extremes of the party together and keep the reforming Whigs at bay. The reform movement had been growing for some time and was finally to sweep away Wellington and the Tories later that year and allow in Grey as prime minister, maker of the 1832 reform bill. Parliamentary reform was, however, just one element in a general feeling of social discontent, made worse by unemployment and economic depression. The Tories were particularly hated in the north west since the Peterloo massacre of 1819 when the Tory government called in the troops to a public meeting of factory workers and eleven people had been killed.

The duke had never believed the stories from the north about dissatisfaction, dismissing it as simply a few radical agitators stirring up the working classes, and considered himself perfectly safe to come and see, and be seen, at the Liverpool opening. In one way it could be argued that railways – to which he was lending his great name by attending the opening – were indirectly hastening the reform movement. 'Parliamentary reform must follow soon after the opening,' wrote a Manchester reformer just before the event. 'A million of persons will pass over it and see that hitherto unseen village of Newton; and they must be convinced of the absurdity of its sending two members to Parliament whilst Manchester sends none.'

The directors knew, even if the duke didn't, how unpopular he was and had made elaborate arrangements for his security. Police guarded the entire thirty miles of the route and all railway crossings had been closed except one at Huyton. (Seat of yet another later PM.) All the same, there was talk of disaster in the air. In his diary, just two days before the opening, Greville records a talk with his brother-in-law in which he mentions the great ceremony due on the fifteenth, but 'fears ruin and the collapse of the Government'. One of the precautions taken to ensure the safety of the duke was that his train should have sole use of one line of the track while the other seven trains would proceed, at six-hundred-yard intervals, on the other line. If this had not been the case, disaster might have been averted.

A cannon boomed to announce the start of the processions and George's *Northumbrian* drew out of Liverpool to the cheers of the crowds, pulling the train containing the Duke of Wellington and the other eighty highly important guests, including Fanny Kemble.

Though the weather was uncertain [she wrote], enormous crowds of densely packed people lined the road, shouting and waving hats and handkerchiefs as we flew by them. What with the sound of these cheering multitudes and the tremendous velocity with which we were bourne past them, my spirits rose to the true champagne height, and I never enjoyed anything so much as the first hour of our progress.

The procession got safely over the Sankey Viaduct, an ideal spot if any saboteurs had had a plan to dislocate the duke's train. The crowds in the grandstands and those below, looking up from the boats on the canal, cheered and applauded. George Stephenson, having one line to himself, was able to stop and start the *Northumbrian* at will without fear of any other train running into the rear, and so allowed the Duke and the other chief guests to take their time exclaiming over the remarkable engineering constructions. The duke was heard to say 'Magnificent', 'Stupendous'. Behind them, on the other line, the other seven trains had to wait patiently for the white flag to signal them on.

It had been arranged that at Parkside, some seventeen miles from Liverpool, the duke's train would take a scheduled stop for water. It had also been arranged 'that at this time the other seven trains would overtake on the other line, thus giving the duke a fine view of each of the trains steaming past.

The duke's train, having taken on water, stopped and waited. Two trains arrived and passed successfully, the *Phoenix* and the *North Star*, and were duly admired by all. There was a slight delay before the third train arrived and while they waited several passengers decided to get out and stretch their legs, including William Huskisson and Prince Esterhazy. This was strictly against the rules. All passengers had been given verbal and written instructions on no account to leave their carriages. Huskisson was standing in the gap between the two rails of the second line, discussing with friends the wonders they'd seen when the duke, sitting in the corner seat of his carriage, caught sight of him and gave a nod and wave of his hand. It was the sign many Tories had been hoping for, wanting the two statesmen to make up their disagreement and become friends once again. The duke opened his carriage, leaned out and shook Huskisson's hand. They'd scarcely begun a conversation when there were shouts that the third train was in sight at last and was about to steam past them on the other track. Prince Esterhazy, with great presence of mind, managed to scramble into the duke's carriage. The other guests either rushed across the track to the far side and got on to the safety of the embankment or flattened themselves beside the Duke's train. Unfortunately for Huskisson he did none of those things. He was confused and frightened and far from agile. According to Creevey, he hadn't been well since attending the late king's funeral. He'd done too much kneeling and developed paralysis in one leg and thigh. He lost his balance and fell and the third train, which happened to be *Rocket*, passed over his thighs. 'I have met my death,' he was heard to shout.

If the space between the tracks had only been wider, six feet as they are today, Huskisson might have escaped. But someone, and it can only have been George, had had the bright idea of making the space between the tracks 4ft 8½ ins, the same as the width of the tracks themselves. The theory was that extra wide loads would be able to run down the middle at off-peak times. (This was agreed to be ridiculous years later and the LNWR had to go to the trouble of altering the tracks.) When therefore Huskisson fell in the narrow gap between the tracks, through panic or paralysis, his legs were splayed across the track, right in the path of the oncoming *Rocket*.

Huskisson didn't die at once, though he might easily have done. There was complete pandemonium with everyone screaming, shouting and arguing, not knowing what to do. Only George took any action. He uncoupled all but one carriage from *Northumbrian* and placed Huskisson inside. Two doctors in the party applied a tourniquet with a handkerchief and George set off at full speed in the direction of Manchester. (He travelled the fifteen miles to Eccles, on the outskirts of Manchester, at an average speed of thirty-six miles per hour, a world record, not that anyone was noting such things at the time.)

William Huskisson died that evening in the vicar's house at Eccles, after dictating a codicil to his will. 'It is an extraordinary fact,' reported the *Manchester Guardian*, 'and evinces the uncommon firmness and self possession of the right hon. gentleman under such awful circumstances, that after he had signed the papers he turned back, as it were, to place a dot over the i and another between the W. and H.' His last spoken words were equally measured. 'The country has had the best of me. I trust it will do justice to my public character. I regret not the few years which might have remained to me, except for those dear ones whom I leave behind.'

Huskisson was aged sixty. He had been an eminent and radical president of the board of trade, a long time supporter of the Liverpool Railway and had now become enshrined forever as the first casualty of the railway age. (Various navvies had been seriously injured, some fatally, in the construction of the Darlington and the Liverpool lines, but navvies don't go down in history.)

Back at the scene of the accident, it took the great men of the day an hour and a half to decide their next move. The seven trains stood idle as the duke and Sir Robert Peel argued that it was only good taste to cancel everything, pack up the celebrations and go home, but the leading citizens of Manchester said that a multitude was waiting for them in Manchester and the mob might take over if they didn't arrive. 'Something in that,' said the duke. So they eventually set off for Manchester, all their best laid schemes and timetables completely ruined, stopping on the way to get the latest report on Huskisson and to pick up George and *Northumbrian*. A lot of coupling and uncoupling and tying of chains took place as the trains were rearranged.

Manchester was indeed in a state of mob rule. The military had been called in to help the police but the crowds had grown impatient with the long delay. When the trains finally arrived the crowds invaded the line and forced the duke and his long procession to crawl into town. The duke had to put up with rowdies banging on his window, shaking their fists, throwing missiles and waving banners right in his face. 'At the Manchester station,' says Smiles, 'the political element began to display itself; placards about "Peterloo" etc were exhibited and brickbats were thrown at the carriage containing the Duke.' Jeaffreson, in his description of the arrival is even more explicit about who was causing the trouble. 'A Lancashire mob is never docile; and just then political discontents had made the lower orders especially unruly.'

The duke, wisely, refused to leave his carriage. When the train did eventually push itself into the station he managed to kiss a few babies which several well-wishers had pressed upon him, but kept safely inside. He was greatly relieved when the procession finally turned round to head back for Liverpool. The journey back was a nightmare, with mix-ups between the trains now that their schedules had broken down, couplings breaking and engines having to be watered and refuelled.

It started to rain, which made the rails very dangerous, but even worse, there were reports that the mob had put sand on the line. They went as slowly as possible, to avoid any crashes, and were soon travelling in the pitch dark. Signalling lamps, or railway lamps of any sort, had yet to be invented. However, they met with only one minor obstacle on the track, a wheelbarrow which was crushed harmlessly, and they finally arrived safely in Liverpool at ten at night.

Apart from the death of Huskisson, it was a successful day, but there was no forgetting the death of Huskisson. The duke personally never forgot and was against railways till the end of his life. In the public mind, that is all most people remember today about the opening of the Liverpool–Manchester Railway. But it was the greatest single day in the history of railways. George had reached the pinnacle of his lifetime's work. The railway age had begun.

# 13

# AFTER LIVERPOOL, THE WORLD

What happened in Liverpool and Manchester before, during and after the grand opening was in the next twenty years mirrored in every town worthy of the name, not just in Britain but in Europe, the USA and throughout the industrial world. The hardest railways were yet to be built. The biggest locomotives were yet to be created. The multi-million-pound schemes had yet to be dreamt up and fought over. George Stephenson had many more wonderful constructions ahead. But for railways, and for George Stephenson, the worst was over. After 1830, railways became matters of public importance, public concern and of intense public interest.

The Liverpool opening, unlike the Darlington opening, was a commercialised event. Public and promoters and souvenir makers, all of them knew that they had witnessed a major event in the progress of industrial civilisation. You don't run off several thousand penny handkerchiefs showing scenes from the Liverpool–Manchester Railway unless you know there's an audience panting for them – and not simply for the purpose of wiping noses. One of them came up at Sothebys in 1945, part of the enormous railway collection built up by the late C.F. Dendy Marshall. It was made of cotton, measured twenty-nine inches by thirty-two and realised £16. It would fetch five times that today. On sale at Liverpool that famous day, and for a long time afterwards, were scores of other articles showing the engines or bridges and aqueducts. You could have bought a papier mâché tea tray, a quart mug, a tobacco jar, a wall plaque, a glass tumbler, a snuff box, all of them a souvenir of the happy day, and most of them with a picture of *Rocket*. The *Rocket* had completely captured the public imagination, becoming the best-known railway engine in the world. It still is.

The makers of commemorative medals, who are still hard at it today, turning out a fresh medal for every conceivable, and sometimes inconceivable event, were exceedingly quick. They had an advertisement in the *Liverpool Courier* on the day of the opening, 15 September 1830. The hand-tooled prose, appealing to the snob in everyone who could afford the price, reads very much like that special brand of highly sincere, vellum smooth, soft sell which accompanies such advertisements in the colour magazines today.

> THE RAIL-WAY MEDAL. – We were highly gratified yesterday with a sight of the very superb metal just published by Thomas Woolfield, Fancy Bazaar, to commemorate the opening of the railway. As a work of art, it is a beautiful and highly-finished production and leaves its competitors far behind, and, being the production of one who is so constantly exerting himself to place before our fair townswomen and townsmen every elegant novelty in his business, we trust it will meet with the patronage so splendid a production deserves. A copy in gold was last evening forwarded to his Grace the Duke of Wellington, Sir Robert Peel and Mr. Huskisson, and we suppose they will be generally worn by those who attend the ceremony this day.

Not every railway company could manage the Duke of Wellington when the railway came to their town, but there were few places that didn't manage some handkerchiefs or the odd commemorative medal. Most of this tat has failed to survive, which is why rare pieces can produce high prices today.

News of the opening travelled fast and many foreign manufacturers produced their own versions of Liverpool–Manchester souvenirs. There was a 'peep-show' of the Liverpool railway produced in Germany – a set of drawings fitted together which pulled out like a concertina to give the impression of travelling down the line. A similar peep-show is known to have been made in France.

It was not only on a commercial level that the Liverpool opening was celebrated. For the first time, serious artists turned their attention to the wonders of the industrial revolution. The water colours by Bury of the Liverpool–Manchester Railway, and the engravings by Ackermann and Shaw, were from the beginning collectors' items, and sets of prints can fetch many hundreds of pounds today. Other well-known artists painted their local railway, such as Richardson in Newcastle, Arthur Tait in Leeds. They introduced an era of documentary illustration which spread from railways, which artists saw immediately as romantic subjects, to other industrial spectacles – bridges, factories, warehouses. It has been suggested that the high quality of many of these industrial paintings encouraged young men to think of becoming engineers, a profession which the better bred families had hitherto rather disdained. Technology suddenly became beautiful, looked at the right way. Perhaps the most beautiful railway painting, which is all emotion and very little technology, is Turner's view of the Great Western Railway, *Rain, Steam and Speed*, now in the National Gallery.

Railways became a literary topic and there is no major Victorian writer, from Dickens downwards, who didn't work at least one railway scene into his or her book. Like Fanny Kemble before them, every writer, amateur and professional, rushed to get their first reactions on seeing a railway into print. Some of the reactions were naturally reactionary. 'Is there no nook of English ground secure from the rash assault,' asked Wordsworth when he heard of a project to bring a railway through the Lakes. But most writers, when they saw their first iron monster, realised that a revolution had taken place. 'We who have lived before Railways were made,' wrote Thackeray, 'belong to another world.'

Up in Liverpool, once the litter had been cleared from the streets, the railway got down to the serious business of railwaying. Here again, unlike Darlington, the effects were immediate and spectacular. By December 1830, fourteen coaches had been withdrawn from the turnpike roads leaving only twelve in operation. The *Manchester Guardian* said the future for coaches was very bleak. In November, the railways had already taken over as the main carrier of the mails between Liverpool and Manchester, a development which heralded the many later improvements in communications directly connected with railways, such as the Penny Post and the electric telegraph. In December the rail passenger trade was doing so well that they decided to reduce fares, bringing first-class fares down from seven shillings to five, and second-class from four to three and sixpence.

The total number of passengers for 1830 – which means only the first three and a half months of operation – was 71,951. In 1831 the total was 445,057.

At the end of December the company announced that in their first few months of operating they'd made a net profit of £14,432. In the doldrum days of 1826 and 1827, when things had looked bad for George and for Liverpool, the railways £100 shares had slumped to £2. The month after the opening the same shares were back to £100.

In its second year of life the Liverpool railway moved on from passengers, cotton and coals to livestock. In May, forty-nine Irish pigs were despatched from Liverpool at a cost of one and sixpence each and arrived safely, if rather noisily, in Manchester. In October, sheep at ninepence each were introduced and then cows. Very soon fresh food, fish and vegetables followed, opening up not just new commercial and economic possibilities but a complete new diet for the industrial masses. Edward Pease had had the poor in mind when he wanted his railways to reduce the price of household coals. The effect of railways on the eating habits of Victorian England has to this day not been properly accounted. As for farmers, who to a man had feared for their pregnant cows and their unborn cabbages with the arrival of railways, completely new and enormous urban markets began opening up for their produce.

George Stephenson had always known their fears were groundless, but nobody had listened to him. Now they were all rushing to his door. The next ten years were the busiest of his whole life as railway promoters besieged him with requests, at home and abroad. Even George was rather startled by the rate of progress. From as early as December 1830, when he wrote this letter (in his own inimitable style) to Michael Longridge, there begins to creep in the first signs that events were beginning to move on without him.

Liverpool Dec: 1830

My Dear sir,

I expect to be able to get off to Scoetland on tuesday next – it would give me great pleasure if I could have you with me. I posiably may take Swanwick with me as I intend to draw up my reports before I return – if I do not see you in Scotland I will return by (way) of Bedlington – It is rely shamefull the way the countrey is going to be cut up by Railways we have no less than eight Bels for Parliament this sissions.

Yours truly,
GEORGE STEPHENSON.

The following year he is even beginning to sound like some of those vested interests who had opposed and thwarted him in the past. In a letter to Nicholas Wood in November, 1831 – a letter dictated to his secretary – he tells how the Liverpool board is trying to keep rivals at bay. 'The Report made by the Directors to the last General Meeting was made as unfavourable as it could with any appearance of truth, in order to throw a damper upon a rival scheme, the L'pool and Leeds Railway, but notwithstanding their attempts, they will not long be able to keep them back.' The ruse was harmless, compared with the tactics he'd personally had to face from the canal companies, but he was obviously getting ready for the scrambling for position which was about to take place.

George himself took pride of place, right until the end of his days. It wasn't in his nature to sit back quietly and let other engineers do it their way. The new engineers might be racing on, cutting up the country, but George was always the first name which any new railway board wanted. With George as the engineer, or as consulting engineer, or even with only a Stephenson pupil at the helm, railway directors knew they had a good chance of getting the necessary backing. George had made a fortune for those Quaker backers in Darlington, Norwich and the City of London who'd invested in his Darlington line and even more for the Liverpool merchants. These Liverpool backers, who followed George's judgements as he moved south through the Midlands, were to prove the most important single lobby amongst all the railway lobbies over the next two decades. One of George's first concerns, after Liverpool, was the Leicester and Swannington Railway (opened 1833) for which the Liverpool party, as it came to be known, put up a third of the capital.

George accepted almost every offer he could, though never for purely financial reasons. He hated to see anyone else doing the job. But, with hindsight, it has to be said that Liverpool was his peak. After that, it was the turn of the younger engineers, notably his son Robert, his pupil Joseph Locke and then Brunel, to make the next great leaps forward.

The leap forward by Locke wasn't without some acrimony. As with the relationship between George and William James, the details are still not clear and probably never will be. Smiles avoids any suggestion of a row but he has to admit the fact that Locke secured a job which George had wanted, and there is a strong indication of a certain coldness which had first appeared during the building of the Liverpool line.

The line in question was the Grand Junction, a line which was to connect Birmingham with the Liverpool–Manchester Railway. There were many ways of doing this and George had been approached by one interested party and had sent Locke, his star pupil, to survey a possible route. Other routes were surveyed by rival promoters but it was Locke's route which in 1833 won parliamentary approval. Locke, naturally enough, hoped to be made engineer, and it looks as though the Grand Junction board thought the same, till George started making angry possessive noises. Locke, in disgust, threatened to back out completely. To keep everyone happy the board decided to divide up the honours, making George engineer in charge of the southern half of the line and Locke in charge of the northern half.

George, as usual, was rather imprecise with his system of estimating and tendering, leaving too much to untried assistants, fully confident that when it came to the actual building he would personally overcome every problem. It was this blind faith which had led him to grief in parliament over the Liverpool estimates. Locke, having benefited by first-hand experience of George's rather haphazard paper work, did beautiful precise estimates and had all the contracts lined up before George, rushing round the country on other jobs, had scarcely begun. The board became impatient and the upshot was that in 1835 George resigned and Locke was left, engineer in chief of the whole line.

Locke went on to build many thousands of miles of railways, in Britain and in France, notably the Paris–Rouen, but from then on he was estranged from the Stephenson camp. (Though he did eventually make it up with Robert after George's death.) Their professional rivalry was well known and fairly heated but the personal feelings, on either side, can only be guessed at. Robert himself had to make that rather dramatic escape to South

America before he could come to terms with his father, and with himself, and they had a bond which was never broken. Locke, without the advantage, or disadvantage, of any blood bond, had absolutely no intention of returning once he'd made the break from George's domineering control.

There is an interesting fragment of a letter, which has recently come into the possession of the Chesterfield Public Library, written by Locke to George in December 1832, before the split finally happened. Between the lines, a feeling comes through of young pupils carefully handling a rather difficult master. George, apparently, had failed to turn up at a dinner party at the Adelphi Hotel, Liverpool, to the puzzlement of Locke and Allcard. Allcard, it will be remembered, was another of George's pupils, the one who drove *Comet* at the Liverpool opening while Locke was on *Rocket*.

> I don't know at this moment where you dined [wrote Locke] and was ignorant until this morning that you felt hurt at our apparent neglect. I beg to assure you that Allcard and myself would have gladly availed ourselves of your company, that we were both disappointed at not seeing you, and that we came purposely on the following day to make up for that disappointment. After that explanation, I am sure you will acquit us.

One of the reasons why George failed several times to get a line he wanted, such as the London–Brighton in 1836, was the fact that he had become rather unbending in his methods. Despite criticism, his initial surveys were always rather superficial. (He surveyed the London–Brighton line by flying visits on a postchaise.) He lost this line to his deadly rival from earlier battles, Sir John Rennie. To the end of his life he always insisted on lines being laid out as flat as possible, as Fanny Kemble had noted, even if this meant going miles out of the way, following valleys rather than going straight up and over the hill. Locomotives were making such advances, in power and speed, that the younger engineers were well aware that they could now tackle the direct routes.

In 1839, in a report on a proposed railway from Lancashire up to Carlisle, George recommended a highly circuitous route to avoid the Lake District mountains, going all the way round

Morecambe Bay and West Cumberland. 'This is the only practicable line from Lancaster to Carlisle. The making of a railway across Shap Fell is out of the question.' He didn't get the job and a railway was made successfully, although using very steep gradients across Shap to Carlisle – and it was made by Joseph Locke. The line is there for everyone to see today and so are George's thunderous assertions as he tried to lay down the law, neatly filed away in the bowels of the Public Records Office (British Rail division) amongst a thousand other reports about our early railways.

To George, the Grand Junction, the London–Brighton and the handful of others, were no doubt little more than minor irritants. He was being offered far more jobs than he could possibly do, many of them far more important. Between 1835 and 1837, so Smiles estimated, George travelled twenty thousand miles by postchaise. His secretaries now began to travel with him to take down his thoughts and his commands in transit. Smiles interviewed one of George's secretaries from this time who said that at the height of the work, George was dictating thirty-seven letters a day. In one session George dictated reports and letters non-stop for twelve hours, till the secretary collapsed with exhaustion.

George's major lines after Liverpool were the North Midlands from Derby to Leeds, the York and North Midland from Normanton to York, the Manchester and Leeds, the Birmingham and Derby, the Sheffield and Rotherham. There were many others, most of them with their own individual histories, lovingly recorded by railway writers over the generations. Lovingly, but rather boringly, at least for the general reader. George's thirty-seven dictated letters a day were all factual, full of prices and figures and measurements. It was only rarely that he dashed off anything personal in his own hand. These individual railway histories are excellent on bridge dimensions, who built which cutting, the size of the first engines, but rather lacking in human detail.

George's own business interests began to widen after Liverpool, which was another reason why he could well afford not to worry too much about his pupils and their own railway successes. Having defeated the established civil engineers, and others who'd doubted his mechanical skills, he now moved on to conquer another field which had loomed large in his boyhood and early days. He became an Owner. He might not have been as grand as the Grand

Allies, not in the way of speech and deportment, but he became just as powerful, controlling the lives of hundreds of miners just as his own early life, and the lives of his neighbours, had been controlled by the Tyneside colliery owners.

During the excavations on the Leicester–Swannington line Robert had noticed rich coal seams, all still untapped. Along with two of his Liverpool gentlemen friends, Joseph Sandars and Sir Joshua Walmsley, George purchased a large estate at Snibston in Leicestershire and started to dig for coal. After a lot of problems, the mine proved a big success. Edward Pease wrote to him from Darlington in 1834, calling him 'my friend George, old and tried', congratulating him on the success of his Leicestershire mining and saying how he still cherished 'so warm an interest in thy happiness and prosperity'. In a postscript to this letter, Edward's son, Joseph Pease, adds a request for employment for a friend who has failed in the iron trade. George had certainly progressed from his Darlington days.

At the end of 1831, excited by the prospect of his Leicestershire mining and Midlands railway interests, George gave up his Liverpool house in Upper Parliament Street and moved into a large mansion called Alton Grange, near Ashby de la Zouche. He lived there for seven years, building a village and a church for the miners beside his Snibston colliery, but the house itself doesn't seem to have occupied his mind very much, not compared with the mansion which he was later to buy. Throughout these seven years he was charging round the country or Europe, spending at least three months every year in London.

The Stephensons, father and son, acquired a London office in 1836, firstly in Duke Street and a year later at 24, Great George Street, and from then on this became the official centre of all Stephenson operations. In that year parliament had passed bills for the building of a total of 214 miles of new railway lines, all under the Stephensons' direction, involving a capital outlay of over five million pounds.

With the opening of the London office Robert took over the main running of the family railway interests, making them much more efficient and streamlined, making sure that all surveys were efficiently carried out. From 1833 he was resident in London, moving down from Newcastle that year with his wife, taking a house in Haverstock Hill, Hampstead. The immediate reason for

Robert's move to London was his appointment, in September 1833, as engineer-in-chief of the London and Birmingham Railway. His salary was to be £1,500 – which was increased by £500 not long afterwards when it was discovered that the projected Great Western Railway had appointed an equally young engineer, Isambard Kingdom Brunel, at a salary of £2,000 a year.

Robert Stephenson was still not thirty. Anyone who might have doubted his capabilities, believing perhaps that his father had been responsible for his rapid rise, was soon to see that Robert in his own right was one of the country's greatest engineers. The London–Birmingham Railway was the biggest engineering achievement that the world had ever seen, at least that's how all contemporary accounts described it. Samuel Smiles, by calculating the man hours and the cubic feet of stone involved, went to great lengths to show that the Pyramids were by comparison a decidedly puny undertaking. George's achievements at Darlington and Liverpool were in their own way much more significant, but in terms of scale, everything about the London–Birmingham turned out to be bigger, better and more breathtaking. It was when the Liverpool line was opened that the penny handkerchiefs and the mementoes started appearing. On the London–Birmingham line, the market was flooded with new views, new souvenirs, after almost every new brick was put in place. It was Robert who built the London–Birmingham line and, as our present hero is his father, only the more significant stages need be outlined.

The idea of an assault on London had been discussed well before the opening of the Liverpool line and George himself had taken part in many meetings and outline surveys, but everyone held back, waiting for the Liverpool promoters to test the water. It took them only three days to make up their minds for on 18 September 1830, George and Robert were commissioned jointly to survey a line from Birmingham to London, though it was Robert who took charge of the survey.

When London heard what was being planned there was an immediate cry from the backwoodsmen, though this time the metropolitan variety, incensed as much as anything by the idea of some uncouth northerners planning to alter the face of London and its environs. Most of the London papers and magazines were apprehensive, devoting leaders or letters to the subject, coming out with the usual worries about pregnant cows and bolting mothers that George and Robert had heard many times in the north east and in Lancashire. There were a few new variations. An anonymous opponent calling himself 'Investigator' brought class into the arguments. 'No one of the nobility, the gentry or those who travel in their own carriages, would, by any chance, go by the railway. A nobleman would really not like to be drawn at the tail of a train of waggons in which some hundreds of bars of iron were jingling with a noise that would drown all the bells of the district.' A certain Colonel Sibthorpe, MP, declared that he 'would rather meet a highwayman, or see a burglar on his premises, than an engineer'. As in Lancashire, Robert had to use subterfuge to survey the necessary lands, doing a furtive Sunday morning visit on one occasion to the estate of a hostile clergyman, knowing that he was busy in church. And once again, the old enemies, the canal and turnpike trusts, were ready to fight to the end. The roads to London from the Midlands, only relatively recently improved by Telford and McAdam, and the canals, such as the Grand Junction, both represented millions of pounds of investments.

Samuel Smiles has a firsthand account, given to him by Robert himself, of the difficulties of persuading one landowner to change his mind.

I remember that we called one day on Sir Astley Cooper, the eminent surgeon, in the hope of overcoming his aversion to the railway. He was one of our most inveterate and influential opponents. His country house at Berkhampstead was situated near the intended line, which passed through part of his property. We found a courtly, fine-looking old gentleman, of very stately manners, who received us kindly and heard all we had to say in favour of the project. But he was quite inflexible in his opposition to it. No deviation or improvement that we could suggest had any effect in conciliating him. He was opposed to railways generally, and to this in particular. 'Your scheme', said he, 'is preposterous in the extreme. It is of so extravagant a character as to be positively absurd. Then look at the recklessness of your proceedings! You are proposing to cut up our estates in all directions for the purpose of making an unnecessary road. Do you think for one moment of the destruction of property involved by it? Why, gentlemen, if this sort of thing be permitted to go on, you will in a very few years *destroy the noblesse*!' We left the honourable baronet without having produced the slightest effect upon him, excepting perhaps, it might be, increased exasperation against our scheme. I could not help observing to my companions as we left the house, 'Well, it is really provoking to find one who has been made a "sir" for cutting that wen out of George the Fourth's neck, charging us with contemplating the destruction of the *noblesse*, because we propose to confer upon him the benefits of a railroad.'

Despite everything, the bill passed through the Commons at its first attempt, though the Lords delayed it for a year. It was finally passed by both Houses in 1833. The company's legal expenses, purely in mounting their parliamentary campaign, had cost them £72,000. There were two reasons why the bill succeeded. One was the brilliant performance by Robert under some very intensive cross-examination – the sort which had floored his father not so long ago. Secondly, the company had silenced the sensitive feelings of the noblesse by the simple exercise of paying them money. Over £750,000 was paid out for land which had originally been valued at £250,000.

It took an army of twenty thousand navvies just over four years to build the London–Birmingham line. It was 112 miles in length, four times the length of the Liverpool line. For this massive enterprise Robert took over a hotel at St John's Wood which he turned into an operations headquarters with thirty draughtsmen producing miles of drawings. There were many formidable cuttings to be made, notably at Tring and Blisworth, and eight tunnels, several of them over a mile long. The most notorious was the 2,400-yards-long Kilsby Tunnel, which was not the longest but was by far the most difficult and expensive, in money and in human life. Trial shafts had indicated that the ground was shale but when digging started they hit quicksands. Robert set up thirteen stationary engines on Kilsby Hill to pump out water. They laboured night and day for nine months, pumping out water at the rate of 1,800 gallons a minute, before the sands were dry and the tunnel could be dug underneath. Smiles estimated that the water pumped out of the tunnel was equivalent to the contents of the Thames at high water between London and Woolwich. The estimated cost of the tunnel had been £99,000. It took over £300,000 to complete it. Almost every structure on the line had similar problems and many of the contractors whom Robert had engaged went bankrupt before the end. The total cost of the line was £5,500,000 – double what had been estimated. The triumphal arch at Euston, now alas gone, celebrated the victory of men over the elements as well as the arrival of railways to the capital.

It opened in 1838 amidst great national rejoicing. Dr Arnold, the famous headmaster, on first viewing a London–Birmingham train as it passed near his school at Rugby, remarked: 'I rejoice to see it and think that feudality is gone forever. It is so great a blessing to think that any one evil is really extinct.'

It could be said, and many people did say, that new evils were brought forward by the now irresistible march of the railways, such as the navvies. It was the London-Birmingham line which saw them grow to military proportions and for the rest of the century they were an ever-present army which settled on many an unsuspecting unspoiled village.

Kilsby, for example, had been a minute village near Daventry. Overnight it became a shanty town as 1,250 navvies arrived to build the tunnel. They took over barns and huts, or erected their own tents and mud huts, and for almost two years completely dominated the area with their tunnelling, not to mention their fighting, their eating, and their drinking. As Terry Coleman observed in his excellent book *The Railway Navvies* (published 1965), navvies were outside the laws, outside civilisation, loved by the contractors, as long as they were sober, but feared by the normal population. Smiles described them as heathens, though he had to admit he was impressed by their capacity for hard work. Thomas Carlyle couldn't find one good word to say about them.

I have not in my travels seen anything uglier than that disorganic mass of labourers, sunk three fold deep in brutality. The Yorkshire and Lancashire men, I hear, are reckoned the worst; and not without glad surprise I find the Irish are the best in point of behaviour. The postman tells me that several of the poor Irish do regularly apply to him for money drafts and send their earnings home. The English, who eat twice as much beef, consume the residue in whisky and do not trouble the postman.

In *Dombey and Son*, Dickens has a long description of the apparent chaos of navvies at work, based on his observations of work on the London–Birmingham line at the Camden Hill cutting in north London. He likened the scene to a great earthquake which had just rent the whole neighbourhood to its centre. 'Everywhere were bridges that led nowhere, thoroughfares that were wholly impassable, temporary wooden huts in the most unlikely situations, a chaos of carts, overthrown and jumbled together.'

The navvies' main tools were picks and shovels, barrows and carts. Their wheel barrow runs, which were set up when they were doing a steep sided cutting, always attracted hundreds of sightseers. It was spectacular, but highly dangerous. Planks were laid up the steep banks of the cutting and the navvy, having filled his barrow at the bottom, ran up the planks, balancing the barrow in front of him, pulled by a rope which went up the bank to a horse and pulley on the top. When he'd emptied his load at the top he ran down again, this time with the rope behind him, the horse taking the main weight of the empty barrow to stop it getting out of control. It was all done at high speed, with the navvies working in a butty (usually a gang of ten men), having contracted for a certain sum to move a certain amount of soil. Naturally, if the horse, or the man with the horse, or the navvy on the barrow, faltered for one second, the navvy could easily fall to his death.

Tunnelling was the most hazardous work. A shift was twelve hours long and when underground they often spent the whole time in foul air, stagnant water and with the constant risk of roofs collapsing or being killed by the haphazard use of gunpowder. The navvies themselves took very few precautions and the contractors thought only of their contract and how many weeks they'd fallen behind. Mechanical diggers, driven by steam, were known in the United States from as early as the 1840s but in England and Europe they were not used till the 1880s. Labour was cheap in Europe – and dispensable. It was not common practice for contractors to keep an account of navvies killed on a job. In Scotland there was not even the need to have an inquest, not if it was a navvy who'd died. Navvies were known for their daring and their daftness, and death was simply part of the job. Three men were killed, one after the other, in the Kilsby tunnel when for a wager they dared each other to jump over the mouth of a shaft.

Under the Truck Act of 1831, the so-called truck or tommy

shops had been banned in England, but the act was aimed at factories not railways. No mention was made of railway labourers in the act. Navvies, as a breed, didn't stir the public awareness until the London and Birmingham. Railway contractors were therefore free to use the truck system and on many occasions they made more money from the truck shops than from building the line itself. It was, on the face of it, reasonable for a contractor, working out in the wilds, to set up a shop in the midst of the navvy encampment where the men could get the necessities of life, like beer and food and boots. But what happened was that a navvy was given his wages in goods – or in tickets to be exchanged for goods – which were only available at the tommy shop. The navvy would take his five shilling ticket to the shop but in exchange he would rarely get more than four shillings' worth of goods. The goods were generally bad and the prices high. They were encouraged to live on credit, spending tickets not yet earned, so it was rare indeed for a navvy to have real cash in his hand. Randies, as the navvies called their Saturday night saturnalia, were usually limited to eating and drinking round the tommy shop. It at least helped to spare some of the villages the worst of the troubles.

Navvies slept in their clothes, without taking their boots off, in their crudely built butty gang huts. Very often each gang hut had one old woman who did the cooking for them, and provided any other services if she was up to it. Navvies didn't get married. If they took up with a woman they left her when they moved on to the next site. The popular press thrived on stories of navvy orgies or woman-selling amongst navvies. A gallon of ale was said to be the going rate.

Some of the more enterprising contractors, to stop their navvies who actually had cash in their hands disappearing for days on a distant randy, arranged for brothels to be set up inside the camps. The girls were available, like everything else, on truck shop terms, with tickets being exchanged before the goods could be touched. There is a very tasteful and euphemistic description of such an enterprise in a contemporary book, published in 1868 by F. R. Condor, who was one of Robert Stephenson's pupils on the London–Birmingham Railway. (The book, *Personal Recollections of English Engineers*, appeared under the pseudonym 'By a Civil Engineer', but Condor later proved to be the author.)

While not given to dancing, like his Continental neighbours, the well paid English labourer is not proof at all times against a weakness for female society, even if it not be of the most unexceptional decorum. Thus, after a pay, some of the most hard working, and therefore, *por tempore*, navvies might wander 'off on the randy' to the nearest cities. To prevent Mahomet from wandering in search of the loadstone in the mountains, the contractor brought the loadstone to his bivouac. He arranged for the presence of some of the objects of Jack's admiration – lodged them, clothed them, fed them, made them as comfortable and respectable as the circumstances of the case admitted, and set down a charge for their blandishments in the paysheet. It came under the head of 'tommy-shop' and reduced, *pro tanto*, the monthly balance of coin coming to the pay table.

High-minded Victorian society was greatly alarmed by the barbaric life of the navvies and on every big railway site there was at least one missionary, sent by some charitable organisation to convert the brutes, trying hard to make them lead decent Christian lives, to sign the pledge of temperance and give up swearing. The coarse language of the navvies greatly upset the missionaries, especially lady missionaries. They maintained that the poor horses didn't like foul language either and begged the navvies not to swear at them.

On most lines, at least one riot broke out which needed the police or militia to break it up. The fights were either between the navvies themselves – with Yorkshire navvies fighting the Irish and Scots – or against the local villagers. In 1846 there was a pitched battle just outside Carlisle, involving over two thousand railway navvies, who'd come from as far away as Penrith and Kendal. The riots spread up and down the line and lasted two weeks till the Westmorland Yeomanry finally restored order.

It was the deaths, not the riots, which finally made the government interfere, particularly the deaths during the building of a notorious three-mile-long tunnel at Woodhead, under the Pennines, in 1838. It was a vital link in the line connecting Manchester to Sheffield and, luckily for George and Robert, it was not a Stephenson concern. The first engineer was Vignoles, an old opponent of George, who was replaced after many disasters and financial collapses by Joseph Locke. George, in his usual opinionated way, declared when the plans were announced that the tunnel couldn't be done. His actual remark was to the effect that he would eat the first locomotive which got through the tunnel. Over a thousand navvies were employed and they lived in miserable, inhuman conditions, nine miles from the nearest village. There were endless delays before the work was finished in 1845, by which time 32 navvies had died and 140 seriously injured. Edwin Chadwick (later famous for his work on the 1848 Public Health Act) revealed many of the scandals, such as penny pinching contractors who had deliberately not provided safe fuses for use with gunpowder as it took extra time. He estimated that in proportion to the total manpower employed, more men had been lost at Woodhead tunnel than at Waterloo. (Woodhead mortality amongst navvies was just over 3 per cent. At Waterloo, only 2.11 per cent of the soldiers died.)

A select committee of the House of Commons was set up in 1846 which talked a great deal about the general state of railway works but didn't do much, though the facts it came across were rather shattering. It was reported, for example, that a total of £16,500,000 was being spent every year on wages for the 200,000 navvies currently employed in building railways. It meant that in just fifteen years, since the opening of the Liverpool line, a new species of the human race had arisen who were now greater in numbers than the genuine armed forces. (In 1846, the effective strength of the army and navy was 160,000.) In most ways the navvies were fitter, stronger, more highly organised and better equipped than the British army who hadn't fought since 1815 and, as the Crimean War was to show, were completely unprepared for any serious action. The navvies might not have looked all that smart and dashing in their moleskin trousers, tied at the knees with string, knotted handkerchief and hobnailed boots, but they were a terrifying sight for every law abiding Victorian.

The men who made the money out of the navvies were the contractors, another new breed, who in an equally short space of time became immensely rich and immensely powerful. They were said at one time to have eighty MPs on their pay role, or at least in their pocket. Several of today's leading contracting firms, such as Cubitts and McAlpine, who did their early work on the Highland railways, can trace their origins back to these first railways. But the two biggest contractors of the day were Thomas Brassey and Morton Peto. Brassey, formerly a land agent, who had supplied some of the stone for George's Sankey Viaduct on the Liverpool line. This time he offered to supply men and materials for one of Locke's viaducts. They went on, with Locke as chief engineer and Brassey as contractor, to build many great railways. At the time of the London–Birmingham line, contractors were still relatively small scale. Robert originally engaged thirty main contractors, splitting up the line between them. But by the 1840s, Brassey was so powerful, controlling over 10,000 navvies, that he could contract for complete railways. By 1850 he'd built one in three of every mile of railway in Britain and one out of two in France. By the time of his death in 1870 he had built 4,500 miles of railway in all parts of the world, 1,700 miles of them in Britain. Peto was equally powerful but his works were not as far flung. He ended up a baronet while Brassey's son, also a contractor, became an earl.

When the English engineers moved abroad, as George and Robert Stephenson and Joseph Locke did, their regular contractors and navvies went with them. It wasn't just British brains which built so many of the world's railway lines – it was British muscles. Naturally it brought out some vigorous flag waving from the more chauvinistic Victorians, delighted by such British examples of Enterprise and Perseverance. Samuel Smiles, while condemning the navvies as heathens, praised their work rate, showing the frogs a thing or two, especially when it came to loading up their barrows:

> While he [the English navvy] thus easily ran out some 3 or 4 cwt. at a time, the French navvy was contented with half the weight. Indeed, the French navvies on one occasion struck work because of the size of the English barrows, and there was an *émeute* on the Rouen Railway, which was only quelled by the aid of the military. The consequence was that the big barrows were abandoned to the English workmen, who earned nearly double the wages of the Frenchmen. The manner in which they stood to their work was matter of great surprise and wonderment to the French countrypeople, who came crowding round them in their blouses, and, after gazing admiringly at their expert handling of the pick and mattock, and the immense loads of 'dirt' which they wheeled out, would exclaim to each other, '*Mon Dieu, voila! voila ces Anglais, comme ils travaillent!*'

The facts about such railways, as opposed to the exclamations, spoke for themselves. The Rouen railway was built by an army of 5,000 British navvies and half of it paid for with British capital. Later, when railways opened up in the New World, Brassey sent 2,000 British navvies to Canada, to build the Grand Trunk, and 2,000 for a line in New South Wales.

*Mon Dieu*, could George Stephenson have guessed for one moment what he had unleashed when he finished the Liverpool line? The railways, with their navvies and contractors and engineers, all of which George spawned, did at least do a lot of economic good. It can even be argued that one of the reasons that Britain in the 1830s and 1840s escaped revolution, while most of Europe tore itself apart, was that we were all too busy building railways. There was work for everyone, if you were prepared to sweat, and the economy boomed. Socially, the conditions of the navvies might have been appalling, but they were in the fresh air, their own masters, and better paid than the sweat shop factories. Railways reduced barriers, joined people and towns together, opened up new worlds, new horizons and gave new opportunities for every class of society.

But there was one rather more abstract result of railways, much more bizarre, which was again directly caused by George Stephenson. When people began to talk of Railway Mania, which very soon the whole country was doing, it wasn't the armies of navvies or engineers or contractors who sprang to mind but the armies of paper speculators. None of them was more bizarre than George Hudson.

# 14

# GEORGE HUDSON AND RAILWAY MANIA

George Stephenson has a lot of things to answer for and one of them is George Hudson. He was a draper's assistant from York who became the Railway King – a Victorian living legend. At the height of his powers Hudson far outshone Stephenson in public acclaim, public fame and social prestige. The newspapers and magazines of the day referred to him as a Monarch, talked about his crown and his court. London society begged for his favours – and his tips. Nobody was unaware of him – Carlyle, Dickens, Thackeray, the Brontës, all refer to him in their private diaries and papers. In the 1840s, during the manic days of railway fever, he became the second most admired man in the kingdom, after the Duke of Wellington. And on one occasion even the Duke of Wellington came creeping to him for a favour.

It was George Stephenson who made George Hudson – in every way. Contact with Stephenson gave him a vital aura of respectability when he was just beginning. The world of instant railways which Stephenson created gave him his millions. What a pity Samuel Smiles never deigned to get to grips with Hudson's life. What terrifying morals he could have pointed. But the Victorians, alas, were so ashamed of their own created monster that when he fell they couldn't bury him quickly enough, vainly trying to hide their own guilt, greed and gullibility.

George Hudson was born in 1800 in a village near York, the fifth son of a yeoman farmer, which was where his peasant shrewdness was said to have come from. It was never more than shrewdness, unaffected by education or even the gift of the gab. He was always a bad speaker, most people finding him incoherent, except when he started reeling off the figures. His father died when he was nine, leaving no money, and he had to make his own way. At fifteen he left home and made for York, where he became apprenticed to a draper. He did well on the counter, well enough to be accepted at twenty-one into his employer's family, marrying one of the partner's daughters, a woman called Elizabeth five years older than himself. When he was twenty-seven, by which time he'd become a partner, he had a stroke of exceeding good luck. He said it was luck, but there were those who said it was his first con trick. A distant relative, a great uncle, became ill and young Hudson immediately rushed to his bedside. The will was made at the bedside, with only Hudson present, and to everyone's surprise Hudson was left everything, a small fortune of some £30,000. Overnight he moved into York's bourgeoisie. To leave no one in any doubt, he ceased to be a Methodist, which was how he'd been brought up, and became very staunch Church of England. At the same time, from being of no political opinion, he became a thrusting young Tory, highly active in the local party, making the right friends and helping all the right local nobility.

In 1833 there was talk in York, as there was in every town in the land, of the coming of railways. Few leading citizens, unlike their counterparts only a decade before, wanted to see their town missed out. A local group was set up to promote the idea of a railway between York and Leeds. Hudson was elected treasurer. An engineer was hired to survey the line and he eventually came up with a scheme using horse power, not locomotives. Despite the success of the Liverpool line, there were still many who thought steam wouldn't catch on. In early 1834 Hudson went on a visit to Whitby to look at some of his property, part of the loot which had come to him from his great uncle. There, by chance, he met George Stephenson who was looking at a possible railway line. Stephenson fired Hudson's imagination with schemes to cover the country with a network of railways. Hudson, whatever else he was, had an equally fervent imagination. He was quick to see the immense possibilities and was converted on the spot. Stephenson was highly impressed by Hudson's breadth of vision and enthusiasm and they became firm friends. Hudson went back to convert the York backers to steam and to build up his local power. He campaigned at the general election for a young local nobleman he'd teamed up with and managed to get him elected. In the process Hudson had distributed around £3,000 in bribes and other inducements. There were accusations in the House of Commons about skulduggery in York but when it came out that Whigs had been no better, hiring thugs to beat up Hudson's paid voters, it was dismissed as just another example of the corruption of local politics.

In 1836 Hudson, realising the growing national fame of his friend Stephenson, got the York committee to change the direction of their line. Stephenson was now working on a line directly through the Midlands and Hudson saw that if Stephenson's line from York could join up with his own line from York they would share in the success of the Stephenson scheme and also get him associated as their engineer. (He tried at first to get Stephenson to change his line, but he wouldn't, and had to change his own plans instead.) So the York and North Midland Railways was launched, with Hudson as treasurer and one of Stephenson's assistants as engineer.

With Stephenson's name to flash around, Hudson soon raised £300,000 and got the bill through parliament. He became chairman of the company, which helped his status in York as the citizens saw how he was putting them on the map. His work in local politics was crowned when he became York's lord mayor.

His reign as lord mayor was noted for its lavishness, mostly out of council funds of course. His banquets were the talk of the north of England as in turn he fêted the local clerical big wigs, the army, politicians, industrial and society leaders. In his speeches he was for ever boasting of his friendship with George Stephenson. When at one time things were flagging with the construction of the railway, he announced that George Stephenson had put £20,000 of his own money into the company's shares and was persuading his friends to do the same. (There is no proof that Stephenson did or said such a thing – more likely Hudson had offered him some shares as a present.) But George did become the engineer of many of the other railways which Hudson was soon creating or annexing. His first step was to take over a rival line, the Leeds and Selby, which he did in 1840, immediately closing it so that all passengers had to use his line. In 1840 George Stephenson was persuaded to join the board of the York and North Midlands, finally establishing his respectability.

In gobbling up company after company, Hudson always seemed to find it surprisingly easy to raise new money and yet keep on paying high dividends on his old companies. His method was simple: he used each intake of capital to pay his old shareholders.

Today this would be highly illegal but Mr Hudson, being a new sort of speculator, was making his own rules. He audited his own books, which helped, disguising the fact that many of his companies could not possibly afford the high dividends he was paying. Naturally, if you were receiving a high dividend, you were keen to invest in any new scheme Mr Hudson might announce. Shareholders meetings consisted of loud and continuous cheers for Mr Hudson.

At the same time he was genuinely cutting costs to the minimum, usually at the expense of safety, and keeping wages low. He was so adept at railway company manoeuvrings that he helped out Robert Stephenson on several occasions. By 1843 he'd become the single most powerful man in railways, controlling lines from York down to Rugby and Birmingham, It was in that year he was first known as the 'Railway King', at last throwing off his image as a cheap, provincial asset stripper. Now he was respectable – and feared – if still a bit of a joke behind his back. On 7 October 1843 the *Railway Times* printed a satirical song about him, saying they were lines to be sung at the grand amalgamation meeting scene of a new opera to be called *Midas*:

> George, in his chair,
> Of Railways Lord Mayor
> With his nods
> Men and gods
> Keep in awe;
> When he winks
> Heaven shrinks
> When he speaks,
> Hell squeaks,
> Earth's globe is but his taw.

In 1844 he came face to face with Gladstone, then president of the Board of Trade, who was against the unrestricted speculation in railways which was convulsing the country and taking up so much parliamentary time. Gladstone got a committee of inquiry set up to which Hudson was called as the most important witness. Gladstone cross-examined Hudson on the possibility of a single powerful capitalist (i.e. Hudson) creating a railway monopoly. Hudson said that amalgamations were good for the country, saving expenses and benefiting each company. The bill which Gladstone was trying to push through, to check railway monopoly, was finally emasculated. Hudson was acclaimed by the railways interests as the victor – beating Gladstone in the House of Commons without even being an MP.

Both Gladstone and Hudson, in their different ways, were to be proved right. Gladstone wanted some sort of state control, which had happened in several European countries, such as Belgium. Britain, by being first in the field, had proceeded in a chaotic, private-enterprise, free-for-all scramble. But it was private enterprise, in Darlington and Liverpool, which had backed railways in the first place. As for Hudson, the eventual monopoly he envisaged (with him in charge of course) was a sensible course for such vast financial operations, though it was a hundred years before a nationalised monopoly in the form of British Rail came to pass.

In 1844, when he opened one of his new properties, the Newcastle and Darlington Junction Railway, he chose the anniversary of Waterloo for the opening celebrations, just to add to the pageantry. He brought up train loads of directors and influential shareholders from London for the celebrations, preceded by a 'Flying Train' which had the country agog and filled acres of newspaper space because for the first time it brought to Newcastle that morning's London newspapers. His train had covered the 303 miles in a record time of nine hours, including stops. People lined the route almost all the way to gape in awe and wonder. As usual, Hudson proposed the toast of 'Old George' at the final banquet, calling him a genius, the true begetter of railways. George Stephenson was there in person and trotted out what was becoming his familiar speech, going over his boyhood memories, of his twenty years in the pits, of his struggles to educate his son and develop his first locomotive.

Hudson had by now acquired a large personal circus, investors, contractors, engineers, lawyers, politicians, nobility, who either depended on him for work or, most of all, for the wink and a nod when a new lucrative scheme was in the offing. He was still using the old dodge of calling up new capital to pay old dividends. It wasn't until 1849, when for the first time a government authorised auditor had to look at all company accounts, that there was any real check on railway directors.

His circus followed him round the country, travelling free on his trains to pack public or shareholders' meetings, cheering his every word. In the north the supporters from his home town of York, where a new street had been named after him, became known as the 'Flying Squad'. One of this group wrote in 1848 that he had sat down to dinner £20,000 richer than when he breakfasted, solely through being in the know about one of Hudson's plans.

Fresh capital was rolling in at such a rate that on one occasion he was paying a dividend of ten per cent on one line before it had even opened. In October 1844 he raised the sum of two-and-a-half million pounds to finance three branch lines without disclosing any details about them! No one knew where they were to be, when they were to be built or even had a guarantee from Hudson that he would ever use the money for railways at all. He went round boasting how he'd kept everyone in the dark.

In 1845 he found himself in a long drawn out campaign against one proposed line that had the audacity to compete with him on his home territory, the London and York Company This was to be a more direct line, via Lincoln, and would be thirty miles shorter than Hudson's more complicated route which went via the Midlands and Rugby. When the line came before the House of Commons, Hudson did all he could to obstruct it, hiring twelve counsel at a cost of £3,000 a day to discover flaws in his rivals' proposals.

The procedure for all new railway companies of the time was that a provisional committee got the line surveyed, got estimates made and produced a list of subscribers showing that at least three-quarters of the necessary capital had already been promised. Naturally, this led to wholesale fiddling of the list of proposed shareholders. Hudson knew all about such fiddles, having done it himself so often, so he brought in an agent called Croucher who went through his rivals' subscription list. With the aid of some House of Commons notepaper, to which he wasn't entitled, he wrote to local postmasters asking them to check the existence and means of all the more doubtful looking subscribers.

As Hudson well knew, a great many of the names turned out to be fictitious. But, even better from his point of view, many of the people who did exist were forced to present themselves before the parliamentary committee. A charwoman's son was revealed to be liable for £12,000 worth of shares, according to the list. A man in the workhouse was down for an equally large sum. Altogether,

£29,000 worth of shares had been applied for by people who didn't exist and £44,000 was down for people who did exist but had no money or property whatsoever. The Lords was forced to throw out the bill. Another triumph for King Hudson. The monopoly of his Midland Railway was safe, though his obstructionist tactics had cost Hudson well over £ 100,000.

During the height of this particular parliamentary battle, it was decided that it was about time Hudson had a testimonial. It was later alleged that this decision had been made by Hudson himself, but there is no proof of this. Hudson was nevertheless delighted. The Victorians loved testimonials. The usual practice was that a committee was formed to honour the great man in question and a subscription list opened. The leading subscribers' names then appeared in large type in the newspapers. The great man would in due course have a statue built or some inscribed silver plate handed over to him at an appropriate ceremony. George Stephenson had recently been so honoured, with Hudson prominent amongst the subscribers.

The testimonial opened for Hudson was rather unusual. According to well-informed rumours, not only had Hudson himself drafted the appeal, he had also drawn up the list of subscribers. He well knew which engineers, contractors and politicians owed him favours and would naturally love to subscribe. He worked out an appropriately handsome sum for each and instructed his secretary to publish the list in the newspapers *before* telling the people concerned. 'Advertise it, that will clinch the matter.'

Only one person dared to refuse when they saw their names in the papers – and that was George Stephenson. He threatened to insert his refusal in the same papers, but so many Hudson directors pleaded with him that such an exposure from Stephenson, of all people, would result in a catastrophic fall in the shares of all Hudson's railway companies, that he desisted. However it seems apparent from then on that he had grown wise to Hudson and his methods, long before anyone else realised the truth. Hudson had earlier become one of Stephenson's partners in a new coal mine and occasionally Stephenson agreed to join the board of a Hudson company, if it looked interesting, or was in his native Tyneside, though basically he was against the amalgamation methods of Hudson, preferring small, privately operated companies all competing against each other, rather than one big national company, which was Hudson's ultimate plan. George always refused resolutely to speculate in any of Hudson's schemes, however much Hudson entreated, even at the height of their friendship.

Not long after the testimonial row, George made clear his new opinion in a letter written to his old friend Michael Longridge. It's dated 22 November 1845, and was addressed from Tapton House. (It belongs to the Institute of Mechanical Engineers, bought by them in 1970.)

> Hudson has become too great a man for me now. I am not at all satisfied at the way the Newcastle and Berwick line has been carried on and I do not intend to take any more active part in it. I have made Hudson a rich man but he will very soon care for nobody except he can get money by them. I make these observations in confidence to you.

It shows Stephenson's tact, not exposing or criticising him publicly, or perhaps he was ashamed at having been taken in by him for so long. At any rate, it looks as if Hudson never knew what Stephenson really thought of him. In public he was still boasting of their friendship, endlessly proposing his health at banquets.

At this stage, in 1845, Hudson was still publicly a rising star, still on the crest of a wave with the best yet to come. The money from his well-publicised testimonial was modestly received by Hudson – and went straight into his own bank account, without a murmur from any of the other eminent subscribers who'd been tricked.

In 1845, a good year for George Hudson, he was elected MP for Sunderland, became Deputy Lord Lieutenant of Durham and finally astounded the nobility by paying the Duke of Devonshire half a million pounds for a 12,000-acre estate and stately home at Londesborough. He built his own private railway station, laying down two miles of track, so that his special train could roll right up to his own front door.

The railway fever which George Stephenson had set going in 1830 came to its height in 1846. For three successive years the nation had been continuously astounded by the amount of money flowing into railways, with everyone convinced each year that it couldn't go on. In 1844 800 new miles of railway had been sanctioned by parliament at a cost of 20 million pounds. In 1845 the total was 2,800 miles at a cost of around 50 million. Then in 1846 permission for 4,600 new miles was granted which would require the astronomical sum of £132 million.

In those three years the number of journals devoted solely to railway matters rose from three to twenty. Journalists were falling over themselves to publicise and tip new shares and people from literally every walk of life scrambled to buy them. Thackeray as a young man, lost all his savings on railways. Emily and Anne Brontë contributed £1 each to Hudson's testimonial, two of the tens of thousands of little shareholders throughout the country who'd made money from Hudson in the past and felt grateful enough to send a little something when they read about his testimonial in the papers. In three months, £30,000 rolled into Hudson's account. But the third Brontë sister, Charlotte, was against subscribing to Hudson's testimonial. She tried in vain to get her sisters to sell out their holdings in Hudson's York and North Midland stock, convinced a slump was bound to come. (Branwell, their brother, was caught up in railway fever to the extent of getting a job in railways, as a clerk on the Leeds and Manchester. He was sacked in 1842 for 'culpable negligence'.)

Having established himself as a country gent, living in the style of a duke of the realm, Hudson decided next to establish himself in London. He bought what was then considered to be the largest private house in London, Albert House, just on the north side of Knightsbridge, where Albert Gate leads into Hyde Park. It cost him £15,000, plus the same again in furnishings and decoration.

Hudson was by now comfortably a millionaire. Along with Crockford, the gambler, he was the first self-made provincial millionaire to move into Victorian London. He'd done it in well under ten years – since that day in 1834 when by chance he'd met Stephenson at Whitby. In 1846 his landed properties were worth £700,000; his industrial interests in such things as Sunderland Docks, Clay Cross collieries and other factories and a bank in York were worth at least a quarter of a million; and then, of course, there were his railway interests which at the end of 1846, judged by the total amount of shares which in that year were held in his name, came to £320,000. 'Get rich quick' was the phrase the Victorians used for Hudson – and all the Hudsons that were to follow.

Once in London he led his life, public and social, in the full glare of publicity with the newspapers reporting his every move.

There was a queue of ducal crested coaches forever outside Albert House when he was in town, waiting for his favours. The aristocracy vied with each other in toadying to him, though their ladies weren't so keen when it came to having him back. Their husbands might fawn on Mr Hudson but they certainly didn't approve of Mrs Hudson. Several years later Lady Dorothy Nevill recollected: 'There were rumours of Hudson, the Railway King, and his wife, but they were never in Society, which, however, was amused by the reports of their doings which reached it.'

Almost every leading diarist of the forties, writing about London affairs of the day, has tales of the Hudsons and their flamboyant style, especially of the vulgarity of Mrs Hudson. Society loved it when Mrs Hudson tried to ape the current fashion for all things French, trying in vain to drag French *bon mots* into her conversation, and best of all when she persuaded George to spend the Easter recess in Paris. Back came the stories of Mrs Hudson sending her maid to buy some shoes from M. Droit and M. Gauche because she'd seen their names on every pair. In a restaurant she was reported as asking the 'gassoon' for 'tire-bottes' for dinner, meaning turbot, only to be given a boot jack.

When Mrs Hudson, back in London, realised that certain ladies were holding out on her, sniggering even, she persuaded several titled if rather impecunious ladies of fashion, such as Lady Parke, to serve as her society bait. Lady Parke sent out invitations in her own name for a grand ball to be held at Albert House. She was there at the door to greet the fine visitors – then introduced them to Mrs Hudson, the real hostess. Mrs Hudson could be just as shrewd as her husband.

When dressing for a banquet, so the story went, Mrs Hudson would tell her maid to 'dress me for ten, dress me for twenty,' depending on the size of the party. But stories about her struggles with French were the best loved. Going to a French confectioner one day to order a gâteau she was asked '*De quel grandeur le voulezvous?*' Her reply was '*Aussi grand que mon derrière.*'

Despite the jokes the Hudsons had certainly arrived. On 21 March 1846, George Hudson was invited by the Marquis of Northampton, president of the Royal Society, to a *conversazione* at his private mansion for Fellows of the Society. Also present was Prince Albert and the buzz went round 'The Prince has asked to be introduced to Mr Hudson!' The introductions took place and

George had a long chat with His Highness about railways, dismissing atmospheric railways, then the talk of the hour, as 'humbug'. The next day the cartoonists had a field day with everyone using the same angle – the meeting of two crowned heads, King Hudson and the Prince Consort.

It wasn't until the following year that Hudson met Queen Victoria herself, when he had the honour of welcoming her at Cambridge on one of his trains. He'd fitted it out regally for her, with great lavishness, lining the walls and ceilings with satin, putting in French furniture. The young queen took his arm along the platform and was reported to have exclaimed, 'Really, this *is* beautiful. Is it not *most* gratifying.' After the return journey Prince Albert conveyed Her Majesty's 'entire satisfaction' at the arrangements. Hudson was obviously well satisfied. He ordered a week's banqueting and entertaining at York Mansion House, where he'd become lord mayor for his third session.

It's impossible to imagine George Stephenson getting involved with such capers and kowtowing to royalty and the aristocracy. He had his chances, as we shall see, but he almost always did the opposite, refusing their offers and their friendship to the point of rudeness.

Perhaps Hudson's greatest social coup was his friendship with the Duke of Wellington. One day his ducal carriage arrived at Albert House and the duke, in great agitation, asked Mr Hudson for his help. His sister, so the duke said, had invested all her savings in a new railway venture. The shares had dropped alarmingly and his poor sister was on the verge of losing every sixpence. (This story is well attested though one wonders if the duke was perhaps relating his own plight, or perhaps a mistress's, rather than his sister's.) George calmed him down, said not to worry, and told him to come back on a certain day.

Hudson started buying a few shares in the company in question and when he'd been doing so for several days the news, not surprisingly, started to come out. The public naturally thought something was afoot. King Hudson must be on the move again, and the shares began to shoot up. When the duke came back on the appointed day he was absolutely delighted. Hudson said his sister must sell all her shares at once. They were bound to go down again. The duke thanked him profusely for saving his sister's fortune and asked if by chance there was anything he could do in return? Hudson said 'Now, thank you.' As the duke was going out of the door, Hudson said well, there was just one little thing. His daughter had been sent to a very exclusive finishing school in Hampstead but unfortunately the other girls were being rather hurtful to her, cutting her because of her origins, daughter of a jumped-up draper's assistant. It would be very nice if the duke just happened to call in on her at school.

Next day, the duke set off in his coach with a large bouquet of flowers. At the school he inquired for Miss Hudson. 'Tell her the Duke of Wellington wishes to see her.' They had a long chat, the flowers were passed over, the duke said what a good friend her father was, and off he rode back to London, leaving Miss Hudson the most desirable girl in the school.

All the same, the wits of the day were still making capital out of Hudson and all the other speculators who'd jumped out of the lower orders and made a killing on railways and then attempted to ape their betters. At the end of 1845 Thackeray started a weekly diary in *Punch* which consisted of the adventures of a footman called James Plush who borrows £20 from a parlour maid and almost overnight makes himself £30,000 from railway speculation. He gives up his job, hires his own valet and other servants, takes a flat in the Albany, dresses like a dandy, becomes a director of thirty-three railroads and decides to stand for parliament. He changes his name to Jeames de la Pluche, Esq., throws over the kitchen maid and says he's going to marry into the 'Harrystoxy'.

The serial, all written in the first person, as if by L. Pluche himself, complete with atrocious spellings, topical jokes and references, was a huge success. Pluche names all his new possessions after the railway lines where he'd made killings, lines that featured high in Hudson's real life, and in the real life of many readers, big and small.

For igsample, the first pair of hosses I bought, [says Pluche in an early episode] I crisn'd Hull and Selby in grateful elusion to my transackshns in that railroad. I have now a confidenshel servant, a vally de shamber. He curls my air, inspex my accounts and hansers my hinvitations to dinner. I call this Vally my Trent Vally for it was the prophit I got from that extent line which injuiced me to ingage him. 'When I ave a great party, Trent' I say to my man, 'we will have the London and

Birmingham plate today (the goold) or else the Manchester and Leeds (the silver).' I bought them after realising on the abuf lines and if people suppose that the companys made me a present of the plate, how can I help it?

There are references to Hudson himself in the serial as Pluche goes on about his famous new friends. 'Last Sunday was a grand Fate. The company was *reshershy*. I had a Countess on my right and my friend George H. . . . the Railway King.'

It was obvious to everyone that Pluche was a parody of Hudson. Pluche gets himself made a deputy lieutenant, just like Hudson, and makes an offer for a house at 'Halberd Gate'. He decorates his chambers with 'potricks of my favourite great man', namely the Duke of Wellington.

There's four of his Grace. I have a valluble one lickwise of my Queen and 2 of Prince Halbert – has a Field Marshcall and halso as a privat Gent. I despise the vulgar sneers that are daily hullered against that Igsolted Pottentat. Betwigxt the Prins and the Duke hangs me, in the Unifirm of the Cinqbar Malitiia, of which the Cinqbars has made me Capting.

Hudson, like Pluche, was a great one for picking up and getting himself decorated with fancy honours. The satire at Hudson's expense was funny but pretty sharp all the same. It showed how Thackeray was to develop later as a novelist – at the time he was writing stories and articles for magazines, *Vanity Fair* was to come two years later. It also shows the freedom and power of the press at the time. It would be difficult for a present day journalist, outside *Private Eye*, to get away with such grotesque caricatures without the Hudsons of today getting it stopped or simply sending in a writ. Such was the success of Pluche's adventures that a pirate version of the story, used without Thackeray's permission, was turned into a play and was performed with great success in the West End. Almost overnight, the railway speculator had become a stock figure which the whole country could appreciate.

Hudson could take the jokes in *Punch* and other magazines but there was one publication who didn't make jokes and, most important of all, didn't engage in the current mania for share tipping. That was *The Times*. They began to thunder, as Gladstone had tried in vain a few years earlier, that railway speculation would finally bankrupt the country. It pointed out that the capital to be invested in railways in 1846, £132 million, was equal to the total value of Britain's annual exports and was greater than the whole public revenue. Other industries were being starved of capital because of the railway mania, not to mention education, health and other areas where money was so urgently needed. While other papers fanned rumours of speculation, *The Times* alone warned of the outcome. Worried by the power of *The Times* and its invective against him, Hudson became one of the backers of a new newspaper, the *Daily News*, which appeared first in January 1846, with Charles Dickens as its editor. Support for a rival made *The Times* even more against him. It was that newspaper which finally did more than anyone to unseat King Hudson from his throne.

The powerful railway lobby based on Liverpool, which George Stephenson had helped to create, was determined to cut Hudson down to size, so were the Peases in Darlington, worried about his encroachments in the north east. They made the most of the fact that the Midland Railway, the mainstay of Hudson's operations, had suffered a temporary fall in shares. But Hudson still had many important friends. The *Standard*, for example, printed a glowing report of a banquet Hudson gave in York, having been given the freedom of the city. The Archbishop of York was there, the Duke of Leeds, eight mayors; George Stephenson surprisingly was also there, and hundreds of other Victorian notables. The *Standard* said Mr Hudson was entitled to give such a grand dinner because after all, he'd provided for the dinners of so many citizens throughout the country.

> Two hundred thousand well paid labourers, representing as heads of families, nearly one million men, women and children, all feast through the bold enterprise of one man, and not feasting for one day or one week but enjoying abundance from year's end to year's end. Let us hear what man or class of men ever before did so much for the population of a country?

In 1847, realising that opposition to him was growing and that several of his companies, bought far too expensively, were now almost bankrupting his profitable lines, he looked round for a new scheme to bring in fresh capital. His whole success had always depended on raising fresh money. This was difficult as railway shares had become unsteady and the public, overwhelmed by three years of railway madness, were being careful, not to say sceptical. Hudson came up with a brilliant idea. He proposed to the government, backed by his colleagues on the Tory front bench, that he should head a commission to set up railways in Ireland, with the government lending two-thirds of the necessary capital. (Having soaked the public he was now trying it on the government.) The arguments sounded good with Hudson maintaining he was doing it all for the public good, a social reform, purely to help Ireland.

'Ireland,' so said Hudson in the House of Commons, 'has been to this country a constant source of anxiety – Government after Government has declared it to be their great difficulty. We have been cobbling and peddling with Ireland, but we have attempted ineffectually to develop its resources.' The arguments sound very familiar.

Hudson declared that railways would make Irish agriculture flourish, would stimulate industry and would employ 130 men on every mile of railway constructed. But the government was against it. It said that the additional employment would be small, only thirty men per mile. Hudson's scheme would cost £16 million, a sum which the country couldn't afford, now that trade generally was receding. (*The Times*' warning that the lopsided investment in railways would affect other industries was beginning to come true.) If the Irish wanted railways, their gentry should put up the money themselves, as had been done in England.

It would have been a masterstroke if it had come off, committing the government to Hudson and handing him £16 million in cash. As it was, he had to return to the problems of his Midland Railway, where he was forced to admit liabilities of £14 million. (According to rumours, the true liabilities were nearer £30 million.) Later that year new legislation was passed to stop Hudson's practice of paying interest on railway shares before the railway was actually opened.

As part of his campaign against his rival, the London–York line, which had now passed parliament, he'd built a line down the east coast, the Eastern Counties Railways, which was proving a disaster. His idea was to build it up sufficiently to take over the

London–York line. He'd managed the publicity – the Eastern Counties was the line Queen Victoria had travelled on to Cambridge – but there just wasn't the traffic in the region to make it pay. The whole line had been a grandiose manoeuvre to outwit his opponents and he was now stuck with paying out dividends of almost four per cent, which he did in 1847, despite the fact that on working receipts the company had acquired liabilities of £13½ million.

Throughout 1847 he was desperately balancing the books, rewriting balance sheets, adding noughts to the profits, grabbing money from one company to pay dividends for another, managing somehow to keep most of his shareholders reasonably happy if not quite as rich as previously. He got himself re-elected for Sunderland at the general election of 1847 and helped his friend Robert Stephenson to get elected for Whitby. (Young Robert was still contracted to many Hudson companies though his father had long since untied himself completely.) The attacks on Hudson, when they came, started on a minor level. He was accused of corruption at York, and Mrs Hudson was criticised in the newspapers for having delayed the express from Darlington to York for twenty-seven minutes one evening so that a pineapple which she'd ordered by telegram could be delivered to their country estate.

The year 1848 was a year of disaster for England and Europe generally. There was a massive trade depression, the potato crop had failed in Ireland, cotton was short from America, the repeal of the corn laws had brought in cheap foreign corn which was bankrupting English farmers, banks were collapsing and shares were tumbling. In Europe, of course, it was the year of the revolutions. Hudson, and all the railway speculators, were being blamed for most of the ills of the home economy. He himself was seriously ill and, even worse, Lord George Bentinck, leader of the Conservatives, resigned, and with him went Hudson's chief parliamentary ally. Disraeli took over. Even though he had occasionally been a visitor to Albert Gate, he'd never cared for the uncouth Railway King.

Yet at the close of 1848 Hudson was, on paper, at the very height of his powers. There were in all 5,007 miles of railways in operation in the United Kingdom, no less than 1,450 of them being under the direct control of Hudson. His empire stretched on the east from Berwick through Cambridge to London, on the west it went to Maryport, in the Midlands it extended to Rugby and in the south west he had one line reaching Bristol. Hudson had by now created three of the greatest railway systems which were to dominate the nineteenth century – the North Eastern, the Midland and the Great Eastern. It was estimated that Hudson had spent a total of £30 million acquiring his 1,450 miles of railway. But now, at long last, he could find no fresh capital.

The exposure of Hudson began on a relatively harmless scale. Two London stockbrokers called Prance and Love, both of whom had lost a lot of money in the York and North Midland line, Hudson's first creation, went up to York and minutely went through the accounts. They found that the company had bought the shares of another company, the Great North of England, at a rate higher than they'd ever been on the stock exchange. At the shareholders meeting in York they revealed that £23 10s 0d had been paid for shares which at no time had been worth more than £21. And the owner of these shares had been no other than their own chairman, Mr Hudson. Hudson made the mistake, a mistake no good con man should ever make, of admitting that it had happened, though he added hurriedly that it wasn't his fault, another director had done the actual buying. Now that it had been revealed, he promised to pay back the profits he had unfairly made. A few years earlier, in times of affluence when he was the nation's hero, he could have laughed it off, been forgiven for a minor slip. In financial terms he'd made £9,000, a relatively minor amount, but the principle of deceit had been established. The meeting broke up in turmoil, but not before Prance and Love had insisted on a committee of investigation. News of the York meeting soon spread to London and shareholders in every Hudson company started asking awkward questions and demanding committees of enquiry.

A meeting of the Eastern Counties shareholders turned out to be even more sensational than the York confrontation. The chairman of their investigation committee was a Quaker called Mr Cash who asked Hudson if he'd ever altered any figures in the annual accounts.

'Well, I may perhaps have added a thousand or two to the next account,' said Hudson.

'Didst thou ever add £10,000?'

'I cannot exactly say what may have been the largest sum I carried to the following account.'

He was asked if he'd ever added a sum of £40,000. Mr Hudson said he wasn't sure. Later, when the full report of the investigative committee was published it was revealed that between 1845 and 1848 the company had paid out dividends of £545,715 even though the total sum earned had been only £225,142. And under the headings 'Secret Service', which Hudson maintained meant payments for parliamentary service, sums ranging from £2,000 to £9,000 had gone without trace. If it had gone into his own pocket, that was embezzling. If it had gone on paying MPs, that was even worse.

From then on the flood gates were open and it became a Victorian witch hunt, with some melodrama from a B movie thrown in for effect. Hudson's brother-in-law, his front man on many deals, committed suicide by drowning.

The charge of bribing MP's became official and he was called before his fellow members in the House to explain his conduct. Hudson's stumbling speech of apology, saying he hadn't meant it, that it had all happened accidentally, was received in silence.

Further revelations from his railway companies showed that he'd paid £40,000 out of the Newcastle and Berwick's account into his own bank, paying himself for land he didn't own. When the lists of his many cases of embezzlement were finally totted up it came to £598,785. That was the sum which was provable.

*The Times* didn't rejoice in its own righteousness. Now that Hudson was down and out, they concentrated their attack on the system which had made Hudson.

It was a system without rules, without order, without even a definite morality. Mr Hudson, having a faculty for amalgamation, and being so successfull, found himself in the enjoyment of a great railway despotism, in which he had to do everything out of his own head and among lesser problems to discover the ethics of railway speculation and management. Mr Hudson's position was not only new to himself but absolutely a new thing in the world altogether. We think the King and his subjects are much of a piece. If they deserve indulgence for their losses, he also must be excused for his difficulties.

But most Victorians were not as kind. Thomas Carlyle called Hudson in his *Latter Day Pamphlets* a 'gambler swollen big' and Macaulay in 1849 described him as a 'bloated, vulgar, insolent, purse proud, greedy, drunken blackguard'.

His home town of York, which he'd worked so hard and so successfully to put on the map, almost immediately turned against him. His name was erased from the Aldermanic Roll and Hudson Street, which had been named after him by a grateful populace, was hurriedly changed to Railway Street.

The whole wrath of Victorian England was brought to bear upon George Hudson but it can at least be said in his favour that he never lied, not once the scandal was revealed. He admitted everything and sold up his northern estates and his London house (which was bought by the French ambassador) to pay as many of his debtors as he could. He was laughed at and jeered, but he carried on till he was forced to flee to Paris, leaving his wife in lodgings, to escape his remaining debtors.

There is an interesting chance encounter in Paris which Dickens records in 1863. He noticed a familiar face by the quayside, 'a shabby man of whom I had some remembrance but whom I could not get into his place in my mind'. It was only on the boat home that a friend told him the man was Hudson, looking for some friend to buy him a dinner. Dickens had remembered Hudson's face from the early days on the *Daily News* when Hudson had been one of the important backers.

In 1868, after twenty years of a pauper's existence in France, a north-eastern MP, deciding he'd suffered enough, opened a subscription for him. It raised £4,800, enough for an annuity of £600, and Hudson returned to England; he died in 1871, and was buried in his home village of Scrayingham, ten miles from York, where he lies to this day. The inscription on his gravestone, near the entrance to the churchyard, can just be read, but with some difficulty.

George Hudson was big and fat and ugly, a most unattractive figure with no charm and no social graces, with no apparent talent for anything except buying and selling railway companies. But he was never a drunk, despite what Macaulay had said, and he was faithful to his wife, as far as was known. Sex scandals at least didn't figure in his life. Most of all, when his fall came, though millions of shareholders, large and small, lost a great deal of money, he never dragged down any of his former associates, neither politicians who'd gained from him nor company officials who'd been his knowing stooges. This can't be said for many of our modern monsters.

In 1971, after over a hundred years in which York had tried guiltily to deny all knowledge of their notorious son, it was decided to change the name of Railway Street, once again, to Hudson Street. The ceremonial unveiling of the reinstated street name was carried out by Dr Coggan, now the Archbishop of Canterbury. At the same time, a pub called The Adelphi was rechristened The Railway King, again in Hudson's honour, all part of what was described at the opening as 'the visual redemption of George Hudson'.

Hudson was the first in a long line of manipulators of the industrial system. Wheeling and dealing from scratch an empire worth £30 million must make him one of the biggest ever. Railways, when George Stephenson introduced them to the world, arrived with a bang and its villains arrived on an equally colossal scale. Meanwhile, our hero and only begetter had been perfectly content to watch the antics of King Hudson from a seat in the wings.

# 15

# GEORGE STEPHENSON'S LAST YEARS

George Stephenson took a rather stately seat in the country, a large, red brick Georgian mansion called Tapton House, near Chesterfield in Derbyshire. He moved into it in 1838 and there he spent the last ten years of his life, though it was only in his final three or four years that he led the life of a retired gentleman, tending the gardens, looking after his estate. Until then he was still rushing round Britain and Europe as a businessman and as a railway engineer, but retirement had obviously crossed his mind as early as 1837, judging by a letter to Michael Longridge.

> I intend giving up business in the course of two or three years when I shall be able to devote more time to my Friends. I have had a most delightful trip amongst the Cumberland Lakes, I should like to have remained a month to fish, I intend going again next year if I have time and have a large party with me. I hope you will accompany us. I want to take in 30 or 40,000 acres of land on the West Coast of England. I think it will be a good scheme.

George by this time could have well afforded such luxuries, but it was business not pleasure which brought Tapton House to his notice. Once again, as with Alton Grange, he'd been working in the area on part of Hudson's Midland Railway and had noticed several rich coal seams during work on Clay Cross tunnel. He had already realised the potential of the district for industrial expansion, with iron and lime in close proximity, all of which could be exploited with the help of the new railway. With four partners, he decided to develop a coal mine and ironworks at Clay Cross, lime quarries at Crich and limeworks at Ambergate. The partners included Joseph Sandars from Liverpool and his new and very good friend, George Hudson, who at the time had recently become lord mayor of York.

Tapton House and its private grounds of around a hundred acres appears to have been included in one of the many leases George took over, buying his way into the district, but when George saw it he fell in love with it and decided to make it his own home. It stands on a hill, high over the town of Chesterfield, about a mile from the centre, a most impressive, imposing mansion, handsome rather than beautiful, elegant rather than ornate, the sort of solid, defiant house that would appeal to George. Today it is a school housing six hundred pupils, which gives some idea of its size.

When his sister Nelly, the one who'd brought up Robert, came down to visit her famous brother the first thing that amazed her were the number of windows. She counted ninety – eighty-nine more than their whole family had had when they'd slept, all of them, in one room at Wylam. It seems a ridiculous size for a canny northerner, with only a wife to help him occupy it, but by now he had rather a large domestic staff, including an old farmer from Killingworth who in earlier years had helped him read and write. He'd been brought down to be in charge of the stables. The house was on top of his business, right beside his railway and therefore in reach of anywhere and, given time, he intended to take up his boyhood country pursuits and develop its large, if neglected, park land.

The views from Tapton House are spectacular, not unlike the views from the Northumberland hills looking down into the Tyne valley, a mixture of unspoiled sylvan greenery and then suddenly, in a huddle, an ironworks or coal mine, a strange chimney belching grey smoke, and then the eye moves on again, up to the untouched Pennine uphills. The good citizens of Chesterfield like to call themselves East Midlanders, but to an outsider their accent is Yorkshire which makes them Northerners at heart. George must have felt at home. The thought of moving south, like Robert, seems never to have crossed his mind. Was he afraid or self-conscious or defiant? Or just happy where he was?

The most striking part of the view from Tapton, then as well as today, is Chesterfield's main, perhaps only, claim to national fame, the crooked spire of its parish church, St Mary and All Saints. The spire went crooked not long after the church was built, back in the fourteenth century, bending itself almost eight feet to the south, as a result of the builders using green timbers which warped in the heat of the sun. They were covered in lead sheets, arranged in a herring bone pattern, which, to the amazement of every architect who has ever looked at them, didn't fall off but rearranged themselves in the new, crooked shape. That's the scientific explanation. The folklore story, which George no doubt was told, as outsiders are usually told, is that one day a virgin was getting married in the church and the spire, never having seen a virgin in Chesterfield before, leaned over to have a better look.

All George's mineral developments prospered and, allied with his railway, account for the industrial success of the district until this day. He built model homes for the miners with garden plots attached, and at his height had one thousand employees working in his Chesterfield companies.

It was from Tapton House that George fought and won two final battles, both vital, both of which would have undermined if not destroyed his entire railway creations. The skirmish with Joseph Locke had meant little, and anyway he'd by now let Robert take the lead in building new railway lines. The two new battles were personal attacks on George's philosophy, which was something he could never take, and both came from Brunel.

Isambard Kingdom Brunel, the son of Sir Marc Brunel, was an exact contemporary of Robert Stephenson and was to prove his lifetime's rival. Like Robert, he was immensely precocious and had many engineering successes to his name, such as the Clifton suspension bridge, while still in his early twenties. But the Stephensons, father and son, and the Brunels, father and son, were very unalike in character. The Brunels had a touch of the Trevithicks, romantic and ingenuous, imaginative and daring. George and Robert were equally inventive but they were much more careful, more practical, meticulous craftsmen, improving on what had gone before rather than throwing the past aside. Brunel, the younger, was particularly original, looking at every problem completely afresh, ignoring, disdaining even, what had gone before. Robert in many ways had less confidence and daring than his father and appears to have worried endlessly, even at the height of his success, convinced, as he wrote to a friend, 'that some fine morning my reputation may break under me like an eggshell'.

Smiles, being sagacious and painstaking himself, and perhaps through being a Northerner (at least a Scotsman), watched all of them at work from fairly close quarters and seems to have preferred the Stephensons. 'The former [the Stephensons] were as thoroughly English in their characteristics as the latter were perhaps as thoroughly French. Measured by practical and profitable results, the Stephensons were unquestionably the safer men to follow.' (Marc Brunel was a refugee from the French Revolution which Smiles, being very British, wasn't going to forget.)

Since then, over the last hundred years or so, most railway writers appear to have had a softer spot for Isambard Kingdom Brunel, a glamorous figure with many glamorous successes to his name. The Great Western Railway, Brunel's creation, has always been a glamour line for railway lovers. Right from the beginning, he questioned the principles for building railways which George had laid down in the north and the Midlands. He decided, for example that wooden sleepers were far better than the stone blocks which the Stephensons had always demanded. Most important of all, he decided against their rail gauge of 4ft 8½ins. This was the gauge George had chosen at Darlington, for no better reason than it had been the wagon way at Killingworth, and was the gauge which had been followed by everyone else. Brunel, down in the remote south west corner of England, chose to be different. He chose no less than seven feet.

The GWR opened in 1838 and Brunel gave elaborate reasons for choosing such a broad gauge. The basic reason appears to have been speed, which led to great technical arguments amongst the experts for many years over whether a train really could go faster on a wide track than on a narrow track. Brunel had the body of his carriages between the wheels whereas the Stephensons had placed their carriages over the wheels so there wasn't a great advantage in volume of passengers or goods carried by the Brunel trains, which to the layman might seem the obvious advantage of increased width. Brunel's point was strength, speed and safety of his much bigger locomotives. They did indeed go faster, though it might have been due to better engineering, and they forced the Stephensons to improve their performances, even though George had by now decided that forty miles an hour was fast enough for any locomotive.

The first locomotive on the GWR was the *North Star*, built by Robert Stephenson and Company at Newcastle, and their first and perhaps most famous engineer was Daniel (later Sir Daniel) Gooch, appointed at the age of twenty-nine. Gooch had previously worked in Robert Stephenson's drawing office, but Brunel, whatever he thought of some of the Stephenson principles, couldn't be said to be blindly prejudiced.

Brunel, however, appears to have been rather blind to the problems which obviously lay ahead, problems which George and Robert had pointed out from the beginning. In 1848, just when George was beginning his genuine retirement at Tapton House, the expanding success of the GWR brought it to Gloucester where it met head on the standard gauge of Stephenson. Along with Railway Mania, the Battle of the Gauges became one of the topics of the day. Thackeray, once again, had a series of short stories about the ridiculousness of it all, about everyone, people, bags, baggages and animals having to decamp from one train and get into another one.

A royal commission, that institution beloved by every British government who doesn't know what to do, was set up in August 1845, and meticulously went through every facet of the problems, putting 6,500 questions to thousands of interested parties. Almost every expert was on the Stephenson side – even Joseph Locke gave evidence in their favour. Brunel and Gooch were almost on their own. The commission reported in 1846 in favour of the 4ft 8½ins gauge. Henceforth they said it had to be used in all public railways in Great Britain.

It was a personal triumph for George, though many commentators, then and now, had brave words to say for Brunel, fighting on his own against the weight of the Stephenson camp and their near-monopoly of the locomotive industry. But in many ways Brunel had been perverse. He genuinely considered his gauge was better, but his dimensions were equally as arbitrary as George's. There is no innate perfect width for a railway train. One width having been securely established, it was surely inconvenient and uneconomic for the country to consider changing it.

If Brunel was perverse in the gauge battle – and it's a word his supporters would never use – there was something paradoxical in his other major battle with George. At the same time as fighting for his broad gauge railway he was advocating a completely new system of rail transport which, if successful, would do away with locomotives of any sort. This was the atmospheric railway.

It must have been highly disturbing for George when he first heard about atmospheric railways. Having usurped the canals and the turnpikes, cutting them off in their prime, it did look for a time as if it could happen in turn to him and his railways before they'd ever reached their prime. The atmospheric system was not Brunel's invention but when he took it up, in the 1840s, his name was enough to make it not just a fashionable cause but a serious and genuine threat.

To put it as simply as possible, the atmospheric system was a method of blowing instead of pulling a train along the tracks. A large pipe was laid between the tracks and air was pumped along it from pumping stations placed at intervals beside the line. A piston connected the head of the train to a slot in the pipe. (Scientifically the principle at stake was more a sucking action than a blowing action, though that was how it appeared: the pumping machines exhausted the air in front of the train, the train therefore being forced into the vacuum which had been created, hence the name atmospheric.) Amazingly, the system worked and was seen to work. It was tried out on a line near Dublin and plans were made to use it at Croydon and elsewhere.

Robert, as was his wont, went into the matter very carefully and inspected every aspect in detail. George, as was his way, dismissed it out of hand. He saw it as just another permutation of the stationary engine principle which he'd beaten once and for all at Rainhill. Instead of having a rope or chain doing the pulling, so he said, it was simply a rope of air and it wouldn't work.

As if the idea wasn't enough of an insult to George, Brunel had the effrontery to propose it on George's homeland, on the railway to be built between Newcastle and Berwick. It was a railway George particularly wanted to build as it would achieve one of his life's ambitions, a direct line from Edinburgh to London. It became George's last great railway battle.

George first surveyed a Newcastle–Berwick line in 1836 but, for various reasons, nothing had happened. It was revived again in 1843 by none other than George Hudson who commissioned George, already identified with the project, as engineer and he was very happy to accept. (It can be seen how George, whatever he was beginning to think privately of Hudson, was therefore forced to continue in public as his friend.) On the other side, advocating a different route and the different, atmospheric, principle, was Brunel and his chief supporter Lord Howick, son of Earl Grey, an enormously wealthy local landowner and MP.

The grand, climactic confrontation of George and Brunel took place in Newcastle with many people hoping for a punch up. There were indeed reports that George had grabbed Brunel's arm in a decidedly rough-house style, but Smiles maintains all was friendly. 'When Stephenson first met Brunel in Newcastle he good humouredly shook him by the collar and asked "What business had he North of the Tyne?" George gave him to understand that they were to have a fair stand-up fight for the ground and shaking hands before the battle like Englishmen, they parted in good humour.'

Both schemes went before parliament and George entered into the fight with enormous gusto and not a little vindictiveness – fighting on a principle, fighting the upstart Brunel and fighting a landed lord, the sort he could never stand. He'd had a running battle with Lord Howick from the beginning – or Hawick, as George called him, confusing him with the town. During his early survey work Lord Howick had tried desperately to keep George's confounded railway well away from his estates. George wrote to Michael Longridge telling him exactly how he felt.

Tapton House, Nov 30. 1843

I am rather astonished at Lord Hawick's observations about the line passing Hawick. It does not go through any of their pleasure grounds. . . . My senses are puzzled in judging how these people can set about making such paltry objections! It is compensation they want, nothing else. . . . This series of objections is a genteel way of picking the subscribers' pockets. It may however be better to keep these observations quiet until we come before Parliament. I have never taken any part in politics but I think I now will and become a Tory; and I shall buy a piece of land in Northumberland to oppose Lord Hawick. I do not like his double dealing work. Is the great thoroughfare through England and Scotland to be turned aside injuriously, for the frivolous remarks made by Lord Hawick? no! the times are changed. I wonder their pulse does not cease to beat when such imaginations enter their brains! these failings are not becoming human beings. I can have no patience with them. However, I suppose we must bend and keep our tempers until we get what we want.

When the battle did reach parliament in 1845, George had a chance meeting with Lord Howick at the Stephensons' London office. Smiles has a very entertaining description of what happened between them, as retailed to him by Robert Stephenson.

On the day in question, George was standing [in the outer office] with his back to the fire when Lord Howick called to see Robert. Oh! thought George, he has come to try and talk Robert over about that atmospheric gimcrack; but I'll tackle his Lordship. 'Come in, my Lord,' said he, 'Robert's busy; but I'll answer your purpose quite as well; sit down here, if you please.' George began, 'Now, my Lord, I know very well what you have come about: it's that atmospheric line in the north; I will show you in less than five minutes that it can never answer.' 'If Mr. Robert Stephenson is not at liberty, I can call again,' said his Lordship. 'He's certainly occupied on important business just at present,' was George's answer; 'but I can tell you far better than he can what nonsense the atmospheric system is: Robert's good-natured, you see, and if your Lordship were to get alongside of him you might talk him over; so you have been quite lucky in meeting with me. Now, just look at the question of expense,' – and then he proceeded in his strong Doric to explain his views in detail, until Lord Howick could stand it no longer, and he rose and walked towards the door. George followed him down stairs, to finish his demolition of the atmospheric system, and his parting words were, 'You may take my word for it, my Lord, it will never answer.' George afterwards told his son with glee of 'the settler' he had given Lord Howick.

George did indeed have the final settling. The Stephenson–Hudson line passed parliament amid much rejoicing in all locomotive circles. In Newcastle eight hundred workmen from the Stephenson loco works paraded in the streets with banners and music. (The atmospheric system did continue elsewhere for some years but was continually breaking down, was found to be uneconomic and finally abandoned. But for a time it did work: perhaps someone, some day, will take it up again.)

George always had great acclaim whenever he returned to Newcastle. He was cheered to the roof when he went back for the banquet organised by Hudson, when the first 'flying' trains arrived from London. He was now being called the 'Father of Railways', even the Inventor of Railways, according to some of the speeches, a title he never argued with. He visited Newcastle on another occasion when it was the venue for a meeting of the British Association, of which he'd been elected one of the vice-presidents. He toured the scenes from his boyhood, like Wylam, taking with him some of the distinguished guests, telling them harrowing stories about his early life and hard struggles.

In London, he never had the same spontaneous acclaim. It was, after all, Robert who brought the trains to London from the north, arriving at Euston, and Brunel from the west into Paddington. George had been personally rather abusive in his battles with Brunel, which Robert never was, and the Establishment generally still considered him something less than a gentleman and a great deal less than an engineering genius. However, George's progress in foreign parts, where he was a prophet showered with every sort of honour, was one long triumphant tour.

As we saw from the early days in Darlington and Liverpool, European and American engineers had long been watching George's locomotives with great interest. When the first locomotives were to be built in France for the Lyon–St Etienne, which started in 1829, two engines were brought from Stephenson's Newcastle works to act as models and George himself received a gift of 12,500 francs for his help and advice. Newcastle was also sending locomotives to the USA from as early as 1828. The oldest complete locomotive which now exists in America, preserved in the Smithsonian Institute, is *John Bull*, built at Forth Street in 1831. America's first locomotive railway was the South Carolina in 1830, five years after Darlington. (But by 1850 America had far outstripped Britain in the extent of its railway system.)

In 1833 Robert Stephenson and Company were exporting locomotives to Germany, plus enginemen to teach them how to run them; then two years later to Russia and by the end of the thirties to almost every European country, but George's relationship with Belgian railways was probably the most fruitful. King Leopold, who'd become the first king of the Belgians in 1831, was determined to introduce railways to his country on a national, rational scale. Being a small, increasingly industrialised country, with important minerals and strategic ports, Belgium lent itself to a master plan rather than haphazard growth, as in Britain.

Locomotives were ordered from Newcastle in 1834 and George and Robert received a royal request in 1835 to come and advise them how to lay out a comprehensive railway system. They were both fêted by the king and queen at receptions in Brussels, which George seems to have enjoyed hugely. 'King Leopold stated he was very glad to have the honour of my acquaintance,' said George in a letter to Longridge. 'He seemed quite delighted with what had taken place in Belgium about the Railways.'

George was made a Knight of the Order of Leopold and visited Belgium on several later occasions, for the grand openings of various lines, each time being handsomely received. In 1848, during one banquet, the director of the Belgian National Railways unveiled before the guests a marble bust of George, crowned with laurels, and under a triumphal arch a model of the *Rocket*.

In the same year, George embarked on the last of his many foreign railway expeditions, this time to Spain where he'd been asked to construct a railway from Madrid to the Bay of Biscay. He was by now sixty-four and the journey there was hazardous enough, quite apart from surveying such difficult terrain. He went with his friend, Sir Joshua Walmsley, and their adventures and near-escapes in crossing the Pyrenees were as hair-raising as Robert's had been in South America. When George eventually struggled back to Paris he was so ill with pleurisy that Walmsley feared for his life, but he recovered, just, to tell Longridge the tale.

Tapton House, 22nd Nov, 1845.

My Dear Sir,

I am now at home and quite well, my recovery has been most extraordinary, the attack I had was pleurisy: I think it was first occasioned by taking unwholesome food at Bordeaux from that place I travelled night and day to Paris: I took very ill there, but still persevered in getting to England; on arriving at Havre I was obliged to have a Doctor who took 20 oz blood from me on board the Steam boat; I was then very weak but still wished to get on to England; the boat sailed at 5 o'clock P.M. I got to London the next day about half past 2 o'clock & there got the best advise; they got two Physicians to me; they put me to bed and cupped me on the right side; how much blood they took by cupping I cannot tell, they then put a blister on my side and gave me Calomel every four hours from Saturday night to tuesday night: I then became so weak that they durst not give me any more. on the Wednesday morning I was considerably relieved from pain and could then eat a little – my rapid recovery since that time has been astonishing, I am now quite as well as I ever was in my life, but I am advised to keep quite for a while.

Yours truly,
GEO. STEPHENSON.

Mich. Longridge Esq.
P.S. I have had a most extraordinary journey in Spain. I crossed the Pyrenees 5 times; and rode on horse back 50 miles amongst the mountains seeking out the lowest pass – we had our carriage drawn up by bullocks on to the mountain passes where a carriage had never been before – we passed just under the snow range. I shall give you an account of my travels when I see you: we travelled 3000 miles in 33 days: stopped 4 days in Madrid. 2 days at the summits of the mountain passes – I was kindly received in every Town where I was known.

Back at Tapton House, George now gave his almost undivided attention to his gardens. At Killingworth in the old days he'd competed with the miners in growing the largest and best vegetables, such as giant leeks, still one of the north east's favourite sports. Now that he was a gentleman, he turned to more exotic vegetables and fruits, such as melons, pineapples and grapes. He built ten large greenhouses, heating them with his own system of hot water pipes. One of his ambitions was to grow pineapples as big as pumpkins which would 'knock-under' those grown by the Duke of Devonshire at nearby Chatsworth. The Chatsworth head gardener, Paxton, and his son Joseph, became close friends of George's but it didn't stop George trying to outdo them at every horticultural show. (Joseph Paxton, later Sir Joseph, went from gardening at Chatsworth to designing the Crystal Palace for the Great Exhibition of 1851. Building larger greenhouses to keep George in his place no doubt helped.) George was particularly pleased, so Smiles relates, when his grapes took first prize at Rotherham in a competition 'open to all England'.

George's ultimate aim was to grow a straight cucumber, an exercise as pointless as three-foot leeks, but one that consumed him for several years. (And led to that barbed joke from William James' daughter – about George taking the credit for everything from cucumbers to petticoats.) He tried different permutations of light and heat and eventually ordered straight, glass cylinders to be made for him at Newcastle. This finally did the trick. Carrying his first straight cucumber into the house to be admired by a group of visitors, he told them gleefully: 'I think I have bothered them noo.'

He also experimented with stock breeding, trying new types of manure and new feedstuff, touring agricultural meetings and telling farmers where they were going wrong. He took up bird-watching again and became highly knowledgeable. He developed a method of fattening chickens in half the usual time. He'd noticed how they could be convinced that each day was really two days by shutting them in dark boxes after a heavy feed. He explained it all to Edward Pease who came to visit him one day, adding that if he were to devote himself to chickens he could make a small fortune. It sounds very much like battery farming.

His wife Elizabeth, not to be outdone, tried to keep bees but she found they wouldn't thrive at Tapton and the hives perished for no apparent reason. George investigated, studying the habits and actions of the bees, and concluded they were too tired to get up the Tapton hill to the hives, having fed themselves on all the flowers at the bottom. The hives were moved downhill and thrived.

This incident is the only story in Smiles, or any other contemporary account, which refers to his wife Elizabeth, to whom he'd been married for twenty-five years. She died in 1845, just before his long trip to Spain, and was buried at Holy Trinity Church, Chesterfield. This was a new church and considered rather 'low', almost Methodist, which she presumably attended, though George is not known to have worshipped there or in any other church. George was left alone in the big house with his housekeeper, a lady called Ellen Gregory. But he had frequent visitors. His relations from Tyneside often came to see him and were handsomely received, usually going home with generous gifts, as did any old mechanic or miner from his past who arrived at his house asking for help. He took great interest in all Mechanics' Institutes and travelled extensively to their dinners where he made his usual speech about his early hard struggles.

Great people also came to see George, though they tended not to be the London greats. Ralph Waldo Emerson, on a visit from America, met him in Chesterfield – at the house of Swanwick, George's former secretary. They discussed Americans, electricity, climate, soil and other subjects on which George had strong opinions and theories, all based on his observations, not on books, for he never went in for reading books, and Emerson expressed himself highly delighted. 'It was worth crossing the Atlantic to have seen Stephenson alone,' he said afterwards. 'He had such native force of character and vigour of intellect. He seems to have the life of many men in him.'

Many distinguished people tried to persuade George to come to them, but he was happiest in his own home or with gatherings of mechanics. Sir Robert Peel, the prime minister, twice invited him to spend weekends at his home at Tamworth. George declined each time but in January 1845, on the third request, graciously agreed. 'I feel your kindness very much and can no longer refuse. I will come down and join your party.' The company was very exalted, including titled lawyers and eminent scientists of the day, and George was worried that his lack of the gift of the gab would let him down. According to Smiles, George was assisted by one of the guests, Sir William Follett, a well-known lawyer, who showed him how to arrange his arguments in a coherent order after he'd been soundly beaten in a discussion with another guest, a Dr Buckland.

One of George's favourite party pieces, when he himself had guests at Tapton, was to bring out a large microscope, draw blood from the fingers of each guest and analyse their globules, discussing the different blood groups which he'd discovered. (His observations were his own, says Smiles, only later did medical science prove they were right.) He liked to go on from a person's blood group to reflecting on their characters, no doubt feeling the shapes of their heads, from which he got other clues.

He took his microscope with him to Tamworth and towards the end of the weekend, his confidence recovered, he invited all the guests to prick their fingers. Everyone except Sir Robert Peel agreed, even though George explained that all he wanted was to see 'how the blood globules of a great politician would conduct themselves'. Peel, apparently, had great sensitivity to pain and when he, as the host, categorically refused to be pricked, George had to abandon his experiments.

George fancied himself on most medical matters and he was fond of giving advice. When Longridge in a letter at one time complained of being unwell, George knew at once what was wrong:

> You have been living high by getting the gout into your hand. I dare say you have had some Turtle soup lately? you must have a poultice put on to every nail and you will find it will do you good, but it must be so arranged that it does not come in contact with the adjoining skin –if it does it will prevent the oil having its proper passage to the growth of the nail which I dare say is flat, looks red and inflamed underneath, and cuts brittle, for want of the liquid I have just mentioned.

There are endless traces in George of a know-all attitude on many subjects. It turned to fury when anyone, such as Brunel, dared to cross him on something where he was irrefutably the master, but his background and early struggles have always to be borne well in mind. He'd won through, despite the prejudices of almost the whole of the scientific world, and naturally thought he had laid down the rules, once and for all.

He never forgot or forgave those who'd opposed him or whom he considered had done him wrong. It wasn't a matter of changing as he got older. He'd always been like this, as his early letters show, convinced he was right. He never took on airs and graces with his new wealth and power, but neither did he assume any humility.

He retained many of his old colliery habits, such as treating his guests to a 'crowdie night', pouring boiling water on to the raw oats for everyone to eat. And if they were from the north he would sing them the old songs he'd learned from his parents – his favourite was 'John Anderson my Joe' – or wrestle with them for old times' sake. He even did his wrestling tricks, so Smiles relates, at Robert's smart Westminster office.

> 'When my father came about the office,' said Robert, he sometimes did not well know what to do with himself. So he used to invite Bidder to have a wrestle with him, for old acquaintance sake. And the two wrestled together so often, and had so many "falls" (sometimes I thought they would bring the

house down between them), that they broke half the chairs in my outer office. I remember once sending my father in a joiner's bill of about 21.10s. for mending broken chairs.'

George always preferred talking to reading and he made it his business when starting on a train journey to go up and down the corridors, searching for an interesting-looking person to talk to. He sat himself beside Lord Denman one day on leaving Euston Station and spent several hours telling him how to mend watches. While waiting in stations, he frequently went over to enginemen and told them how to do their jobs more efficiently, or demonstrated to labourers the correct way to use a shovel and fill a barrow.

Thomas Summerside, who worked under George for many years in Tyneside and in later life, published a memoir in 1878 which has several stories of George telling people how to conduct themselves. A young hopeful came to Tapton one day wanting George's help, wearing a gold chain and a fine ring. George, always a modest dresser, despised all finery. 'Let me advise you never to put on such trinkets as these. I never did and had I done I should not have been the man I am.' He was equally suspicious of anyone's fine learning which had been gained from books or universities. 'Never judge a goose by its stuffing,' was one of his favourite sayings.

George was once staying at a hotel when he was engaged in conversation by a gentleman and his wife. Neither of them recognised George and the wife even had the audacity to ask George, no doubt rather dismissively, who he was and what he did for a living.

Madam, I have in my time dined with a hedger in the hedge bottom off a red herring and also sat at the table of Royalty. I used to be called plain George Stephenson but now my title is George Stephenson, Esq, of Tapton House, Chesterfield, Derbyshire; but the result of my observation is that we are pretty much alike, but for our raiment.

The lady turned to her husband and said 'My dear, this is the *great* George Stephenson, with whose son ours is employed.' Mr Stephenson replied 'And a simpleton he is, just like his mother.'

George's attitude to the aristocracy was complex. He could boast of their acquaintance at one time, then despise them the next. 'It is but a short time ago since I dined with the Earl of Carlisle,' he said to Summerside on one occasion, 'and there were brought to meet me a Duke, Earls, Lords and other gentlemen. Fine difference, Summerside, to what there used to be.'

His Belgian title pleased him, though he never used it in England. But when he was twice offered a knighthood in his own country by Sir Robert Peel he turned it down. He was also offered a safe parliamentary seat at South Shields but his refusal of this was more understandable, never being interested in politics nor a fluent public speaker. In the case of the knighthood, perhaps he felt it would mean that he'd given in and joined the Establishment still knowing, or at least feeling, that he wasn't really accepted and that they were simply trying to corrupt him. Perhaps if his wife had been alive he might have accepted. Abroad, it was different. He was accepted for what he had done not for what he was and any honours had no strings attached, real or imaginary. Abroad, no one noticed his Geordie accent. Abroad, no one made jokes about 'coos' behind his back.

In a letter he wrote in 1847, in reply to someone asking him how he would like to be described in a dedication, it looks as if he'd become invertedly snobbish about his refusal of honours.

Dear Sir,

I have received yours of the 23rd inst. In reply to it I have to state that I have no flourishes to my name, either before it or after, and I think it will be as well if you merely say Geo. Stephenson. It is true that I am a Belgian Knight, but I do not wish to have any use made of it.

I have had the honour of Knighthood of my own country made to me several times, but would not have it; I have been invited to become a Fellow of the Royal Society; and also of the Civil Engineers Society, but I objected to these empty additions to my name. I have however now consented to become President to I believe a highly respectable mechanics' Institute at Birmingham.

I am, Dear Sir,
Yours very truly,
GEO. STEPHENSON

The organisation to which he'd consented to be president was the Institution of Mechanical Engineers, who are very proud to this day that he was their first president. They'd started the year before, 1846, in Birmingham when a group of railway engineers had been watching some trials near Bromsgrove. A shower of rain drove them into a platelayer's hut, so the story goes, and they fell to talking about how unfair it was that the civil engineers were always lording it over them. As they were a completely new trade, nay a new profession, it was about time they had their own professional body. George, who was always interested in anything mechanical, readily accepted their invitation to be president. One of their first meetings was held at Tapton House. As we well know, he never cared for the lordly Civil Engineers and their haughty Institution.

In an early edition of his biography, Smiles states that George had applied for membership of the Institution of Civil Engineers but was informed he must supply proof of his professional qualifications and write an essay. George, of course, had no qualifications, never having passed any examination nor having been apprenticed to a qualified engineer. George was so hurt by their attitude that he never forgave them and instead accepted the offer from the Mechanicals.

It's the sort of story George might have told to friends at Tapton House, boasting how he was self-taught and unqualified, not good enough for the likes of the Civils, who wouldn't let him in if he tried, the sort of boasting which self-made people often delight in, once that everyone knows they're in fact much more successful and rich and powerful than their enemies could ever be. In his young days, he might well have applied, and technically they would have had to turn him down; but by 1846 he wouldn't have bothered to apply unless out of devilment, and if he had they would no doubt have waived the rules and given him some sort of position. By this time, many members of the Civils' council, which included his son Robert, had been his former pupils or assistants. And they weren't all his enemies.

Smiles dropped the story from later editions, apparently because the Civils denied they'd ever turned him down. George in the letter quoted above says, rather contradictorily, that he'd been offered but turned down a Fellowship of the 'Civil Engineers' Society', which can only refer to the same body. Nonetheless, the story of George, the greatest engineer of his age, not being good enough for the Civils, was one that was often repeated, long after

George's death, and it was one which never ceased to annoy them. George, no doubt would have been very amused.

In April, 1848, there occurred a minor incident, not mentioned by Smiles, which shows George in not such an amusing light. There appeared in the letters column of the *Darlington and Stockton Times* a letter signed by someone called 'Nemo' which was a fulsome panegyric to the work of Edward Pease, about all the good he had done to Darlington, but how little recognition he'd received. Nemo, just to clear himself, adds that he is not related to Pease and has never met him. He just wants to see him honoured as

. . . the man who first conceived the idea, and so successfully carried out the completion of the first railway for the conveyance of goods and passengers. That man is Edward Pease, Esq., and that Railway is the Stockton and Darlington Railway . . .

George was absolutely outraged and immediately wrote to Nicholas Wood in Newcastle, instructing him to put the record straight.

Tapton House,
April 10th 1848.

My Dear Sir,

I am going to give you a little work to do if you like to, but if you don't then send back the enclosed observations.

I am disgusted with a letter which has been published in the Stockton & Darlington Times of April 8th which I enclose you.

You are the only man living except myself who knows the origin of Locomotive engines on the Stockton & Darlington Railway. I shall be obliged if you will take the matter up and shew that Edward Pease is not the man of Science who has done so much for the country.

I am My Dear Sir
Yours faithfully,
GEO. STEPHENSON

P.S. When are you going to bring Mrs Wood and your daughter here? I have grapes now ripe and the Duke of Devonshire has not.

The Northumberland Record Office, who have kindly allowed this letter to be published, have also a copy of the full letter as written by Nemo but nothing from Nicholas Wood in reply. Whether a reply from him was ever published, it is George's reaction which is significant. (His PS is also very much in character.) There must have been many people in the north east who were genuinely disgusted when George gave his self-made speech at places like Newcastle, all of them fully reported in the papers of the day, without ever mentioning the work of the engineers who had gone before or the help he'd had from people like Losh or the Grand Allies, or the work done by Pease or William James and many others. Unlike his son Robert, there was never a murmur of contradiction from George whenever the purple passages started flowing at the Hudson inspired banquets in honour of the Inventor of Railways.

Smiles reports several of George's speeches in his biography, speeches he personally listened to, presumably during Smiles' period as editor at the *Leeds Times*, from 1838 to 1842.

On more than one occasion, the author had the pleasure of listening to George Stephenson's homely but forcible addresses at the annual soirées of the Leeds Mechanics' Institute. He was always an immense favourite with his audiences there. His personal appearance was greatly in favour. A handsome, ruddy, expressive face, lit up by bright dark-blue eyes, prepared one for his earnest words when he stood up to speak and the cheers had subsided which invariably hailed his rising. He was not glib, but he was very impressive. And who, so well as he, could serve as a guide to the working man in his endeavours after higher knowledge? His early life had been all struggle – encounter with difficulty – groping in the dark after greater light, but always earnestly and perseveringly. His words were therefore all the more weighty, since he spoke from the fulness of his own experience. His grand text was – PERSEVERE; and there was manhood in the very word.

If there had been examples in George's speeches of his magnaminity, Smiles would surely have been quick to quote them. Many people did note George's lack of generosity towards other engineers, whether ex-pupils who'd moved on, rivals who dared to contradict him or offer different solutions, or engineers in the same field whose inventions he'd definitely followed. It was this lack which particularly upset the professional engineers of the day who so studiously stuck to the gentleman's code of crediting everyone first, putting oneself last. As far as George was concerned, he had done everything by himself. Looking back, he probably could not remember anyone whom he considered had really helped him. All he no doubt remembered was that they'd all been agin him. Given the man, his manners are more understandable. In our present age, unnecessary humility is often viewed with suspicion as being insincere. The 'I am the greatest' syndrome is much more accepted. In George's day, humility was a virtue.

Despite the ill-feeling George attracted, it didn't worry him too much or give him sleepless nights. There is every evidence that he was exceedingly happy in his old age, content with himself and with life. He had certainly more than fulfilled all his ambitions, proved everyone wrong, and received more than sufficient worldly recognition of his greatness. He achieved wealth and power and fame and lived long enough to enjoy all three, which can't alas, be said for every great man.

Summerside, in his little book of memoirs, has suggested by one oft-repeated anecdote that George Stephenson was mean – and Rolt appears in his book to accept this. George often gave Summerside and other members of his staff a box of grapes or peaches from his greenhouses, always adding: 'Mind! Fetch the box back.' The boxes, as Rolt notes significantly, were worth only a few coppers. It sounds more like common sense, not meanness. Replacing humdrum objects can be a bother for both rich and poor. George was no doubt canny. His instances of financial generosity revolved mainly round the families of his brothers and sisters, all of whom he provided for till the end of his life. His generosity didn't extend to the world at large but he was certainly not greedy. Hudson, at the height of his powers, was continually rolling up at Tapton in his private train, trying but failing to induce George to invest money in railway shares which he guaranteed were going to double overnight. George often took shares in a railway if he was building it, though more often than not he would waive his fees until the line was paying, but he never speculated in other shares.

He kept completely out of Railway Mania, even while the rest of the world was going wild. In April 1846, before the signs of any crash, he advised a friend: 'I hope you have kept clear of the mania of wild Railway schemes – thousands of people will be ruined as I have learned that many have mortgaged their little properties to get money; of course their property will be lost up to the amount of money they have got.'

When shares did start falling Robert urged his father to sell out the ones he did have and at least get his money back. 'No,' he said. 'I took my shares for an investment and not to speculate with and I am not going to sell them now because folks have gone mad about railways.' Smiles, in a rather endearing chapter heading, describes Stephenson as 'Essentially Unsordid'. It would appear to be true.

George married for the third time in February 1848, just six months before his death. It was to his housekeeper, Ellen Gregory, daughter of a Bakewell farmer. They had obviously been very fond of each other for some time as is shown in a letter in his own hand, now preserved in the Science Museum in London. (They have a transcription which says the letter begins 'My dear Glen', which of course should be my dear Ellen, but the handwriting is very bad.)

24 Great George Street,<br>Westminster, 1847

My dear Ellen,

    I have just got Mr. Marks letter which gave me much pain to hear your illness I do hope you are better. I shall not leave here until Tuesday morning so that I can have a letter before [leaving?] London to say how you are. you cannot write in time for me here I shall hear from you at Tapton if you are no better I will come down to to [sic] you but do not let me come unless you feel very ill.

    I shall be home to be with you by the end of the week.

I am my dear Ellen<br>Your loving friend<br>GEO. STEPHENSON

Summerside was surprised by news of the marriage and says in his book that he never remembered seeing Ellen on his frequent visits to Tapton.

I learnt from her brother that which very much surprised me, viz, that after the death of her husband, although the furniture, plate, etc, and £800 per annum were left to her, she found it too little; and even contemplated coming to Matlock to reside, in order to economise. She wrote to her step-son, Mr Robert Stephenson, for an increase of her allowance, but he significantly referred her to his solicitor. I only name the above by way of contrast, knowing that it will strike all the intimate friends of his second wife who would know that her watchword was frugality, economy and saving.

Three wives, then, and very little to say about any of them, nice or otherwise: Fanny was older, was always ill and died early: Elizabeth was a Methodist who kept bees and for twenty-five years was a frugal but very retiring wife: Ellen arrived late, was much younger, and liked his money.

George Stephenson died at midday in his bedroom at Tapton House on 12 August 1848, after a severe attack of pleurisy, a recurrence of the illness he'd contracted in Spain. He was sixty-seven. He was buried at Holy Trinity, Chesterfield, the church where his second wife Elizabeth had been buried, beneath a simple stone slab. Later, his name was added to a tablet bearing his wife's name and Robert presented a memorial window in his father's honour to the church.

According to the *Derbyshire Courier* of 18 August 1848, the funeral was an exceedingly impressive occasion with all the Chesterfield shops closed from midday for the cortege as it came down the hill from Tapton House, followed by 'hundreds of people, including some who'd come a long distance'. The Mayor of Chesterfield and the Archdeacon of Derby were present, plus many local councillors, but looking through the names there were no national figures, apart from Robert Stephenson. Even George Hudson didn't turn up. He was very busy that day trying hard to explain to irate shareholders why he couldn't pay them any money. He managed to quieten them, for a few minutes at least, by calling for silence in his great grief at the sudden loss of his dear friend.

Someone who did make the effort to come a long way was Edward Pease, now aged eighty-one, and he recorded his impressions of George's funeral in his diary.

*Wednesday, Aug. 16* Left home in company with John Dixon to attend the interment of George Stephenson at Chesterfield, and arrived there in the evening. When I reflect on my first acquaintance with him and the resulting consequences my mind seems almost lost in doubt as to the beneficial results – that humanity has benefited in the diminished use of horses and by the lessened cruelty to them, that much ease, safety, speed and lessened expense in travelling is obtained, but as to the results and effects of all that Railways have led my dear family into, being in any sense beneficial, is uncertain.

*Thurs. Aug. 17* Went in the forenoon to Tapton House, late G. Stephenson's residence, and received from Robert a welcome reception; had a serious friendly conference with him, under a feeling expressed to him of my belief that it was a kindness to him his father was taken, his habits were approaching to inebriety; his end was one that seemed painfully to feel no ground, almost, for hope. I fear he died an unbeliever – the attendance of his funeral appeared to me to be a right step due to my association with him and his son. I do not feel condemned in doing so, yet gloomy and unconsolatory was the day. In the church I sat a spectacle with my hat on, and not comforted by the funeral service.

It's hard to know what Pease meant by George's 'Inebriety'. Smiles always insists how sober George was, though to a Quaker like Pease, anyone who took drink would be a drunkard. (To a true Quaker, anyone who condemned anyone else, as Pease was doing, was also sinning.) Perhaps he was referring to George's general character. When the obituaries appeared, there were indeed constant asides to his well-known faults ('And who will pretend he was without them,' as the *Derby and Chesterfield Reporter* observed), but few went into exact details.

One paper said that the cause of his death was 'spending too many years in the impure air of a hot house in a praiseworthy but imprudent rivalry with the Duke of Devonshire in the cultivation of certain exotics. Whether peer or commoner, Stephenson could not bear that any man should be his superior or equal in whatever he undertook.'

The *Civil Engineer and Architect's Journal* ran an enormous obituary–biography which came out in installments. It generously praised his achievements, though it recognised that he hadn't been a friend of theirs. 'From prejudice against some of the members, he refused to belong to the Institution of Civil Engineers.' They referred to his feud with Brunel as being bitter:

To those who applied to him for countenance for new projects he was not always so considerate; he was wrapped up in his own schemes and looked upon others with ill-will. His feelings towards Brunel were shown with a warmth and bitterness unbecoming, and it extended to all the supporters of the atmospheric system. The locomotive was his cherished idol, and woe to those who interfered with its worship. A very coarse scene took place when Mr. Hudson brought before him a plan of Mr. F. W. Beaumont, the engineer, for common road locomotives; and many more might be quoted. His temper was too apt to give way, unless he had the field wholly to himself.

His plainness of mind and speech as often verged on simplicity as on coarseness, and he ever had more respect for the man than the coat, an example more uncommon in those who have risen from the ranks than it is even among those of higher birth. He was never ashamed of his own works and of his fellow-workmen, and was most proud that he had been a working-man and not a lazy man.

After the final chapter appeared, they printed at great length a letter of correction, sent anonymously, saying that Edward Pease was the true Father of Railways and that it was 'his patronage and support that brought George Stephenson before the public'.

In all the public references to him, then and for the next few years, there was a general feeling of unforgiveness about his faults which could explain the lack of any real stars at his funeral. But what the *Derby and Chesterfield Reporter* said about him, in their final summing up, was certainly agreed by all. 'Take him for all in all, we shall not look upon his like again. Nay, we cannot, for in his sphere of invention and discovery, there cannot again be a *beginning*.'

# 16

# AFTER GEORGE

George Stephenson left £140,000, almost all of which went to Robert his only son. Robert had little need of it by then. In financial terms, Robert became wealthier than his father had ever been. Smiles at one stage talks about him as the first engineer to become a millionaire, though there is no proof that he ever had such an amount of money. Jeaffreson, Robert's biographer, says that at his height he earned £30,000 a year as an engineer. In terms of prestige, popularity and social position, Robert became better known in his lifetime than his father, which is strange, considering he is hardly known to the public today.

Robert's career had been very much tied up with George's, but he went on to specialise in different fields and they were very different in character. He was more concerned with money than George. He worried about it, losing money during Railway Mania and, worst of all, becoming involved, completely honourably, in one of the nastier railway disasters of the day, the Stanhope and Tyne fiasco. This is a long complicated saga stretching over many years which began in 1834 when Robert, as engineer of the line, agreed to take shares in the company in lieu of his £1,000 fee. In 1839, having almost forgotten such a relatively minor railway, the company went bankrupt, £400,000 in debt. Robert, through the vagaries of the company law at the time and through other people getting out well in time, turned out to be the only shareholder with any assets. He felt morally involved, despite what friends told him, and tried to save the company by personally raising £20,000. It meant realising all his own assets, which he'd spent many hard years earning, including £4,000 which he borrowed from his father. George Hudson finally came to the rescue in 1840, doing several sleights of hand with other railway companies tied up in the disaster, and eventually settled the matter. However, it had cost Robert £20,000 and it meant he had to start financially from scratch once again. It also meant he was associated, whether he liked it or not, with many of Hudson's ventures, repaying his favours.

Hudson, it has to be said, did create and amalgamate some fine railways and commission some fine constructions. He was vice-chairman of the company for which Robert built the High Level bridge over the Tyne, one of his greatest achievements. Robert, like his father, built many railways, from the six-mile long Canterbury and Whitstable line which opened in May 1830 (four months ahead of the Liverpool–Manchester, but its main power was stationary engines) to the 112-miles long London–Birmingham. But he moved on after this to specialising in bridges, for which there was an urgent demand due to the huge increase in railways. The whole problem of bridges had to be rethought, now that they were needed to carry the full weight of heavy locomotives and trains, charging across them at high speed.

The High Level Tyne bridge was opened in September 1849, by Queen Victoria. It was 1,372 feet long, resting on five great sandstone piers, contained 5,000 tons of iron and cost £243,000, and was one of the marvels of the age. It is still in full working condition today. The following year the queen opened another of Robert's bridges, this time over the Tweed, the Royal Border bridge at Berwick. The Tyne and Tweed bridges were the final links in the London–Edinburgh line and the queen, on behalf of a grateful nation, offered Robert a knighthood. He refused. No doubt he felt that as his father had declined, and as he normally bowed to his father, he must do the same.

The railway company had commissioned John Dobson, Newcastle's famous town planner, to design the station in Newcastle – still one of the handsomest stations in the country – and this too was opened by Queen Victoria in 1850. An inaugural banquet was given there, on the station platform, in honour of Robert, and his speech was absolutely typical of all his public utterances – quiet, restrained, modest, bending over backwards to thank everyone, mentioning all his assistants by name.

If you would read the biographies of all your old distinguished engineers, you would be struck with the excessive detail into which they were drawn; when intelligence was not so widely diffused as at present, an engineer like Smeaton or Brindly had not only to conceive the design, but had to invent the machines and carry out every detail of the conception; but since then a change has taken place, and no change is more complete. The principal engineer now only has to say 'Let this be done!' and it is speedily accomplished, such is the immense capital, and such the resources of mind which are immediately brought into play. I have myself, within the last ten or twelve years, done little more than exercise a general superintendence and there are many other persons here to whom the works referred to by the Chairman ought to be almost entirely attributed. I have had little or nothing to do with many of them beyond giving my name, and exercising a gentle control in some of the principal works.

Robert was also responsible for the famous rail bridge across the Menai Straits, the Britannia bridge. Telford had built his road bridge across the Menai in 1826 and his suspension bridge principle was still the only known method of achieving a large span, but where Robert was planning to cross was 1,511 feet from land to land, too long for a suspension. After many experiments with different models and materials, extensive investigations and research, Robert created what became known as tubular bridges. The bridges consisted of enormous wrought iron tubes, so large that the trains passed through them, with the tube itself providing the main supporting power. The Britannia bridge, opened in 1850, had a highly dramatic completion with sections of the iron tubes having to be floated out at high tide, leaving only an hour for them to be put in position before the tide turned and swept everything away. It was done successfully, just, though Robert himself suffered endless agonies.

Robert did other bridges on the same principle, including one across a branch of the Nile, but the most stupendous of all his tubular bridges was the one over the St Lawrence at Montreal. This had every conceivable problem, the worst being the icing up of the river for six months which threatened every year to destroy the previous year's work. The navvies sent out by Brassey and Peto got frostbite in winter and sunstroke in summer. It was designed in Robert's London office, all the ironwork was built in England and then shipped out to Canada. It was a colossal undertaking in every way, being 6,588 feet long, dwarfing all his British bridges, and it cost over £1,400,000. It was opened by the Prince of Wales, later Edward VII, in November 1859, six weeks after Robert's death.

Robert attracted world wide attention throughout all his bridge-building exploits and crowds gathered at every stage and artists did paintings of almost every pier being put in position. They were concentrated miracles, which one could take in at one view, as long as one stood well back, whereas a railway line was somehow diffuse, once the miracle of seeing a steam locomotive had been experienced. Both the public and the professions acclaimed his achievements. The section on Iron Bridges in the 8th edition of the Encyclopaedia Britannica, still produced in those days from his old university town of Edinburgh, was written by Robert Stephenson.

At the height of the drama of floating the tubes across the Menai for the Britannia bridge, Robert was joined by Brunel, who'd arrived to comfort and keep him company during the agonising wait till all had been finished. Robert, in his turn, turned out to be with his friend during the first fruitless attempts to launch Brunel's famous liner, the *Great Eastern*. Robert heard of the problems during a dinner party at home but left almost at once to go down to Blackwall where he stood with Brunel all day in deep mud and a freezing wind till the attempt was abandoned. Robert went back to bed, with inflammation of the lungs, and was seriously ill for ten days.

Throughout all the rows, over the gauge and other topics, Robert was on his father's side, but he never ceased to be a personal friend of Brunel's, even when they were direct rivals themselves for the same contracts. This endeared them both to the general and to the engineering public. 'Two nobler adversaries the world never witnessed,' said Jeaffreson.

After George's death, Robert took up his friendships with many people who had apparently left the Stephenson camp for ever. Both Joseph Locke and Vignoles gave personal testimonies on Robert's behalf at various tribunals. In 1846, while George was still alive, William James Junior wrote to Robert and other eminent engineers about a testimonial to his father. Robert signed the testimonial at the head of the list, followed by almost every other distinguished engineer of the day such as Brunel, Locke, Rennie and Vignoles. William James' daughter, E.M.S.P., prints the full list in her 1861 book. The testimonial never came before the public because, so she alleges, George was so furious when he heard that Robert had signed that he took steps to stop the whole testimonial. (All that Robert managed was a small present, sent through the Liverpool and Manchester Company.)

In October 1848, the *Mechanics' Magazine*, George's old critic, revealed the existence of the document, now that George had just died.

> This document assigns to William James that prominent place in railway history which George Stephenson was habitually fond of ascribing to himself (after the death of his precursor) and on it are subscribed the names of nearly all the most distinguished railway engineers of this railway age, including, in a foremost place, that of ROBERT STEPHENSON! Need we press the weight to be assigned to such testimony as this.

The testimonial was never resurrected. Robert presumably had thought better of it, once and for all; having upset his father in his lifetime, he didn't want to raise the controversy again. George was clear cut in all his hatreds and his likes but Robert, though basically kind and generous, worried about his actions, relationships and decisions.

Robert had every possible honour offered to him, and accepted most of them. He became MP for Whitby in 1847 and served with distinction, though he made few speeches and then mainly on engineering matters. (He pronounced the Suez Canal scheme, having travelled the whole distance on foot, to be impracticable.) In 1855 he was elected president of the Institution of Civil Engineers. The emperor of France made him a member of the Legion d'Honneur, King Leopold of the Belgians made him a knight and in Norway he got the Order of St. Olaf. At home he was an FRS and in 1857 received an honorary degree at Oxford, along with his friend Brunel and Dr David Livingstone, an impressive trio for one day's ceremony.

The saddest blow he had to bear, while still at a relatively early stage in his career, was the long illness and death of his wife Fanny. They'd had several very happy domestic years together since moving from Newcastle to their London house in Haverstock Hill. She was a strong personality, much stronger than any of George's wives, and Robert leaned on her heavily. 'She ruled her husband,' says Jeaffreson, 'without ever seeming to rule him, and was much liked by all his friends.' She was fond of social occasions and took an equal part in entertaining Robert's distinguished friends, such as Professor Wheatstone, the co-inventor of the electric telegraph. She was obviously a rather lively lady – and so was a young girl cousin of hers who stayed with them for some time. In a long, rather boring letter to one of their mutual relations Robert had said that 'we are all tolerably well at Hampstead'. She had grabbed the letter and added a much more pertinent PS.

> My dear Uncle, – Cousin Fanny would have filled up this part but she is in bed with a sick headache. Tell Mr Hardcastle Mr G. Stephenson's brother Robert is dead, the new groom has been thrown from his horse and both horse and man are at presently perfectly useless. This is what Mr Stephenson calls being tolerably well at Hampstead.

Robert always worked very hard, doing two hours' study every morning before breakfast, reading the latest scientific magazines and books. Under his wife's direction, he took an interest in poetry and collecting works of art, but scientific subjects were always his first interest. On Sundays he accompanied her to the parish church in Hampstead and in the afternoon walked with her on the Heath. Not long after they came down to London she persuaded him against his real wishes, to apply to the College of Heralds for a coat of arms. The family was traced, rather indirectly, to some Scottish Stephensons who'd once had arms and having been dished up with a crest and other garnishings, Mrs Stephenson had them painted on dishes and other objects. Jeaffreson recounts how, long after his wife's death, Robert was still regretting being pushed into such snobbery. 'Ah, I wish I hadn't adopted that foolish coat of arms,' he said, his eye chancing to fall on an object ornamented with his arms. 'Considering what a little matter it is, you could scarcely believe how often I have been annoyed by that *silly picture*.'

Perhaps if she had lived longer she might have persuaded Robert to have accepted the knighthood when offered, though by then she might have agreed that he was successful and famous enough not to need a title, compared with the days when they first arrived in London and she was trying to find a social position.

She died in October 1842, after two years of great pain, bad years for Robert anyway as he had been facing near bankruptcy through the Stanhope disaster. The bad headaches had been finally diagnosed as cancer. 'My dear Fanny died this morning at five o'clock,' wrote Robert in his diary. 'God grant that I may close my life as she has done in the true faith and in charity with all men. Her last moments were perfect calmness.' Her last request to Robert was that he should marry again. He was only thirty-eight. Fanny had been unable to have any children and it had been a great disappointment for both of them. Robert would have loved a son to take on the family concerns. He knew that his own success had given his father boundless pleasure throughout life.

Robert never remarried and instead looked for solace elsewhere, most of all in work but also in drugs. Once his wife died, he couldn't bear to remain in their Haverstock Hill house and moved almost at once to a house in town, nearer his office, at Cambridge Square, Hyde Park. He had scarcely moved all his furniture in when a fire destroyed much of the new house and he himself had a narrow escape from the flames. The drugs are never mentioned by name but one assumes it might have been opium, a popular escape used by some of the intellectual classes of the day. It could have been cocaine, which was what Sherlock Holmes injected himself with.

He was habitually careless of his health [wrote Smiles], and perhaps he indulged in narcotics to a prejudicial extent. Hence he often became 'hipped' and sometimes ill. When Mr Sopwith . . . succeeded in persuading Mr Stephenson to limit his indulgence in cigars and stimulants, the consequence was that by the end of the voyage he felt himself, as he said, 'quite a new man'. But he was of a facile, social disposition and the old associations proved too strong for him.

F. R. Condor says that very early on Robert was addicted to calomel, a form of mercury, which he took during the anxious days on the London and Birmingham. Condor was the engineer who worked with Robert and he gives several personal observations of him in his memoirs.

Robert Stephenson, in those days, almost lived on the line, and the personal appearance of that fortunate engineer is not unfamiliar to many of those whose eyes never rested on his energetic countenance, frank bearing, and falconlike glance. It is rarely that a civilian has so free and almost martial an address; it is still more rare for such features to be seen in any man who has not inherited them from a line of gently-nurtured ancestors. In the earlier days of Robert Stephenson, he charmed all who came in contact with him. Kind and considerate to his subordinates, he was not without occasional outbursts of fierce northern passion, nor always superior to prejudice. He knew how to attach people to him; he knew also how to be a firm and persistent hater. During the whole construction of the London and Birmingham line, his anxiety was as great as to lead him to very frequent recourse to the fatal aid of calomel. At the same time his sacrifice of his own rest, and indeed of necessary care of his health, was such as he would have soon destroyed a less originally fine constitution. He has been known to start on the outside of the mail, from London for Birmingham, without a great coat, and that on a cold night; and there can be little doubt that his early and lamented death was hastened by this ill-considered devotion to the service of his employers, and the establishment of his own fame.

When his fame was finally established, Robert treated himself to a yacht, his one great luxury which gave him much pleasure in his last years and was the only real sign of his millionaire status. He never had a country home preferring, as a widower with no family, the company of friends at his London club, or on his yacht. His first yacht, the *Titania*, was launched in 1850 and his second, with the same name, in 1853. She was 184 tons, ninety feet in length, and had palatial sleeping quarters. He took large parties of friends for long cruises. To keep the crew occupied, and to help a friend he once allowed it to be used for a scientific expedition. It was highly suitable for such a trip as Robert had it fitted with every scientific device.

An old school friend, a Mr Kell of Gateshead, who was a guest on one voyage, gives a very glowing description of life on board in a letter of October 1857.

My old friend and school fellow came down in his schooner yacht, Titania, with a crew of sixteen men, a good cook and a first rate cellar. We had an ample supply of astronomic and mathematical instruments and one person on board, at least, knew how to use them. We made repeated observations at one place in Loch Ness at a depth of 170 fathoms. . . . At Hollyhead, we devoted a day to the Britannia Bridge. Judge Keogh gave us some amusing reminiscences of his discussions in the smoking-room with Bright, Cobden, Stephenson and other friends from both sides of the house. There was a capital library on board, and a gimbal lamp at each bed head and each man before going to bed selected a book. At seven in the morning a cup of coffee was served in bed to each man, who then read or snoozed till nine; when the decks having been washed, the brass hand-rails and passages all cleaned, he dressed and came on deck.

Robert felt free from his business worries once on board, from meetings and from people queuing up to see him. 'I find nothing gives me actual freedom from attack but getting out of the way of the postman. The sea is my only alternative. Ships have no knockers.'

He frequently took guests round home waters as well as the Mediterranean. Going round the north of Scotland he would point out places he'd visited on expeditions as a student at Edinburgh. Round Wales he would sail past the Menai bridge and go over the drama of its construction. Sailing down the east coast of England he would stop at Sunderland, perhaps going ashore to retrace old steps.

On one occasion he took his guests to visit Wylam, as his father before had done, and to Killingworth to look at the sundial and then round Newcastle. When he heard that the Newcastle Literary and Philosophical Institute, scene of his boyhood studies, was £6,200 in debt he paid half the sum on condition that they lowered their subscription from two guineas to one. This grand gesture might indicate that he was all for educating the poor and underprivileged but from his House of Commons speeches he appears highly reactionary, opposing the education reforms of Lord John Russell. 'It is all nonsense Lord John preaching education for the working classes. What the artisan wants is special education for his own particular speciality.' Brunel was even more extreme, declaring that he preferred his enginemen illiterate as it stopped their minds wandering from the job in hand.

While in London, Robert's favourite clubs were the Athenaeum and, being a strong if independent Tory, the Carlton Club. He was also active at the Geographical Society and the Royal Society Club. His last visit to the latter was in August 1859 when he had dinner with Rowland Hill.

Robert's last long voyage was at the end of 1858 when he went on his yacht with a few friends to Egypt as a guest of the Pasha, grateful for his bridge work on the Nile and for the railway he'd built from Alexandria to Cairo in 1856. They took their time getting there, stopping at Malaga, Algiers and Malta. In Cairo he met up with his old friend Brunel who was on holiday and, despite poor health, rushing round the town on a donkey. The two of them had Christmas dinner at the Hotel d'Orient, Cairo, in 1858, the last time the two great engineers of the Victorian age dined together.

On his return, Robert's health grew worse. He hated going home to his large house in the evening, always lingering in his club, always wanting 'a little more talk and just another cigar'. His spacious home was hung with fine paintings by Lucas and Landseer, furnished with marbles he'd purchased from the Great Exhibition, but his memories were all in the past. 'It is the Robert Stephenson of Greenfield Place [Newcastle] that I am most proud to think of,' he told a lady visitor who complimented him on his London house.

Jeaffreson says that his natural good temper had begun to give way to a 'passing peevishness and irritability on trivial provocations'. Those who knew him put it down to bad health. 'Few suspected how he struggled against melancholy and how he looked forward to death. The quiet of his house, when it was without guests, he could not endure. Often he walked about the lonely rooms and sat down to yield to sorrow which in the presence of others he courageously suppressed.'

In a photograph of Robert, taken towards the end of his life, one can see how tired and aged he looked, his eyes baggy, his brows furrowed. His father was at least spared the indignity of being photographed.

Brunel died in September 1859, and Robert followed him a matter of days later, dying at his home in Gloucester Square on 12 October 1859, four days before his fifty-sixth birthday. It was said at the time that never before had the death of a private person struck so deeply into the feelings of the country. He was given the ultimate honour, for a British subject, of being buried in Westminster Abbey. The queen expressed her personal regrets and in consideration of Robert's 'world wide fame' and 'the country's great loss' she gave permission for his funeral cortege to pass through Hyde Park to the abbey, another unusual honour, never before given to someone not a member of the royal family, let alone a commoner. It was almost as if the Establishment were putting old George in his place once and for all, accentuating by comparison the humbleness of his provincial burial, or perhaps it was the nation making up for it, turning on the pomp and circumstance to mark the end of the Stephensons. Whatever any subconscious reasons, the funeral became a public occasion. Everyone of any note, in politics and science and society, crowded into the abbey – two thousand tickets were issued but three thousand people crammed in – and the entire route was lined with silent worshippers. Joseph Locke, the old rival of George's, and now president of the Institution of Civil Engineers, was one of the distinguished pall bearers. On the Thames, Tyne, Wear and Tees, shipping lay silent with flags at half mast. Throughout Tyneside, all business ceased at midday and the fifteen hundred employees of Robert Stephenson and Company marched silent through the streets to a memorial service at St Nicholas.

When his will was proved, Robert was found to have left just over £400,000. Most of it went in legacies to his engineering friends and colleagues, to his relations, and to worthy institutions, particularly in Newcastle, such as £10,000 to the Royal Infirmary and £7,000 to the Lit. and Phil. There was one bequest of £2,000 which, rather surprisingly, considering his lack of interest in the church, went to something called The Society for Providing Additional Curates in Populous Places.

His grand funeral was doubtless seen as the end of an era, coming as it did so quickly after the death of Brunel, but in comparing it with George's more modest final rites it has to be emphasised that Robert was a national figure and was genuinely loved by all his contemporaries. A public testimonial had been raised for Robert as early as 1839, £1,250 being subscribed in a matter of days. (And George Hudson wasn't even on the committee.) George Stephenson's own testimonial came much later.

Jeaffreson explains the difference in popularity between them as being a matter of north and south.

The fine old man, whose kindest teacher had been adversity, was not duly appreciated in the metropolis. His manners were rugged and far from prepossessing and his personal connections were for the most part in his 'old country'. For one inhabitant of London who visited the Liverpool and Manchester line, ninety nine were familiar with the works of the London and Birmingham Railways. It is therefore easy to account for the fact that the Father of the Railways system saw his son publicly honoured whilst he himself had been comparatively unnoticed.

Robert had complete universal acclaim in his lifetime, though he would no doubt have preferred a more humble domestic happiness. His acclaim was justified, but it is an acclaim which is now almost totally forgotten. George, however, came into his own not long after his son's death.

It took about ten years, after Robert himself had died, before the George Stephenson industry moved into full force, and it was probably Samuel Smiles who gave it the first big push. His 1857 biography was an instant success with the public. It came out eventually as part of his series on the lives of the great engineers, The Life of George Stephenson being volume 3. (The first two volumes included the lives of Sir Cornelius Vermuyden and Sir Hugh Middleton who presumably must have been known to at least some Victorians.) Smiles travelled extensively for his Stephenson book, going back to Wylam to interview old school friends, old associates like Edward Pease and old friends like John Dixon. He didn't interview Nicholas Wood because Wood demanded a present worth £3,000. (Wood's information, says Smiles in his own autobiography, 'was not worth 3,000 farthings'.) Robert Stephenson had been surprised at the idea of a biography, saying that nobody in the literary world would be interested, but he gave every assistance, read the manuscript and added a weighty and lengthy appendix on the state of the railway system in 1857.

The book was obviously greatly influenced by Robert, unwittingly or not. When he sent a bundle of letters about William James to Smiles he added a covering note.

There is a bundle of James's which characterise the man very clearly as a ready, dashing writer but no thinker at all on the practical part of the subject he had taken up. It was the same with everything he touched. He never succeeded in anything and yet possessed a great deal of taking talent. His fluency of conversation I never heard equalled, and so you would judge from his letters.

Smiles produced a comprehensive piece of journalism, over five hundred tightly packed pages, and it was immediately attacked by some of George's old rivals for being a white wash, painting a glowing account of his character and giving the Stephenson side on almost every technical issue. The public, however, loved it and it was reprinted many times and sold one hundred thousand copies by the end of the century. It appeared in several guises including an abridged version called *The Story of the Life of George Stephenson*. The facts of George's rise to fame, his perseverance and self-help were irrefutable but Smiles made the most of them to prove his own philosophy of life which he outlined in his even more successful book *Self Help*. This had been turned down before he wrote the Stephenson book but his publisher now jumped at it and it sold 250,000 copies, becoming a moral bible for the Victorian age.

The Band of Hope was one of the first organisations to see the moral appeal of George's life and they were issuing potted histories of his life and hard times at a penny a sheet from 1859. One of the most popular paintings in Victorian times shows George as part of a beautiful family group. It still sells well today – the Science Museum has post cards of it – but it is a completely false picture as hardly any of the people were alive together at the same time in real life. Little Fanny, who died at three weeks, is shown looking about five years old, standing with her mother, who also died young, with George's next wife, his mother, his father and Robert as an adult, all of them striking suitably lyrical but impossible poses.

So great was George's new-found popularity, now that everyone knew the full and wonderful story, that there was a movement to have his remains removed from the little church in Chesterfield to Westminster Abbey. This so incensed William James' daughter that it appears to have been the main reason why she published her vitriolic attack on him in 1861. His body, however, was not removed.

The various subscriptions, and talks of subscriptions, which had occurred just after his death, all came to life again in the 1860s, having either fizzled out or disappeared. A handsome statue of George, which had been talked about immediately after his death, was finally erected in Newcastle in 1862, almost outside the Literary and Philosophical Society, not far from the High Level Bridge. In Chesterfield, they didn't get their memorial completed until 1879 but it too was suitably handsome – a large red brick building in the centre of the town, the Stephenson Memorial Hall. An appeal had been launched for some sort of memorial twenty years previously, to build a home for miners, but had failed. This time the subscription list was terribly impressive, headed by the Duke of Devonshire (£500) and the Duke of Rutland (£100). It included George's former secretary, F. Swanwick (£100), who still lived in the area.

Combined with the sudden rush of national affection for George was an increasing awareness that the railway, which many people still alive had first seen appearing with some trepidation, was a great British invention, just one more sign that Victorian England ruled the waves. When railway anniversaries started cropping up, they were seen as great excuses for national celebrations, for steam and for George, Father of it all.

The first railway anniversary was in 1875, the Jubilee of the Stockton and Darlington. The North Eastern Railway, which had taken over the Stockton and Darlington in 1863 (the S & D being worth at that time £4 million) contributed £5,000 towards the celebrations and Darlington Corporation a further £1,000. As Jeans said in his 1875 history of the Stockton and Darlington, which came out to mark the jubilee, it was a problem knowing exactly what to do. 'A railway jubilee is an event of character so unique that there is no precedent to guide those who are concerned in its celebration.'

The problem was solved by unveiling a statue to Joseph Pease, and presenting a portrait of the said Joseph Pease. Mr Henry Pease, whose idea it was to have a jubilee celebration, served on a committee which contained Mr W. R. Pease, Mr J. W. Pease, Mr A. Pease and Mr H. F. Pease. There wasn't a Stephenson in sight. Pride of place in an exhibition of old engines was *Locomotion* number one which had continued running strong from the opening day in 1825 until 1850, when it went into Mr Joseph

Pease's collieries for seven years before ending up on a pedestal opposite Darlington Railway Station.

Over a thousand VIP visitors were invited, including bishops, lords and members of the cabinet and on Monday 27 September 1875, they were fêted in a large tent erected specially in a cricket field, there being no hall in Darlington big enough for such an assembly. 'The banquet will be purveyed,' so the announcements said, 'by King and Brymes (late Birch and Birch) who purvey the Lord Mayor's banquets at the Guildhall.'

For the ordinary populace there were fireworks, processions, displays, and for the children of the town a tea party in the marquee, two days after the VIPs. Special trains ran from King's Cross and there were specials to Darlington from all over the north east. Thousands of handbills about the jubilee celebrations were printed which can still be bought at most railway enthusiasts shops for only a pound or two.

The Peases and their Quaker friends had always dominated the town of Darlington so it wasn't surprising that they should still be so prominent. Edward came from a large family, had eight children himself and Joseph, his eldest son, in turn had eight children. They were everywhere and they seemed to live for ever. Old Edward Pease, who'd come to George's funeral despite his years, had many more years to go. He was fit and well when Samuel Smiles came to interview him in 1854, at the age of eighty-eight. He'd had a few qualms over the years, wondering what sort of monster he'd brought into the world, but Smiles must have convinced him he'd done a great job, according to what he wrote in his diary.

*Fri.*, *Oct. 20* – S. Smiles was with me to obtain particulars for a memoir of the life of George Stephenson. It appears to me that Railways will be a favour to the world, and I do not regret, but far otherwise, that my time, care and attention was so closely occupied for many months. Except with the help of a faithful secretary, R. Oxley, the care and charge of providing all materials and all the costs for the waymen's wages rested on me. If I have been in any way made a humble instrument of use in the creation, all the praise, and I render it, is due to my God.

Three days later, Robert Stephenson came to see him:

*Mon, Oct. 23* – My friend, Robert Stephenson the engineer, to spend two or three days with me – a man of most highly gifted and talented power of mind, of benevolent, liberal, kindly, just, generous dispositions, in company most interesting. My dear Sons John and Henry dined with me. At tea at my son Joseph's, a considerable and interesting company. At home to sup, and after it some social interesting subject occupied us to near eleven.

The evening pleasantly spent nearly alone, expressing to Robert Stephenson my anxious desire that smoking and taking wine might be carefully limited. Oh my soul, be upon the watch.

One of the aspects that worried Edward about railways was how much he himself had made, even though he could console himself by remembering that he'd simply been trying to help young Robert.

*Dec 28, 1848* – . . . Pecuniarily, I have cause to admire how an effort to serve a worthy youth, Robert, the son of George Stephenson, by a loan of £500, at first without expectation of much remuneration, has turned to my great advantage. During the course of the year I have received £7,000 from the concern at Forth Street.

It will be remembered that Edward Pease put £1,600 into Robert Stephenson and Company in 1823 (apart from helping Robert with his own stake). Receiving £7,000 annually after twenty-five years for an investment of £1,600 is certainly pecuniary.

In 1857 there was a movement in Darlington to have a testimonial to Edward Pease and to erect a statue in his name but he categorically refused to allow it. He died the next year, aged ninety-one. Joseph Pease, his son, had long since been the controlling influence in the Pease railway, colliery and banking concerns which had by now grown to an enormous size, mainly thanks to Joseph himself who wasn't as guilt ridden about money as his father. In 1830 Joseph had bought up enough local collieries to be known as the largest colliery owner in the whole of the South Durham coalfield. The S & D had similarly expanded, though it soon had competition from Hudson to face, but perhaps Joseph's most inspired investment was to buy five hundred acres of swamp land lower down the Tees in 1829. He saw this as a better site for a port than Stockton and also as an ideal site for new iron smelting works, using the recently discovered Cleveland iron mines. This swamp, which he got for a few pounds an acre, is now Middlesbrough, still one of the most important iron and steel towns in the country.

In 1832, Joseph Pease entered parliament, becoming the first Quaker MP. MPs previously had to take an oath to the Established Church but Joseph was now allowed to affirm. He still retained other Quaker ways, never taking his hat off when entering the House of Commons (instead an alert door-keeper always took it off for him, thus solving the problem). His son Joseph Whitwell Pease (later Sir Joseph) was also an MP for many years. There is a story told in the Pease family of the time in the Commons cloakroom when he put his hand in his coat pocket and found a gun. The Quakers, of course, were against all firearms. The mystery was solved when he discovered he'd picked up the wrong coat. The House of Commons coat pegs were in alphabetical order and next to him was Parnell.

Joseph Pease died in 1872 and Henry, his younger brother, became the leading Pease and the inspiration of the jubilee celebrations. He too became an MP and carried on his father's tradition of beseeching world leaders to give up war. In 1853 he went to Russia and had a long interview with the tzar and then to Paris where he saw the emperor.

The Peases kept up their expansion in business, helped by their relations the Barclays and other bankers, and in politics. By the end of the century there had been ten MPs in the family and not long afterwards their total in the Lords went up to three – Lord Gainford, Lord Daryngton, Lord Wardington. They also managed three baronets. The family is going strong to this day, many of them still in the City, though few of them are now Quakers.

The Stephensons, by comparison, have almost disappeared. They had no more distinguished members after Robert, the last and only member of his father's line. There were many cousins and they were active in Robert Stephenson and Company for many years but none became public figures. Robert Stephenson and Company eventually moved their works to Darlington and were finally taken over by larger combines. Today they are lost in GEC.

George Stephenson, meanwhile, kept marching on, in fact and in fiction. For the centenary of his birth in 1881 over fifteen thousand people turned up at a festival in his honour at the Crystal Palace. Belgium sent a large deputation and in every foreign country where George or Robert had sent locomotives or built a railway some form of commemoration took place. In Rome, the station was bedecked with flowers and the Italian papers contained potted histories of George, most of them based on Smiles. In Germany there were long editorials, One of them likening his deeds to those of Napoleon and Bismarck. In England there were fireworks and processions in all the main towns and railway commercialisation, which had first raised its tentative head at Liverpool in 1830, erupted in a flood of sheets, posters, books, poems, mugs, plates and other suitable or unsuitable objects. Many books came out to mark the event and there was even a book brought out in 1886, edited by William Duncan, which contained reports of all the 1881 George Stephenson celebrations up and down the country.

In recent decades there has been a lessening of public interest in George Stephenson, though Chesterfield did remember the centenary of his death in 1948 with a buffet tea. The 1975 celebrations for the 150th anniversary of the Stockton and Darlington Railway did do a lot to revive interest in George himself. Smiles made him into a Victorian legend and today the Victorians and their legends are back in favour.

His face and his engines often appear on railway medals and stamps abroad, when they are celebrating some anniversary, but many countries have their own pioneer engineers and their own railway sagas which are taught to children at school, forgetting that many of their railways, if not their engines, owed their inspiration to George. In Britain, every child does learn the name of George Stephenson but even educated adults soon forget what exactly it was he did, thinking perhaps he was the one who watched the kettle boil or wrote *Kidnapped*.

In the engineering and railway worlds his works are of course still well known to everyone, and they still argue about where he got his tubular boiler from. But, as ever, it is his engines and railways which have been constantly analysed and argued about at length rather than Stephenson the man.

Professor Jack Simmons of Leicester University, the leading academic in the field, says that before the war there was a slight period of debunking of the Stephenson legend. Railway writers, tired of the perfect picture of him as painted by Smiles, began to find a few warts. L.T.C. Rolt, with his theory about the relationship with William James, even if that particular row now can't be proved, was one of the first not to treat George as a plaster figure in a glass case.

'There are many things we still don't know about George Stephenson, as a person and as an engineer,' says Professor Simmons. 'I would like to know much more about the early days at Killingworth, from about 1814 onwards. He'd done so much by the time 1820 came, and he became involved in the Stockton and Darlington line, yet so little is known about it.

'There is also something strange about the way he seemed to give up railways around 1845. Something appears to have snapped in him. It was the height of the mania, yet he kept out of it. Something made him withdraw and I think whatever it was happened around 1842–3. Perhaps he was worried by Hudson's success, jealous of Robert even, or perhaps he just physically suddenly aged and decided to retire? I've never seen anyone attempt an explanation.

'We know him best from the late twenties and by then he was rather overbearing and arrogant, though it was understandable, when you know what went before. I think the incident of the Safety Lamp resolved him not to let such a thing happen again, to make sure he always got the credit where it was due and not give it to others.

'He did become a megalomaniac. You should have a look at what he said to the people of Sheffield in 1836. He was unscrupulous in attacking his opponents' plans. He told Sheffield that unless they did things his way they would be excluded for ever from Railways! He did get rather carried away at times.

'By the time we know him best, when he was rich and famous, his mind had set. His experiences had been learned a long time ago and he could be inflexible. He never quite got over his early triumphs. He was out of his depth when he got into any arguments with other people, such as the Parliamentary débâcle. He went harsh and rigid when opposed or when the situation got out of hand. He had created railways on his own and he naturally felt self-important. He was the perfect self-made man and he displayed all the classic self-made-man patterns. He was jealous and afraid of others. He was not a generous man, that is very clear.

All these faults are understandable. Smiles completely hid them, yet they are to be expected in such a man who's faced the struggles he'd faced.

'It's good that his character is now being filled out more, after all these years. The attacks on him by the professional engineers, which happened from the very beginning, have proved very little. There had been rival claims made by many other people for many of his successes. Most of them are nonsense. Nobody can pretend that George Stephenson was other than he was – the pioneer of railways.'

# Postscript:

# THE GEORGE STEPHENSON TOUR

The end of steam came to Britain in 1968. Overnight, everything to do with steam became an art form. As an art form, railway mania is one of the world's growing pastimes. The nostalgia, and the prices, appear to be limitless. In Britain alone there are estimated to be two million railway enthusiasts who will buy or read or watch almost anything to do with their particular passion from the age of steam.

There are many places and objects associated with George Stephenson which can be seen today – some fascinating, some not worth the visit. True Stephenson pilgrims will go round them all. The layman might simply be interested in knowing what happened after George moved on.

WYLAM ON TYNE

George would be surprised to see his birthplace today. The industrial revolution has not left Wylam a wreck, as one might imagine, but a rather quaint country village with stone built cottages and some smart new desirable detached residences occupied by people like Tyne Tees TV executives who commute into Newcastle, nine miles further down the Tyne. As long as you stand with your back to the direction of Newcastle and its suburbs, which are moving steadily west every year, you can see gently rolling hills and a pretty river valley. The pits and ironworks have gone and George's cottage now stands in rural seclusion about half a mile east of the village. You get to it along the river banks, following a path out of Wylam village, past a notice saying 'University of Newcastle, Private Fishing'. The cottage is set back slightly from the river bank, right beside the overgrown relics of the old North Eastern Railway line. There are several Victorian railway notices still standing *in situ*, the sort which can cost £50 a time from the sharper London antique stalls.

It's quite a handsome cottage, bigger than I'd expected, and in good condition, though of course in George's day, he and his family occupied only one room. A plaque over the door states that this is George Stephenson's birthplace, but most of the wordage is taken up with the names of long forgotten councillors who put up the plaque. The cottage was bought by the North East Coast Institute of Engineers and handed over to the National Trust in 1948. The present curator (Mrs Stephenson – no relation) welcomes visitors from April to the end of September who want to see round the house. Ring 0191 200 7146. She also does teas.

KILLINGWORTH

Killingworth is no longer a colliery village but it's far from rural. It's a new industrial estate with very little character, part of Newcastle's northern sprawl. Stephenson's cottage, Dial Cottage in Great Lime Road, stands out like an antique at Woolworths, a beautiful white-washed cottage in sparkling condition, obviously lovingly cared for. At the front is the famous sundial, put up by Robert and his father. Over the front door is a plaque which reads 'George Stephenson, Engineer, Inventor of the locomotive engine, lived in this house, 1805–1823.' William James' daughter would have had apoplexy.

When I called in 1975, the owner, a Mr Cook, came to the front door in carpet slippers and invited me in. He turned off his colour TV, much to his son's displeasure, and made me sit down. He's a Mancunian who retired to Newcastle some years ago after working locally as a traveller for a knitwear firm. He said he had to be called Cappy and wouldn't reveal his real christian name. 'Even my wife calls me Cappy. Cappy Cook of course!'

He saw the house advertised for £4,500 in the *Evening Chronicle* in 1961. As a railway enthusiast he was immediately interested and offered £3,600, but expected that the council or some such body would offer more and open it to the public. 'I still don't know why they didn't. Perhaps one day when I'm gone it might be open to the public.'

As it is, the public are constantly traipsing to his front door. 'What I can't stand are the nosey buggers who just peer through the windows, thinking it's a museum. If they knock and ask and seem genuinely interested, I let them in. I had a man from California last week. He was in London on business but broke his journey to come all the way up here to look at this cottage. I've had Dutch, Japanese, Germans, Yankees, all sorts. The other day I had two Australians waken me up at 11.30 at night.

'I get regulars coming every year. The Duke of Wellington's butler, he's been coming for years. He worked for the previous Duke, not the present one. He's getting on now. He's a Henderson and tells me he's related to Fanny, George's first wife.'

He's done a lot of work modernising the cottage and filled it with his own railway knick-knacks, such as a model of the *Rocket* which actually works. 'I don't know who put the plaque up. I've looked in all the books. It should of course be pioneer, not inventor. George himself started off in just this end of the cottage, but as he got on he enlarged it himself and took over the rest. This is the room in which he nearly blew himself up when he was experimenting with his safety lamp.

'I try and keep the cottage as nice as possible. The previous owner told me that the council was going to bulldoze it down at one stage. Can you believe it? They did that to Robert's old house in Newcastle. A friend of mine got the scraper from the front step.

'What I can't understand is why no one's never written a play about George. His life would make a great film. They've made films of some dafter people who did nothing at all in their lives.

'He was probably not as nice as he's usually made out. I've a suspicion he was a dogmatic old bugger, pretty bad tempered I shouldn't wonder.'

NEWBURN

Newburn Church, where George was twice married, is still there, just off the west road out of Newcastle. It's a well-known Tyneside church with a handsome Norman tower, Saxon additions and contains many stones from Hadrian's Wall. It has associations with the Delaval family and with William Hedley, the *Puffing Billy* engineer, engineer at Wylam Colliery and one of the many locomotive pioneers who paved the way for George Stephenson. Hedley was a benefactor of the church and there's a window in the south aisle in his memory – but no mementoes of George, apart from his signatures in the church register.

The church doesn't boast about its Stephenson connection –

there's only a passing reference to him in the official history of the church – and doesn't attract many railway visitors. They would find it hard to get in anyway as the church is always locked to protect it from vandals, a sad situation for such an architecturally interesting building, especially as it is extensively written about in Pevsner's book on the buildings of Northumberland. The vicar didn't have a key – he was new and had only just arrived in the district – but I tracked down the church warden, Thomas Gillespy, who was very helpful.

In George's day, so the church warden said, the church came under the Bishop of Carlisle, who appointed the vicars. It wasn't until 1882 that the diocese of Newcastle was created, St Nicholas' Church in Newcastle being promoted to a cathedral. He brought out the church's marriage registers, which go back to 1665, and looked up George's two marriages. He agreed George's signature on his first marriage was rather rough and childlike but refuted any suggestion that George could in any sense be classed as illiterate.

'He went to night classes when he was grown up, to a man in Walbottle. My grandmother went to the same man and she always said he was very good.'

NEWCASTLE
There are several original letters and documents by and relating to George and Robert at Newcastle's Central Library, in their local history room, and out at the Northumberland County Records Office in North Gosforth. The latter also has the manuscript of Nicholas Wood's notes taken at the Rainhill trials.

The Central Station, where Robert was fêted, is as imposing as ever, having recently been cleaned up. Not far away in Neville Street is the statue of George, dressed for some reason like a Greek, the one erected by the city fathers in 1862. The Lit. and Phil., also nearby, is still going strong and its subscription fee hasn't gone up by very much since George enrolled Robert a hundred and sixty years ago. He paid three guineas a year. They have one of his first safety lamps in a glass cage and copies of the reports and newspaper cuttings about the safety lamp row.

While in Newcastle in 1975, I went to see the chairman of the North Eastern branch of the Stephenson Locomotive Society. The SLS, as it's known to all fans, was founded in 1909 and is the oldest railway society in the world. (A boast worth making when you consider that there are 900 different railway societies.) It was not named directly after George Stephenson but after a locomotive called *Stephenson* which used to run on the London, Brighton and South Coast line. The society was begun in Croydon by seven enthusiasts to encourage a love for railways.

It had almost thirty branches throughout the country and many in Europe and America. Each branch had its monthly meetings, dinners and endless trips for members and friends to look at old locomotives, sheds, stations, signal boxes, and anything else to do with railways. There was a monthly magazine, usually about thirty-two pages thick, which carried the society's news plus irate letters from members who are incensed by terrible mistakes made by other members, such as labelling 'The Merchant Venturer as leaving Box Tunnel whereas it is clearly emerging from Middle Hill Tunnel.'

The chairman of the North Eastern branch was a retired Newcastle jeweller called Leslie Charlton. He and about thirty local members met once a month at the Central Station. They don't hang around the platforms but congregate in room 36, one of British Rail's staff meeting rooms, to watch slides of old engines and other excitements.

Despite the intensity of their printed words when they take each other to task in their journals, railway enthusiasts are very gentle, warm-hearted people. Some groups of enthusiasts are suspicious of the outside world, turning themselves into cold cliques, but railway fans, treated kindly, fall over themselves to be helpful, absolutely confident that the passion which has taken over their lives will soon dominate yours. They're almost messianic in their fervour, desperate for converts, seizing any chance to spread the good word.

Mr Charlton dropped everything when I called on him, though I'd arrived out of the blue with no advance warning. He rang his son, a commercial traveller and railway enthusiast, who rushed round by car and offered to take me to Killingworth to look at where the colliery used to be. It took a long time to get there, and back, because they each got so carried away with telling me about their love for railways that they kept on stopping the car so they could tell me face to face and enthuse all the better.

Mr Charlton senior explained that his speciality has always been works locos – the engines owned by private companies.

'Most enthusiasts have always liked the locos that pulled the passenger trains best, but now they're all dashing round trying to photograph the old works that I photographed years ago. There aren't many passenger locos left these days so they're turning to works locos before they get broken up.'

The biggest new development amongst railway fans, I gathered, is stereo. LP records of railway noises have been selling in their thousands for years but now with stereo, members compete to produce the most deafening effects.

'I've got one friend,' said Mr Charlton, 'who's extended his lounge so that it's now twenty-four feet long, just to improve his stereo. He puts on the Big Boys, like old *Ohio* and *Baltimore* locos, and you should hear them! They start quietly in one end of his lounge, in the distance, then they get louder and louder till they tear right over you!'

The car was stopped again so they could both savour the memory of it all. Not just the memory. They continually talked in the present tense about steam.

'Steam's live, that's the attraction. That's what we love about it. You feel you can do anything with steam, if you understand it. You've got to understand steam.

'You work together to control it, to get the best out of it. Your fireman could ditch you by putting on too much or too little. If you were driving, you could kill him by going too hard at the wrong time. It takes two people, a partnership, to get the best out of steam, to get to the heart of its power. When two people are working in harmony with steam, you can do anything. Now diesel, huh. One man turns it on, and that's all there is to it.'

'What I like about steam is its smell,' said his son. 'That's the biggest attraction to me. It's a sort of hot, oily smell. Not the sort of oil smell you get from that stuff you put in the car. This is real oil. It was a most peculiar scent.' They sat breathing in heavily, remembering long forgotten whiffs.

Today, the Stephenson Locomotive Society has 600 members. Meetings are held in twelve centres around the country, and they still have a magazine, now published monthly. The General Secretary is Brian Gilliam (telephone 020 8501 1210).

LONDON

London, as ever, has most of the good things in life and much of George Stephenson's life has ended up there.

The Institution of Mechanical Engineers has to be the first stop, just to see how they remember their first president. I expected a dusty old office run by a man and a Smike-like boy trying hard to keep alive the spirit of steam. The organisation sounds so Victorian and artisan whereas the Institution of Civil Engineers, the one which was so much smarter and snobbier in Stephenson's day, would seem to have a better chance of being up to date and relevant. Civil engineers means roads and bridges, motorways and flyovers. Mechanicals means machines and makes you think of blue overalled mechanics and fitters.

Their headquarters is at 1, Birdcage Walk, a smart address at least, beside Horse Guard's Parade, just round the corner from Whitehall, very handy for Buckingham Palace. (I imagined a couple of rooms stuck away at the back of someone else's building.) It turned out to be the handsomest, poshest building in sight, one I'd passed many times thinking it must be part of the Foreign Office. And the Mechanicals own all of it. As a site it must be worth millions of pounds. Inside, it oozes quiet affluence with massive carved staircases and corridors, thick carpets and antique furniture, uniformed lackeys hovering discreetly to direct the bustling business men who've flown in from all over the world, come to meet in one of the many committee rooms. There's a staff of 180 and a membership of 80,000, *all* of them very far from blue collar workmen.

Mechanical engineers are still basically occupied with machines. Steam just happens to be the first ever mechanical means of transport. After that came the motor car, the aeroplane, the jet engine, the hovercraft and now the space ship – all of them created by mechanical engineers. But transport is only one of the many branches of mechanical engineering. The institution has departments for energy, environment and sustainability, mechatronics, medical engineering, tribology, power industries, pressure systems – anything in fact where a machine of some sort is used. They have just started to allow membership to incorporated engineers, i.e. 'technician' grades. They get very upset when the papers talk about 'engineers on strike again' when what is meant is fitters. To be even the humblest novice member of the Institution of Mechanical Engineers you have to be a graduate or hold an acceptable diploma in some aspect of mechanical engineering. To be a Member with a capital letter, and therefore allowed to put M.I.Mech.E. after your name, you have to be an established engineer holding a position of authority. When you've really made it, or as their guide book says, 'when you are a well established mechanical engineer holding a post of greater responsibility', then you might be elected a Fellow and allowed to change your visiting card to F.I.Mech.E.

The institution is a professional body, looking after the rights and interests of its members. Until recently it set its own examinations, but now a general council of all engineers looks after that. But it does guard its prestige very carefully, investigating at least two bogus claims a week from scoundrels masquerading as M.I.Mech.E. George Stephenson would certainly never have got in today.

However, they're still highly pleased with their first president. There are Stephenson relics and references all over the place. Members can buy an institution tie inscribed with the *Rocket* motif. There's the Stephenson room, used for committee meetings, which is festooned with Stephenson memorabilia, drawings and paintings, patents taken out by him, a paper knife used by the great man, his brass rule, a watch. They have his will framed and hung up for all to see, and a desk arranged as it was at Great George Street, plus various specifications and drawings thought to be in his hand. (Graphic panels explain his work and its importance).

The institution's library has the greatest surviving collection of letters relating to Stephenson, either gifts from collectors and families over the years or purchases which the institution itself has made, either privately or at auction at places like Sotheby's. One of the librarians pointed to a portrait of one benefactor who in the 1930s gave the institution a present of £100,000. In another corner he pointed out a solid silver replica of the *Rocket* – the only known model made in silver – and worth a small fortune.

All Stephenson documents are accessible via the institution's website. Like the vast majority of Stephenson letters, they were dictated to secretaries and refer to purely railway business. But the Phillimore collection does include George's bank pass book and a cheque for £72 16s 3d, both from the Glyn Hallifax Mills bank. In a collection of letters and documents called the Crow Collection I found a shirt collar which once belonged to Stephenson, folded flat and arranged in a plastic folder like one of the letters. It's signed by him, presumably for laundry purposes. If only collars could speak.

The Institution of Civil Engineers is round the corner in Great George Street, the street where Robert and George had their London office, and is an equally imposing building and an equally thriving professional organisation.

The Civils have never quite forgiven Smiles for that story about them turning George Stephenson down for being unqualified. As late as 1956 they were still worrying about it, judging by a publication they produced that year called A *Study of an Alleged Slight*. It refutes once and for all the charge that they thwarted his desire to be a member, saying that such a story about such a great national figure can be 'little more than a tax on the reader's powers of credulity'.

They have a handful of letters by George and Robert (one from Robert to Brunel) but perhaps their most interesting Stephenson relic is a scrap album which George compiled. It contains newspaper cuttings that took George's fancy and show his wide and rather esoteric range of interests. The subjects include: Hawkes's Newly Invented Portable Cockle for Hot Air Beds; Purity of Flours; Witchcraft; Divorce in France; Sir Walter Scott; Wings of Insects; Interesting Anecdote of a Cat; Piracy; Brazilian Diamonds; Advice to Young Ladies; The Jewish New Year; Curious Musical Instruments; Goat's Milk at Lisbon; Paganini's Departure from Dublin; Gretna Green Marriages; Opening a Mummy. Newspapers today see very tame by comparison.

The most extensive collection of railway documents are in the British Transport Historical Records, now cared for by the Public Record Office at Kew.

They have the official documents, minute books, plans and other materials of more than 1,000 railway companies, all arranged on more than 15,000 feet of shelf space. They're immaculately preserved and catalogued and open to the public (once you have applied for a reader's ticket), though a great many people are not fully aware that they exist. Many railway enthusiasts haven't quite realised that the government, in the shape of the Public Record Office, is now the guardian of British Rail's history.

They are particularly strong on Robert Stephenson, having seventy letters written by him, plus documents about Robert Stephenson and Company. Their original material on George is limited, though they have six letters from him and the records of all the companies he worked for.

The officer in charge when I called was Derek Barlow, author of the standard biography of Dick Turpin, currently working on a history of London banyos, the eighteenth-century gentlemen's bath houses, many of which were also brothels. He was born in Darlington and collected engine numbers as a boy. 'You'd hear the noise first, feel the rail shimmering, then see the smoke, inhale the smoke and with a woosh, the great monster would be bearing down upon you. My goodness, it was terribly exciting. I can understand the fascination of all trains, even today's rather grubby, impersonal diesel engines. You can see and feel an irresistible force. You don't have to be Freudian to say it's sexual.'

The mecca for all railway fans of every age is the Science Museum in South Kensington. It's a child's delight but must be an attendant's nightmare. Everything is so invitingly displayed, great hulking engines and trams and machines, stretching up to the ceiling, and all of it welcoming you to climb or clamber over, to press buttons and start machines and models. It's always crowded with kids, many of the bigger ones treating it as an adventure playground, running round in hordes, fighting behind machines, trying to light cigarettes, till the keepers grab them.

The *Rocket*, their most famous single railway exhibit, isn't as big an attraction as one might expect. Most casual visitors pass it by. It looks rather small, black and ugly, not painted up the way it was at Rainhill. Surrounded by much bigger, more glamorous machines, both steam and electric, *Rocket* seems dwarfed and rather left behind.

The *Rocket* ran successfully on the Liverpool–Manchester line until 1836 when it was bought for £300 by James Thompson of Kirkhouse, near Brampton in Cumberland, who was agent for the Earl of Carlisle's collieries. He ran it on his four-mile colliery railway till around 1840, during which time it is supposed on one occasion to have covered the four miles in four minutes, carrying the Alston election results, but no engineer today believes this was remotely possible. It was exhibited at the 1851 Great Exhibition and in 1862 finally ended up in South Kensington, though by that time many of its original parts were missing.

Apart from the original, the Science Museum has also on exhibition nearby a full-sized replica of *Rocket* which was made for them by Robert Stephenson and Company (by then moved to Darlington) in 1935. There seems to have been quite a trade in *Rocket* reproductions in the 1930s, big and small, started by Henry Ford in 1929 who had a working, steaming reproduction made for him personally at a cost of £2,451 – five times what Robert Stephenson and Company had charged to make the original. Two others, at around the same price, went to the Museum of Peaceful Arts in Chicago and the Museum of Science and Industry in New York.

There are several personal objects on display at the Science Museum which belonged to George, such as a calico bag made from the dress of his first wife (so it says, and who are we to disbelieve), a snuff box, a magnifying glass and some locks of his grey hair. They've framed one of his rare handwritten letters, the one written to his third wife, 'Dear Ellen', which the transcription maintains reads 'Dear Glen'. Locked away from public sight they have a good collection of other railway documents, reports, cuttings and letters, many of them to do with Robert Stephenson. (Volume 18 in the brown holders, should anyone be working on a biography of Robert Stephenson, a work long overdue.) Being taken to see them was like visiting prison. A lady attendant, brandishing a large bunch of keys, took me down several corridors, unlocking doors as she went, including the office door of the Assistant Keeper in charge of Rail Transport. His door is always locked on the outside, just in case any railway enthusiast, carried away in a mad passion, should try to break in, hoping to find more grey locks of George's hair.

The Science Museum is government run and staffed by civil servants and is the sister museum to the big new national railway museum opened at York in September 1975, around the time of the 150th Stockton and Darlington celebrations. This has taken over British Rail's transport museum which used to be at Clapham, and a smaller museum which was already in York. The new York museum is very much an entertainment museum, catering for family parties, plus research, leaving the Science Museum to be more technical. But York does have a working model of the *Rocket*, unlike the Science Museum.

CHESTERFIELD

Robert is still lying in state in Westminster Abbey, if you can fight your way through the crowds. He has a large brass plate on the floor and it's always thronged with people. Not because of Robert but because next to him lies the most popular single person in the abbey, so an usher told me – David Livingstone. They did meet in real life, getting their Hon. degrees together that day in Oxford, but Livingstone, like George Stephenson, went on to be a Victorian legend while Robert, to most visitors, is just another name on the floor.

To see George's final resting place, however, it is necessary to go back north to Chesterfield. I had a lot of difficulty getting into Holy Trinity Church, Chesterfield, to look at his grave. I was misdirected first of all by a know-all passerby who took me to a gravestone at the front of the church and pointed to the name, George Stevenson. He'd taken many a visitor to look at it, so he boasted. George's spelling was bad, but it wasn't that bad. The dates of this wrong George, by a further coincidence, are almost the same dates at the real George Stephenson, who lies inside the church.

I could hear an organ playing so I gently tried the church door handle, in case there was a service in progress. It was locked. I pushed and then banged. I went round other doors and they were all locked, with the organist playing louder and louder. I found the vicarage and the vicar's son came out and he too banged at all the church doors and shouted 'George, come out!' George, he said, was the young assistant organist and often got carried away on his organ. I'd better come back later, say in about three hours.

The church, when I did eventually get inside, still has a Methodisty air about it, which was what Mrs Elizabeth Stephenson liked – whereas the parish church, the one with the crooked spire, is still exceedingly High. George is buried under the holy table at the east end of the church, the simple stone grave slab, 'GS 1848' being obscured by a cloth hanging down from the table. Above is the east window, decorated with the initials GS, which Robert presented. On a wall is a plaque to George and his wife.

The Clay Cross Company, which George founded, has now closed. They had many mining records from his day and took pleasure in calling the company magazine *The Rocket*. Most of their archives have gone to the Institution of Mechanical Engineers in London.

The Stephenson Memorial Hall is still standing, red brick and solid, right in the heart of the town. Nearby is Stephenson Place. Few people in the town refer to it as the Stephenson Memorial Hall as it is now occupied by the museum. The local library has several letters from Joseph Locke to George and one from Edward Pease, but very little original matter relating to George himself, though they have one letter in his handwriting which looked interesting but was hard to read. It was to a local lady who had written to him complaining about her coal supply and with it he'd enclosed a letter which he said was the sort of letter she should have written to him, if she really had a complaint about his coal.

They have a form of passport signed by Lord Palmerston, dated September 1816, which is simply a letter introducing George Stephenson, the celebrated Engineer, hoping he will be helped when visiting Munich. The dates are about right for such a trip but the letter looks very amateurish and badly written, without any Government or foreign office stamp. Perhaps George wrote it for himself.

They also have a massive genealogical table of the Stephensons which someone has done for them, naming hundreds of descendants of George's brothers and sisters, many of them in the USA. This table states that George's father was definitely Scottish, either born in Mount Grenan, Ayrshire, or in Jedburgh.

Chesterfield's museum has a few dafter things, like a sleeping bonnet, said to have been worn by George Stephenson, though there was a long correspondence from people saying an important man like G. Stephenson wouldn't have worn a bonnet in bed. There are three of his waistcoats and a table from Tapton House, not on display but in a storeroom.

The other half of the Stephenson Memorial Hall is today Chesterfield's Pomegranate theatre. There was a rehearsal in progress but the stage manager stepped out to tell me that he, and four other grown men, had recently heard footsteps along an empty stage and saw, with their own eyes, a heavy door swing open and close, yet nobody was near it. 'Lots of strange things happen in this theatre, and I know who causes them. George.'

The strangest, and nicest, Stephenson object in Chesterfield today is Tapton House. It was a school and is now an adult education college. Tapton House is much as it was when George lived there – a large, handsome Georgian mansion, standing on a hill in its own lavish grounds, completely unspoiled, uncluttered, unaltered. The grounds consist of a thirty-acre public park, Tapton Park, and are also used as the school playing fields. It was given to Chesterfield Corporation in 1931 by the last owners, the Markham family, and a highly enlightened education director at the time, a Dr Stead, decided to turn a school into the house, not a house into a school, which is what usually happens when a council gets lumbered with a stately home.

Each room has been left as it was, each Georgian window exact, the plaster decoration in the corridors untouched, the wedgwood blue decorations in the front hall are exactly the same, the polished wooden stairs all gleam. Rooms in a Georgian mansion, being naturally large and rectangular and spacious, lend themselves to classrooms, but they've kept classroom apparatus to a minimum. School inspectors with a passion for visual aids must be very shocked. I toured the twenty classrooms when it was still a school with Mr Pearson, the headmaster, and saw few signs of it being an educational establishment, apart from the desks. There are few maps on the walls, no diagrams, no charts, the classrooms have no names or numbers written on them and even the headmaster's office has nothing on the door to signify its use. Most surprisingly of all, there is no graffiti, either inside or outside the school, and I looked in the boys' lavatories. Does he beat them all?

'You couldn't transpose this sort of school into another building and expect it to work. We have a tradition which has been built up over many, many years and everyone understands and respects it. I never call it a school. Nobody does. It's a House and we try to keep it like a home. Directions and labels and notices would ruin it. It would turn it into a shop at sale time.'

Each classroom had a number, though every child has to memorise it, and there is one room known by a name, the Stephenson Room, now a first year classroom and the room in which George died. A few years ago his sixth form girls restored it as it must once have been, borrowing a four poster, some antique furniture and Victorian clothes. The school has only one George Stephenson letter – a note to his friend Paxton, the gardener at Chatsworth, who wanted George to arrange an introduction to George Hudson, the Railway King. They have one Robert Stephenson letter, again to Paxton, this time about a dinner engagement. They have a couple of paintings and a bust but few other Stephenson objects. What Mr Pearson was trying to do was keep alive the spirit of the house as George left it. George would be very pleased. In 2004, at long last, a statue of George Stephenson went up outside Chesterfield Station.

DARLINGTON

In 1975 the celebrations to commemorate the 150th anniversary of the railway put Darlington once again on the railway map of the world, but in a normal year, Darlington as a town is pretty bored by railways. Their football team, which the rest of the country tends to look upon as a bit of a joke, as they're usually around the bottom of the Third Division, is known locally as the 'Quakers'. It's doubtful if many of their fans today know much about Edward Pease. At one time the railway-men's galas were the social events of the year, but the last railway works has closed. Their railway history now means little to the man in the street, despite the activities of certain officials who've been trying to drum up some enthusiasm for many years.

But the success of Darlington's Railway Museum, opened in 1975, situated at the old North Road Station, has brought in a lot more railway fans and people on the George Stephenson trail, for it is here you will find Locomotion No. 1. For many years it used to stand on the platform on Darlington Station, confusing all those who queued up, trying to get on, or waited for it to depart. *Locomotion* was the first locomotive on the world's first public railway. It's much bigger than one might expect, gleaming black and rather fierce looking. There are horse-like stirrups at the side where the driver climbed up and then perched on top, on a little platform running beside the boiler, right amongst the works. It must have been very perilous, completely exposed to the elements, easily brushed off by any obstacle or a high wind, or perhaps caught up in the cogs and cranks or burned by the boiler. The fireman was relatively safe, hanging on at the back and much lower down. In front of the driver, as he crouched on top of the engine, was a rope attached to a brass bell at the front, so he could warn the public of his approach.

Beside *Locomotion* is another engine, *Derwent*, which is painted green and black, and dates from 1845. You can see how much engines developed in just twenty years. *Derwent* looks very much the sort of loco which became the prototype for the following fifty years.

In the middle of the town in Tubwell Row, was a small, rather homely museum which had a room devoted to the Stockton and Darlington Railway. It has now closed and the contents transferred to the Railway museum.

One of Darlington Railway Museum's best possessions, and one which is reproduced in many books on the history of railways, is the well-known painting by John Dobbin of the opening of the Stockton–Darlington Railway on 27 September 1825. It's a pretty work showing groups of fine ladies and gentlemen standing by their coaches and horses, looking up as the packed train, pulled by *Locomotion*, goes over a viaduct. It's meticulously done, loaded with rather lush detail and probably a bit too glamorous to be true. Dobbin was too young to have done the painting on the opening day and is thought to have done it several years later, perhaps from rough sketches, helped by hindsight and a good imagination. But it's a fine work. I wanted to buy a print or even a post card, but they hadn't got one. Even the smaller provincial museums sell post cards of their best treasures. I tried across the road in an art shop but they hadn't got one either, though they wished they had.

I then went to Northgate, looking for number 73, the house where the momentous first meeting took place between George Stephenson and Edward Pease. Northgate was a fine Georgian row of merchants' houses in the 1820s, judging by contemporary drawings, and Mr Pease's was about the last one on the way out of the town. Today it's just another small town high street, dominated by Woolworth's, British Home Stores and other chain stores. Above a cafe called El Vino's, a cafe rather less salubrious than its noted London namesake, just beside an army recruiting centre, there is a plaque which notes the site of Pease's house.

There's only one member of the Pease family still living locally. All the rest have long since departed with their peerages to their grand country estates in the south. Most of them are not even Quakers now, though they're still strong in their traditional City pursuits. Lord Wardington, one of the present Peases, is a stockbroker.

In Crown Street stands Darlington's Public Library, very well organised and with many records of the Stockton and Darlington Railway, and of the Pease family, all beautifully catalogued, far better arranged than many a library in a town four times its size. The guide book to their collection of S. & D. material is twenty pages long – more impressive in fact than some of the actual material.

The most expensive single undertaking for the 1975 celebrations was to renovate the old North Road Station, originally built in 1833 as the first station on the Stockton–Darlington. It was rebuilt ten years later and today is still one of the finest examples of early Victorian railway architecture. It had been unused for the last ten years, having ended its days as an unmanned halt, with railway enthusiasts having stolen any railway bits of note and vandals destroying most of the rest. The cost of refurbishing it, making it the home of Darlington's new railway museum, was estimated at £250,000.

In 1925, *Locomotion* had once again been at the centre of celebrations, but they did a bit of cheating. Smoke came out of the chimney, as it should, but it was caused by an oily waste burning in the chimney. The motive power came from a petrol engine hidden in the tender. For 1975 they decided to build a fullscale working model of *Locomotion*. It was then realised it would cost £30,000, but Mike Satow, coordinator of the 150 Joint Committee, said he would organise it personally – and get it done for nothing. Mr Satow is a retired ICI executive, formerly managing director of ICI in India, and an expert on Indian railways. He turned the project into a vast training scheme for engineering apprentices and talked twenty-eight different firms in the north east into letting their trainee engineers produce different bits of the engine. By the end of 1974 he couldn't get into his garage, as all the bits had started to arrive, but by April 1975 it was ready for a public assembly.

The new *Locomotion* proved to be the star attraction of the 1975 opening ceremonies, pulling many vintage coaches and coal wagons.

LIVERPOOL

Until the 150th celebrations in 1980, Liverpool hadn't been very much interested in George Stephenson. Yet Liverpool figured highly in the family saga. It was from Liverpool that Robert sailed to South America and then, three years later returned. And of course it was at Liverpool docks that the *Rocket* arrived by sea from Carlisle, all ready to be assembled for Rainhill and its journey into history.

Liverpool's Central Library, in its local records office, has a fine collection of Liverpool–Manchester letters and documents which are visited by railway scholars from all over the world, especially America. It's a collection that's growing all the time. Unlike some local libraries, they're always interested in buying more documents about their past. In 1968 they acquired that remarkable original handwritten letter from George to his son Robert at the mines in Columbia. In July 1973 they bought at Sotheby's a collection of letters by and to William James, the original surveyor of the Liverpool–Manchester line.

The 1980 Liverpool celebrations made local people aware of their unique railway history and one of the many tangible results was the rehabilitation of Edge Hill station. Some of the buildings were restored and it was hoped to make it a permanent Visitor Centre and a Rail Trail. The buildings, for so long overgrown, are incredible, a memento of the lavishness of the railway age, and well worth a visit.

As with the 1975 celebrations in Darlington, Mike Satow organised the building of replicas – three in all for the Rainhill Trials' reconstruction run in May 1980. On a smaller scale, souvenir manufacturers produced thousands of little replicas. There were the usual commemorative plates, medals and mugs, just as there had been in 1830. Any old junk produced back in 1830 for the original opening is now of course a valuable antique, prized by collectors everywhere. By 2030, for the 200th anniversary, anything from 1980 will have a charm and a price. So hold on to everything, even this book. . .

# APPENDIX

## THE MYSTERIOUS LETTER FROM ROBERT STEPHENSON TO WILLIAM JAMES

The original of the letter, now in Liverpool, is very faint and difficult to read. The following is a transcript of the entire letter, for which I am grateful to Naomi Everts of Liverpool City Libraries (who have kindly allowed me to reproduce the letter).

Newcastle 18th April 1824

Mr. James.

Sir,

I beg leave to inform you that I have for some time back been in treaty with one of the Mexico Mining Compy as Engineer and the Superintendence of a Railway, having had perhaps more general practice than any other person in that line in the Kingdom, but in consequence of the great disapprobation of my Wife and large family, which must ever be my chief care I am obliged to relinquish the very liberal offer which has been made me, in consequence of this alteration taking place, it has for the present left me in want of a situation. I therefore take the liberty to inform you, that I consider myself fully competent as an Engineer, and have lately made some useful discoveries in the Locomotive Engine, and should you be in want of assistant, I flatter myself, I could be very useful and should be glad to engage with you, should this meet your approbation shall produce the strongest testimonial proofs of my assertions.

Your reply will much oblige
Sir
your most Humble Servant
(Signed)         ROBT. STEPHENSON.

Thomas's Court,
Forth Street.

Rolt assumed that this letter was written by Robert Stephenson, George's son, and refers to it in his book (*George and Robert Stephenson*, Longman, 1960, page 96), using it as an important piece of evidence to support his theory that Robert, the son, was being loyal to James and was upset by George getting James' job on the Liverpool line.

This letter was one of a bundle of letters to William James which was first discovered on 13 September 1930, at 5, Rochester Road, Coventry. An attempt was made to transcribe some of the letters at the time, although all of them were kept in private hands. This particular letter was amongst several ascribed to Robert Stephenson, George's son. Rolt, when using some of the information in the letter, accepted that it was written by Robert the son.

In July 1973, Liverpool City Libraries bought the bulk of the collection at Sothebys for £1,326 when they were stated to be the 'property of a lady' (one of William James' daughters had married and settled in Coventry). In November 1973 I visited the Liverpool City Libraries, in the process of researching this book, and was allowed to read the entire collection which they were still in the process of arranging and transcribing. I noticed that in a bundle marked as being written by Robert Stephenson, George's son, there was one dated 18 June 1824, Newcastle. I pointed out to Mrs Evetts, who was doing the cataloguing, that young Robert was at that date on the high seas heading for South America so the letter must be from his Uncle Robert, George's brother. She agreed a mistake had been made and put the letter, which wasn't at all important, in the correct bundle.

The following year, in writing my chapter on Robert leaving for South America, I was having difficulty in making out certain words in various photostats I'd taken from the William James letters. In particular, the letter from 'Robert Stephenson' written on 18 April was very confusing. I could make out the request for 'a situation', as Rolt had done, but I couldn't understand his reference to 'wife and large family'. Young Robert wasn't married at this time, though he might for some reason have been referring to his stepmother as the 'wife'. I wrote to Mrs Evetts to ask if she'd finished transcribing the letters. Not only had she done so but, perturbed by my discovery of the wrongly ascribed Robert letter, she'd gone through every 'Robert Stephenson' letter in great detail and had discovered that one other letter had been wrongly catalogued, the one written on 18 April which had been puzzling me.

She had several reasons for deciding that Robert, George's brother, was the author: 1) The reference is clearly to 'my wife'. Young Robert, an only child, was not married at the time, while Uncle Robert was and had a family, not to mention his numerous brothers and sisters. 2) The letter is addressed in much more formal terms than the other letters from Robert, the son, to William James, who was an old and very close friend. 3) The signature at the end corresponds to the one already wrongly ascribed, the 18 June letter, and not to the other known letters by Robert, the son. 4) Checking in the Jeaffreson biography she found that Robert was fully occupied in London at the time, very excited by his plans for Colombia, and wouldn't be likely to be contemplating another English job. For these reasons she reattributed the letter to Robert Stephenson (b. 1788), brother of George.

In checking the authorship of the letter she wasn't aware that Rolt had placed such importance upon it. When my doubts crept in I'd already begun to re-examine Rolt's theory, feeling convinced that if there had been a row over James, George wouldn't have been so cheerful or have kept in such close contact with Robert, seeing him off almost happily at Liverpool. George Stephenson sounds the sort of person who would have cut his son off for ever if there had been a serious row. It was completely by chance that I approached Mrs Evetts with my doubts, just as she herself was deciding the letter had been wrongly ascribed.

There remains the minor mystery of why Robert, George's brother, wanted to leave the Newcastle works, and his dear brother who'd done so much to help him, and work instead with William James, one of his rivals.

As this Robert Stephenson achieved none of the international fame and fortune which his same-named nephew had, it's unlikely that many people will be longing for the mystery to be cleared up, though someone one day will doubtless earn himself a Ph.D. by explaining all.

# BIBLIOGRAPHY

ORIGINAL MATERIAL – Letters, documents, reports, relics.

## LONDON

INSTITUTION OF MECHANICAL ENGINEERS: Brandling Papers; Crow Collection; Phillimore Collection; Longridge Letters; Thompson Collection.

INSTITUTION OF CIVIL ENGINEERS: George Stephenson scrap book.

PUBLIC RECORDS OFFICE (BRITISH TRANSPORT RECORDS): Railway Company Records.

SCIENCE MUSEUM, South Kensington: George Stephenson relics; Robert Stephenson and Company records; *Rocket*.

## NEWCASTLE

NEWCASTLE CENTRAL LIBRARY, LOCAL HISTORY DEPARTMENT: George Stephenson letters; Contemporary newspaper files.

NORTHUMBERLAND RECORDS OFFICE: George Stephenson letters; Nicholas Wood diary.

LITERARY AND PHILOSOPHICAL SOCIETY: Geordy Lamp documents.

## NORTHUMBERLAND

WYLAM. GS's birthplace cottage, owned by the National Trust, open Thurs, Fri, Sat and Sun afternoons, April–Nov. Also does teas. Tel. 01661 853 457.

PERCY MAIN. George Stephenson Railway and Museum – small, preserved railway, just two miles of track, plus loco museum. Open May–Sept. Tel 0191 200 7146.

## CHESTERFIELD

Statue of George Stephenson outside the railway station. Tapton House, where he died, is now an adult education college.

# BIBLIOGRAPY

## DARLINGTON

PUBLIC LIBRARY, LOCAL HISTORY DEPT.: Pease Letters; Stockton and Darlington Railway Company Records.

DARLINGTON RAILWAY MUSEUM, NORTH ROAD STATION: *Locomotion* No 1, plus other engines and relics, including Hackworth's 'Derwent', 1845 .

## LIVERPOOL

CITY LIBRARY, RECORDS OFFICE: Liverpool and Manchester Railway documents; William James letters.

## YORK

NATIONAL RAILWAY MUSEUM, LEEMAN RD: working replica of *Rocket*.


BOOKS – Contemporary and Near Contemporary

Booth, Henry *An Account of the Liverpool and Manchester Railway* (Liverpool 1830)

Bowen Cooke, C. J. *British Locomotives* (Whittaker 1893) Condor, F. R. *Personal Recollections of English Engineers* (Hodder and Stoughton 1868)

Jeaffreson, J. C. *The Life of Robert Stephenson*, 2 vols (London 1864)

Jeans, J. S. *History of the Stockton and Darlington Railway* (London 1875, reprinted by Frank Graham, Newcastle, 1974)

Kemble, Fanny *Records of a Girlhood* (London 1878)

Knight, H. C. *The Rocket* (London 1877)

Mackay, Thomas *The Autobiography of Samuel Smiles*, completed 1889 (John Murray 1905)

Pease, Sir Alfred (ed) *The Diaries of Edward Pease* (London 1907)

E.M.S.P. *The Two James's and the Two Stephensons* (London 1861, reprinted by David and Charles, 1974)

Pease, Mary *Henry Pease* (London 1847)

Smiles, Samuel *Life of George Stephenson* (John Murray 1857 – first edition)

Smiles, Samuel *Lives of the Stephensons* (John Murray 1864)

Summerside, T. *Anecdotes, Reminiscences and Conversations of and with the Late George Stephenson, Father of Railways* (London 1878)

Wood, Nicholas *A Practical Treatise on Railroads* (London 1825)


BOOKS – Modern and Near Modern

Bailey, Michael R. *Robert Stephenson, the Eminent Engineer* (Ashgate, 2003)

Carlson, Robert *The Liverpool and Manchester Railway Project, 1821–1831* (David and Charles 1969)

Coleman, Terry *The Railway Navvies* (Hutchinson 1965)

Darby, Michael *Early Railway Prints* (Victoria and Albert Museum 1974)

Dendy Marshall, C. F. *Centenary History of the Liverpool and Manchester Railway* (The Locomotive Publishing Co. Ltd 1930)

Dendy Marshall, C. F. *A History of British Railways down to the Year 1930* (O.U.P. 1938)

Emden, Paul *Quakers in Commerce* (Sampson Low 1939)

Gard, R. M. *Northumbrian Railways from 1700* (Northumberland Records Office, Exhibition Catalogue 1969)

Gard, R. M. and Hartley, J. R. *Railways in the Making* (University of Newcastle, Archive Teaching Unit No. 3, 1969)

Jarvis, Adrian, *George Stephenson* (Lifeline Mini Biographies, Shire Publishing, 2004)

Lambert, Richard *The Railway King, a Biography of George Hudson* (Allen and Unwin 1934)

Nock, O. S. *The Railway Engineers* (Batsford 1955)

Parsonage, W. R. *A Short Biography of George Stephenson* (Institution of Mechanical Engineers 1937)

Reed, Brian, *The Rocket* (Loco Profiles, No. 7, 1970)

Rolt, L.T. C. *Isambard Kingdom Brunel* (Longman 1957)

Rolt, L.T. C. *The Cornish Giant (Richard Trevithick)* (Longman 1960)

Rolt, L.T. C. *George and Robert Stephenson* (Longman 1960)

Simmons, J. *The Railways of Britain* (Macmillan 1968)

Skeat, W.O. *George Stephenson, the Engineer and his Letters* (The Institution of Mechanical Engineers 1973)

Smith, Denis, ed., *Perceptions of Great Engineers* (Newcomen Soc., 1994)

Swinglehurst, Edmund *The Romantic Journey, the story of Thomas Cook and Victorian Travel* (Pica 1974)

Tomlinson, W. W. *The North Eastern Railway* (Newcastle upon Tyne 1914)

Thompson, L., *History of Tapton House* (Cranley, 2000)

Warren, J. G. *A Century of Locomotive Building by Robert Stephenson and Co.* (Newcastle upon Tyne 1923)

Westcott, G. F. *The British Railway Locomotive* (Her Majesty's Stationery Office 1958)

# INDEX

GS = George Stephenson. RS = Robert Stephenson

# INDEX